Do
This

Liturgy as Performance

◆ RICHARD D. MCCALL

University of Notre Dame Press

Notre Dame, Indiana

Library of Congress Cataloging-in-Publication Data

McCall, Richard D., 1947–
Do this : liturgy as performance / Richard D. McCall.
      p.   cm.
Includes bibliographical references and index.
ISBN-13: 978-0-268-03499-3 (pbk. : alk. paper)
ISBN-10: 0-268-03499-0 (pbk. : alk. paper)
1. Liturgics.   2. Performance—Religious aspects—Christianity.
3. Liturgy and drama.   I. Title.
BV178.M37   2007
264.001—dc22

                                                    2006039808

For

TERRY

Contents

◆ I ◆

Introduction

The Varieties of Liturgical Performance

For centuries Christians have explained their repeated enactment of the Holy Eucharist as an attempt to remain faithful to Jesus' words at the Last Supper: "Do this in remembrance of me."[1] Justin Martyr (c. 100–c. 165), whose *First Apology* and *Dialogue with Trypho* are two of the oldest explanations of the Christian meal, traces its celebration to these very words: "The apostles, in their memoirs which are called gospels, have handed down that they were commanded to this: Jesus took bread, and, after giving thanks, said 'Do this in remembrance of me; this is my body." And again, "[T]he offering of fine flour . . . was a type of the bread of the eucharist which our Lord Jesus Christ commanded us to offer in memory of the Passion He endured."[2] This "argument" would be repeated over and over again by apologists and theologians East and West and would survive into the modern period in the debate between Protestants and Catholics over the place of the Eucharist in the life of the church.

The unfortunate consequence of this obsession with the so-called "institution" of the Eucharist by Jesus at the Last Supper would be a medieval legalism that required such warrant for all sacramental acts and that reduced liturgical performance to the minimum needed to adhere to Jesus' command. On the positive side, however, the ordinance to do something may have ensured that Christian spirituality could never be reduced to mere doctrinal orthodoxy or passive assent. Built into the very warrant for sacramental worship is a verb of performance. Hidden in that performance is a vision of life in Christ that is not a state of being but rather an act, an act of the worshippers who *en*act a cosmos and a community that is nothing less than God's act of creation.

But the ordinance calls not just for any doing. Rather, it is a doing of remembrance ("Do this for my *anamnesis*"). We shall have occasion further on to examine more deeply this most polysemous word. Suffice it to say that any attempt to enact remembrance contains the seeds of what can be called drama. The church may never have intended to invent a dramatic liturgy. Certainly the early house Eucharists were simple occasions of reading and prayer and meal. Nonetheless, Christians inherited from the Jewish prayer tradition the habit of invoking God's active involvement in this present moment by remembering thankfully God's mighty acts in the story of God's people. Narrative remembers act; act fulfills narrative.

There is a seemingly irresistible temptation to speak about the liturgy of the Christian Church as somehow "dramatic." Theodore of Mopsuestia was not the first, but he was certainly the most systematic of the fourth-century theologians to describe the actions and the participants in the Holy Eucharist as representative of something other than what they appeared, in their liturgical functionality, to be. He tells the catechumens that in the offertory procession they must see Christ being led to his passion and in the deacons who enact it "the invisible ministering powers when they carry up the offering."[3]

Dionysus the Pseudo-Areopagite and Maximus Confessor in the East and Pseudo-Germanus and Amalarius of Metz in the West, to name only a few, developed this perspective to the extent that for Amalarius in the ninth century the liturgy was to be understood primarily as an enactment of allegorical, tropological, and anagogical acts after the model of scriptural exegesis developed by the Anglo-Saxon Bede. While not confining his vision of the liturgy to a simple dramatization of the life of Christ, "Amalar furnishes an elliptical view of salvation history, with an array of overlapping images designed to symbolize, and make present, the mighty works of God in Christ."[4] However much Amalarius would be censured during his lifetime, his "allegorical" and dramatic method of liturgical exegesis would dominate popular sacramental teaching until the last century.

Such a dramatic analysis of the liturgy has not, however, been confined to the "official" teachings of the church. Medieval drama itself, in the form of the Passion and mystery or cycle plays of the fourteenth through sixteenth centuries and in such unique plays as the Croxton *Play of the Sacrament,* has been seen by scholars as nothing less than "commentaries" on the liturgy of the church, liturgical "expansions" in dramatic form of the basic acts of the liturgical year and the Mass.[5] Moreover, modern approaches to the history of the medieval drama, beginning with Karl Young and widely disseminated in the work of O.B. Hardison, take as their starting point an understanding of the Mass, the Office, and the liturgical calendar as dramatic enactments.[6] The debate among these scholars is less over whether there is a dramatic element to the liturgy than over what exactly constitutes "drama" and its differentiation from "liturgy." Is it the presence of costumes or impersonation or scripts or stage directions or an audience that separates a "play" from a "liturgy"? Or is it something else that "frames" the action and tells us in one case, "This is a play" and in another, "This is a liturgy"?

Recent theories of semiotics and performance, especially in the work of M. M. Bakhtin, Roland Barthes, and Umberto Eco, deriving from the linguistic theories of Ferdinand de Saussure and Louis Hjelmslev, have opened an even broader horizon for looking at the nature of the act or constellation of acts that forms the basis not only of drama and liturgy but of social acts, political acts, and even reality itself as it is enacted moment by moment as "once-occurrent Being-as-event."[7] The word *performance* has come to denote not only "a show put on by a performer for an audience" but also a many-faceted model for approaching all of that reality which can only be, for human beings, symbolic and enacted in our institutions, relationships, art, and rituals.[8] The basic structures of enactment in drama and in liturgy still fall on points along this continuum; but these points can be seen as part of a larger field that includes the enactment or performance of language[9] (and thus of culture) and of sociopolitical relationships,[10] not to mention the ontological status given to the *act* in the systems of Martin Heidegger, Alfred North Whitehead, and M. M. Bakhtin.[11]

Thus both *drama* and *liturgy,* the only two poles of enactment available to Theodore or Amalarius, have become terms in a far richer field of action, one that purports to enact a reality that, for both Theodore and Amalarius, could only be "imitated" or represented, at most made present anamnetically in the liturgy. For them the question was: "How can the divine reality be represented effectually in the rites of the church?" The question for the postmodern liturgical theologian might well be stated: "What is the place of the rites of the church in a world that is itself a performance, a continuing enactment that comes to be in the act?"

That the drama of medieval Europe "developed" from the liturgy of the church sometime during the tenth century has been the dominant assumption of twentieth-century scholarship at least since the publication in 1903 of E. K. Chambers's seminal *The Medieval Stage*. Asserting that the "dramatic tendencies of Christian worship declared themselves from an early period," Chambers sees his task as describing "a most singular new birth of drama in the very bosom of the Church's own ritual."[12] The child brought forth, which was to be the father of the great medieval cycle plays and the grandfather of Shakespeare, Chambers believed to have been the simple trope *Quem quaeritis?*

> Whom do you seek in the sepulcher, followers of Christ?
> Jesus of Nazareth who was crucified, O heavenly ones.
> He is not here, he has arisen as he foretold.
> Go, announce that he has risen from the sepulcher.

———

> [Quem quaeritis in sepulchro, Christicolae?
> Iesum Nazarenum crucifixum, o caelicolae.
> non est hic, surrexit sicut praedixerat.
> ite, nuntiate quia surrexit de sepulchro.]

The development of scholarship concerning this liturgical/dramatic interface begun with Chambers was taken up by his most important "successor" Karl Young, and became finally the subject of a critique begun by Hardison and continued by a number of scholars during the past thirty years.[13] More recent musicological scholarship has provided the most essential correctives to this literary history.[14]

In every case there are spoken or unspoken assumptions on the part of the literary critics and historians concerning what liturgy is, what drama is, and what, if anything, can be called "liturgical drama" or "dramatic liturgy." The widespread assumptions both that the liturgy of the tenth-century church was in some way "drama" and that the liturgical drama (e.g., the Visit to the Sepulcher, *Visitatio sepulchri*) "gave rise" to the later cycle plays have been corrected by subsequent studies of medieval performance and especially by musicological studies of medieval chant.

Nonetheless, some writers do not define clearly just what differentiates a "dramatic" liturgy from a "drama," liturgical or otherwise. In fact, it would seem that some recent work done in the field of political ritual (e.g., Ernst Kantorowicz's *The King's Two Bodies* and Geoffrey Koziol's *Begging Pardon and Favor*)[15] might suggest a new and more fruitful line of inquiry in the attempt to place both liturgy and drama in the historical context of the ritualizing behavior of the period from the ninth to the thirteenth centuries.

It seems fair to say that speculation about the dramatic nature of the medieval Mass drew impetus from the supposition that the drama "evolved" from the liturgy by way of the *Quem quaeritis* trope and other so-called liturgical dramas. That the liturgy is "enacted," that it is "commemorative" or anamnetic, even that it has a performative ritual structure might all have been said about it without attempts to discover in it the seeds of the drama, were it not for this simple trope and the historiography which dictates that like must beget like and simple forms must evolve into more complex forms. A corollary implicit in this historiography is that later forms reveal the nature of their antecedents.

Thus the Darwinian program, when applied to the history of the medieval theater, assumes that drama could develop only from a liturgy that was somehow already embryonically "drama" itself. Hardison's opening essay in *Christian Rite and Christian Drama in the Middle Ages* drew attention to this prejudice and argued for a fresh look at the evidence. It was his contention that, as with so many other historical documentary traditions (including, we might add, the early Eucharistic Prayers), there is no demonstrable "evolution" of simpler into more complex forms. I would further affirm, along with scholars of the medieval drama, that there is no necessity for the liturgy to *be* a species of drama in order for it to invite dramatic exposition, commentary, and counterpoint. Rather, both liturgy and drama can be seen as subcategories of a larger human activity that has come to be called performance or enactment.

The organization of the argument in what follows presents an approach to the liturgy as a species of performance. This approach takes seriously the postmodern critique of methodology in general insofar as methodology tries to abstract itself from the context of the work under discussion or to fit all specific instances into the procrustean bed of a self-consistent theory. What I have attempted is less a method then an approach, a species of discourse that organizes its observations according to a schema but that refuses to reduce the work observed to the schema. To apply this approach, one would not simply analyze a liturgy by mapping it to a predetermined grid of structure or language. Rather, in the final chapters I have attempted to demonstrate how one would speak of the liturgy using a certain kind of discourse — one grounded in the language of so-called "performance theory."

However, I have also attempted to bring the wide-ranging diversity of what might be more accurately described as performance *theories* into a useful relationship by demonstrating their interrelated positions in a larger definition of performance. To accomplish this I suggest that each of the many performance approaches speaks to one of the so-called "four causes" from which Aristotle gathers up his famous definition of tragedy in chapter 6 of the *Poetics*.

In deriving a similar definition for liturgy, I do not claim that liturgy is tragedy or even drama or that liturgy can be reduced to a template. Rather, I attempt to gather up a definition of liturgy that does justice both to its similarities to and its differences from other kinds of performed events. To differentiate liturgical action from the popular meaning of "performance" as a display of virtuosity by one person or group of persons for an audience, I present various twentieth-century redefinitions of this term derived from linguistics, semiology, literary and dramatic criticism, and the behavioral sciences. But to avoid the theatrical overtones of the word, I often refer to the *enactment* of the liturgy, reserving the term *performance* to a more technical sense of the style or manner of that enactment.

After having examined some of these approaches, I organize them in a schema by which they can most profitably and appropriately be applied to a performance event considered not simply from the point of view of one approach but from the perspective of all four causes that Aristotle imagined to be at work in any made thing. By using this schema I derive a definition of the liturgy as performance.

I then attempt to apply the performative definition to an actual liturgical enactment. This approach would, of course, be applicable to any liturgy at any period for which we have evidence of the actual performance. I have chosen, by way of example, the celebration of the Mass at Rome in the early eighth century according to the Gregorian Sacramentary and the actions described in *Ordo Romanus I*. This enactment had far-reaching effects on the subsequent development of the performance of the liturgy in the West as the ordo and the sacramentary were disseminated, copied, modified, and imitated throughout the Carolingian Empire. As we shall see, moreover, the enactment described in the first Roman ordo may be the most appropriate working out of the words of the Roman Canon to be achieved in its long history. Later and more elaborate performances, such as those of the late Middle Ages, perhaps never again achieved the theological wedding of word to gesture that we find in this seminal enactment.

Finally, it must be borne in mind that the approach I am proposing must rely heavily on narrative recreation of the event—the mind's eye and ear must first attempt to see and hear what was enacted in order to approach the meaning of the event. Even better would be a recreated performance followed by each participant's description of the experience. The symbolic acts of the liturgy have a history and a context and can only be understood both as what they have been and as what they are in the present moment. And, like all real symbols, they can never mean just one thing.

✦ 2 ✦

Performing Liturgical Interpretation in the Medieval West

İn any search for the earliest relationship between the liturgy and the drama per se, it may be noted at the outset that nothing that might be called "drama" is in evidence in the Western Church before the tenth century. Western Europe was effectively without mainstream drama from the moment that Christianity gained political influence in the fourth century. As early as the second century, the decadence of late Roman drama and the reputed immorality of its practitioners had made the theater one of the professions that had to be abandoned before receiving baptism. Augustine, as is well known, prided himself for having left behind the life of the theater.

What is, perhaps, more surprising is that the Gothic tribes that constituted the locus of evangelism and the ever-growing center of Western Christendom from the fourth through the ninth centuries found the Roman theater decadent and repulsive. Their own tradition of minstrel storytelling had never included mimetic role-play, and they quickly rejected the excess, bawdry, and licentiousness of the Italian *histriones*.[1] Thus, by the early sixth century, the theater in the West survived only among the folk and in the occasional traveling mime or pantomime. Any sense of "official" drama must be seen as having been confined to the elaboration of the ceremonies surrounding the liturgy of the church.[2]

The rekindling of the dramatic instinct in Western Europe is usually considered to have begun in the ninth century with the elaboration of parts of the Mass and Office by means of tropes.[3] Not in themselves dramatic, these additions to the Introit and Kyrie of the Mass and the Antiphons of the Office allowed the introduction of nonbiblical, and nonofficial, expansions of the basic texts to emphasize the theme of a season or feast. Thus the Introit to the Easter Mass, by the end of the ninth century, had been expanded by the addition of the *Quem quaeritis* trope, which tells the story of the visit of the Marys to the sepulcher on Easter morning. Although such a trope would have at first been sung antiphonally by the two sides of the choir or by the choir and a cantor, it does not take a great stretch of the imagination to see how easily such a "script" would lend itself to dramatic enactment.

Indeed, the tenth-century *Regularis concordia* drawn up by Ethelwold, bishop of Winchester, contains specific stage directions and costuming to be used by the Benedictine monks as they enacted this little play at the third nocturn of matins on Easter morning.[4] While the third lesson was being chanted, one of the monks, dressed in an alb, would "approach the sepulcher without attracting attention and there sit quietly with a palm in his hand. While the third respond is chanted," St. Ethelwold continues, "let the remaining three follow, and let them all, vested in copes, bearing in their hands thuribles with incense, and stepping delicately as those who seek something, approach the sepulcher. These things are done in imitation of the angel sitting in the monument, and the women with spices coming to anoint the body of Jesus." What followed was a chanting of the aforementioned dialogue by the "actors," culminating in the recovery of the cross, which had been hidden on Good Friday, and the singing of the Te Deum. Ethelwold justifies this bit of drama on the grounds that it is instructive: "Since on this day we celebrate the laying down of the body of our Savior, if it seem good or pleasing to any to follow on similar lines the use of certain of the religious, which is worthy of imitation for the strengthening of faith in the unlearned vulgar and in neophytes, we have ordered it on this wise."[5]

This simple liturgical performance, along with others that would be elaborated particularly around the great feasts of Easter and Christmas, would eventually come to have great popular appeal. But it would not be until the twelfth century, with the building of the great Gothic cathedrals and cathedral schools, that these originally monastic endeavors would be staged for the people.[6] The naves of the great churches were transformed

into a playing area surrounded by "mansions" representing the various locations of the liturgical drama, which began, in many instances, to include
multiple scenes taken from the Bible and elaborate machinery for special
effects. Hardin Craig believes that these essentially Latin plays were, nevertheless, products of the efforts of a variety of people, not all of whom were
clerics. "That the provincial, often no doubt parochial, population and the
members of schools and colleges did participate in the religious drama is
beyond question. The records, often casually preserved, are fairly plentiful,
widespread, and varied."[7]

The earliest manuscript evidence for the *Quem quaeritis* exchange used
as part of a play dates from midcentury, and the earliest evidence for any
sort of "staging" is found in the *Regularis concordia* of St. Ethelwold, written
c. 970. Moreover, as Dunbar Ogden and others have demonstrated, parts
of the *Quem quaeritis* and *Quem quaeritis in praesepe* were, in some instances,
enacted in areas of the church where there was no possibility for the inclusion of spectators.[8] Although eventuating in, for example, the display of the
grave-clothes to the waiting worshippers, such enactments would seem to
retain more similarities to the ritual action of the silent Canon of the Mass
than to anything we would ordinarily call drama.

There is no evidence for medieval drama during the early Carolingian
period, although certainly the growing interest in ceremonial may be seen to
contribute to a taste for enactment in both political and ecclesiastical ritual.
Thus it is from the period of Louis the Pious (early ninth century) that we
get the first coronation ordines, the prayers of which, modeled on episcopal
consecration prayers, present a self-conscious appropriation of Old Testament typology to the king and the "Christian empire" of the later Carolingians.[9] The political ritual that constituted the Carolingian political myth,
however, seems to have derived from ecclesial ritual rather than vice versa.
Thus the anointing of the king apparently derived from the "new" practice
of anointing the hands of priests and was accommodated to kingly anointing through prayer-images of the anointing of David by Samuel.

Later, the Cluniac reform movement of the late tenth and early eleventh
centuries included an expansion of the liturgical action within the monastic
communities affected. Such an expansion may be seen as a part of the kind
of "dramatic" impulse that included the *Quem quaeritis* dialogue. Lanfranc's
monastic constitutions, written for his new community at Canterbury, indicate a "filling in" of the time between matins and lauds with often-elaborate

processions to stations at the side-altars of the cathedral. These very side-altars, derived from the Frankish love of Roman liturgical books with their stational Masses, may themselves have given impetus to the kind of processional staging using *platea* (playing space) and *sedes* (constructions representing particular locations) that would become the norm for medieval drama when still performed within the confines of the church building.

Nonetheless, in the centuries before the *Quem quaeritis,* "drama" did not influence the liturgy so much as liturgy became more *enacted.* O. B. Hardison's thesis in *Christian Rite and Christian Drama in the Middle Ages* is that the Mass and the "Lenten Agon" followed by the rites of Holy Week and Easter *are* the drama of the early Middle Ages, but a drama that *is* the liturgy. The interpretive writings of Amalarius of Metz are just that: interpretive writings, "criticism," and not, as Christine Schnusenberg would suggest, "dramas."[10]

Hardison speculated that the *Quem quaeritis* grew from a dramatic post-baptismal moment in which the newly baptized at the Easter vigil were taken to the now empty "Easter Sepulcher." Were this picture accurate, we would have a moment in which a dramatic act commented on the baptismal liturgy.[11] In fact, the neophytes could be seen as playing the *role* of the Marys when they were asked by a deacon, "Whom do you seek, O followers of Christ," to which another replied on their behalf, "We seek Jesus of Nazareth, O heavenly ones." The neophytes, in this reconstruction, were then told that he was not there and that they must "go, tell his brethren that he is risen." At this point, according to Hardison, the neophytes returned to the church, and they or someone on their behalf made the first Easter proclamation. Such an event would seem to represent liturgy-becoming-liturgical-drama in the tradition, found in the fourth-century Holy Week rites described by Egeria at Jerusalem, of involving the worshippers.

Clifford Flanigan, however, has refuted Hardison's picture and repositioned the *Quem quaeritis* as a trope on the Easter Mass Introit.[12] For him it becomes a *commentary* to make clear that the words of the Introit psalm are to be understood as the risen Christ addressing his Father. The trope, that is, serves a celebratory and a didactic function. In any case, in the tenth century, the *Quem quaeritis* lines appear in the Introit of the Easter Mass, in some locations in pre–Easter Mass processions, and at Winchester and in Germany in a little play, the *Visitatio sepulchri,* positioned just before the Te Deum at Easter matins.

That text, along with the Magi Play *(Officium stellae)* and the Shepherds' Play *(Officium pastorum)* at Christmas and the *Ordo prophetarum* in Advent, proliferated throughout the Continent; but I do not believe they can be said to influence the development of liturgical rites beyond the fact of their inclusion in them. Their use seems to have been both didactic (as in Ethelwold's statement in the *Regularis concordia* concerning the edification of neophytes and of the unlearned) and liturgical (see Ogden on the *Quem quaeritis* above) by the eleventh century.

The eleventh century witnessed the controversy over eucharistic doctrine revolving around Berengar of Tours. Lanfranc, who opposed Berengar's more symbolic understanding of the eucharistic presence, also replaced the cross with the Host in the ceremony of the *Elevatio* (its lifting up from the place in which it had been "buried" on Good Friday) on Easter. This may indicate, as it would in the future, a connection between ritual, drama, and the increasing piety of vision that some would see as a central element of medieval social life. That is, spectatorship was to become, by the late Middle Ages, a major social complex governing legal punishment as well as ecclesiastical ritual.[13]

Finally, another drama of the period, the twelfth-century vernacular Anglo-Norman *Adam,* may have been influenced by liturgical sources but was apparently *not* performed as part of the liturgy, was spoken, not sung, and, thus may have been the first actual "early medieval vernacular drama." The sung liturgical drama continued to be part of the Easter and Christmas celebrations, and its continuance might be seen as filling the void left by the loss of the great dramatic liturgies of Holy Week in an age that relied more and more on liturgical presentation *to* the people rather than enactment *by* the people.

The liturgical drama of the tenth and eleventh centuries can be characterized as "processional." One wonders whether, if the people of God had never moved into large basilicas, there would ever have been a liturgical drama. Four early forms that survive, the Visit to the Sepulcher (*Visitatio sepulchri* with its *Quem quaeritis* lines), the Office of the Star *(Officium stellae),* the Office of the Shepherds (*Officium pastorum* with its *Quem quaeritis in praesepe* lines), and the Procession of the Prophets *(Ordo prophetarum),* all involve one or more movements that mirror or comment upon liturgical movements of the Mass of the High Middle Ages—namely, processions, sung dialogues, and the solemn exposition of objects.

Although the *Quem quaeritis* exchange did not derive from the Easter vigil (as Hardison believed) but was, as Karl Young, Clifford Flanigan, and Susan Rankin contend, a trope on the Introit of the Mass,[14] it nonetheless indicates a processional movement at its core. Indeed, it appears at the same period of history both as a trope on the Introit and as a processional before the Mass. It is a short step (and not necessarily one always taken) between singing the trope during the entrance rite and assigning "roles" to the singers who, at any rate, are walking toward the altar. Certainly the altar would have been, in this model, the earliest focus for the "Sepulcher." It was on the altar, after all, that the early *Depositio* (burial) and *Elevatio* (lifting up) of the Host took place during the rites of Maundy Thursday and Easter. Thus the earliest form could have been nearly indistinguishable from the troped Introits of other feasts except for the already existing paraliturgical rites surrounding the burial and "resurrection" of the Host.

By the time of Ethelwold's *Regularis concordia* (c. 970) the *Quem quaeritis* dialogue, at least at Winchester, had been "moved" to a place following the third nocturn of matins, immediately preceding the Te Deum. Here we see the first evidence of something that does not otherwise appear in the liturgy of the tenth and eleventh centuries, namely, the hint of impersonation on the part of the "performers" and the playing out of an action. Moreover, the locus for the "drama" may no longer be the altar but rather the sepulcher of the patron saint of the church or a replica of the Holy Sepulcher.

Thus liturgical, processional expansion may be seen to give way to representational action in a sort of setting. The participants are to walk to the sepulcher "as if searching for something." They wear rudimentary (though ecclesiastical) costumes and carry thuribles representing the oils to anoint the body of Jesus. This is clearly something "extra" that is like the liturgy in its use of movement and ecclesiastical costume but unlike the liturgy in its avowedly representational and presentational mode. What we witness here is the use of the words of the *Quem quaeritis* trope as the dialogue of a play, the *Visitatio sepulchri*.

However, the line is a fine one. Although no ordo of the period directs the participants in the liturgy to "represent" anything or anyone, Amalarius of Metz and Honorius of Autun certainly provided the contemporary imagination with a complete set of representational parameters for Mass and calendar. It is no wonder that Hardison is so taken with Amalarius's allegorical analysis of the liturgy. Such an approach represents a sort of middle ground, a fine line between anamnesis and mimesis, between liturgical en-actment and dramatic representation.

The point is, perhaps, even more finely drawn in the Christmas "dra-mas," clearly influenced by the *Quem quaeritis in sepulchro.* Here the shepherds are asked, *Quem quaeritis in praesepe,* "Whom do you seek in the manger?" They reply that they are looking for Jesus, the Son of God. What they and the rest of the congregation are then shown is, often, a statue of Mary and the Christ Child. Here, as in the Easter drama of the Fleury Playbook, the holy people of God *(plebs sancta dei)* are included as "actors"; they are brought to see Christ and even invited to lay the gifts at the manger.

This would seem to represent a middle way between liturgy and drama proper, a stage in which, just as in the liturgy of the period, enactors (the priest, a deacon, the cantor) speak (chant) on behalf of the people, who are brought to a place where Christ is revealed (either as empty tomb or as Child of Mary). This acting-on-behalf of the people is at the heart of the so-called clericalization of the tenth and especially eleventh centuries. How-ever much abused it would be after Lateran IV, it seems to have begun as a vision of a Christian society in which each order, *oratores, pugnatores,* and *labo-ratores,* performed its specific role in the body on behalf of the others. The exchange among these orders was governed by rituals of gift exchange,[15] and these may be taking place between the *oratores* and the other orders dur-ing the Mass and, in this case, in the early liturgical dramas.

The last form we might examine in this brief summary of the period, the *Ordo prophetarum,* the Procession of the Prophets, is performed dur-ing, and derived from, the Advent focus on the precursors of Jesus. These forms are almost entirely presentational and didactic. They present a pro-cession of Old Testament prophets who then engage in debate with unbe-lievers on the truth of Christ's Messiahship and Godhead. They are appar-ently derived from a sermon attributed to Gregory the Great. This form becomes almost entirely presentational and representational and, as far as I know, was never "performed" away from the spectators, as was, on occa-sion, the *Visitatio sepulchri.*

Although I do not wish to overstate the case, these liturgical enactments may have preserved vestiges of popular participation in the Mass in a pe-riod in which the actual liturgical action was becoming increasingly remote from the people. But the great Gothic cathedrals with their impermeable rood screens were still in the future, and these "plays" seem very much a part of the liturgical world in which they developed. Let us examine a specific instance of the transformation of a liturgical action into one that has become presentational or performative while still a part of the liturgy. This transformation may shed some light on the relationship between the two types of performance that we are examining: the liturgical and the dramatic.

The final 150 years of the last millennium—the age, in the West, of the Carolingians and the Ottonians, the age of Alcuin and the reforms of Benedict of Aniane—were a watershed in the liturgical life of the Western Church. Like a great lens, the Frankish Church would gather the prayers and practices of public worship inherited in all their diversity from the fathers of the church, from the ages of Gelasius and of Gregory the Great, and from the Eastern Empire and focus them into the images of the missals, pontificals, and rituals that would give form to Christian liturgy for the next thousand years. The vast number of sacramentaries, ordines, and other *libelli* (little books) that have survived from this period, in the characteristic Carolingian minuscule of the Frankish scriptoria, formed the basis of the worship of evolving Europe and returned, finally and much altered, to their place of origin. In the form of the Romano-Germanic Pontifical of the tenth century, Europe gave back to Rome the distilled essence of two centuries of devotion to the ways of Rome. Such devotion did not, however, preclude an even greater attachment to the poetry and drama of the Franks, the Gauls, the Germans, and the Goths. That pontifical, from which would arise the *Missale Romanum,* is as much a product of the experience of evolving Europe as of the city that, during the same period, was seeking the ecclesial hegemony of the West.

Nowhere is the cross-pollination of the old West with the new more evident than in the prayers and rites surrounding the blessing of the paschal candle on Holy Saturday, the *sabbato sancto* of the sacramentaries and ordines of the eighth and ninth centuries. In these rites we can trace the confrontation of the rites practiced in the papal city with the desire for lush poetry and dramatic expression (however frequently self-abnegating) that is the mark of the Gallican and Frankish spirit as revealed in the surviving forms. Moreover, that tendency to dramatic enactment, which, during this same time, was giving rise both to the allegorical interpretations of Amalarius of Metz and to the germination of Western drama in the *Quem quaeritis* trope, can be seen in the development of the vigil liturgies from the Gelasian Sacramentary (c. 750) to the Pontifical of Poitiers (c. 875).

There would appear to be two important characteristics of the Gallican and other non-Roman Western liturgies that most clearly distinguish them from the Roman. The first, which has been used repeatedly by scholars to characterize the Gallican rites, is the expansive and poetic language of these liturgies, apparent in the imagery of flowers and bees found in the Exultet. It is this language, found in the Beneventan, Gallican, and Milanese prefaces to the Easter Proclamation, that Alistair MacGregor, in his recent study of the Holy Week rites, sees as the locus of Jerome's objections to these blessings.[16] They are, he believes, the product of a development and expansion of the simple prayer of thanksgiving found in the Apostolic Tradition, a prayer that represents that opposing character of precision and simplicity lauded by Edmund Bishop as the "genius of the Roman rite."[17]

A second characteristic of the Gallican liturgies is less noticed but, I would contend, no less important for the growth of Western culture. It is a distinct fascination on the part of the composers and developers of these rites for what can only be called the dramatic. This dramatic bent is exhibited not only in the use of poetic language in the Gallican Mass but in the ever-growing tendency to see in every action and gesture of the liturgy a meaning and to enhance these meanings by designing liturgical actions to carry them at every possible opportunity. Even liturgical actions that entered the Frankish rites as a result of the northern fascination with things Roman and of the Carolingian program of Romanization eventually were transformed into dramatic actions replete with symbolic meaning for the clergy and people, who found themselves embraced by the multiple meanings of the Holy Week liturgies.

Given that there was a Roman ceremony of the rekindling of the lights at the Easter vigil baptisms, what is of interest to us is a detail, given in Ordo XXIII and in others, concerning the participants in this action. On Holy Saturday, according to this ordo, around the seventh hour, the clergy enter the church. The deacon and subdeacon then hasten to the sacristy, where "two *regional subdeacons* each kindle one of the little torches from the candle which has been hidden since Friday, and they come before the altar."[18] These two *regionarii,* subdeacons who were organized in Rome according to regions (referred to in Ordines XXIV, XXIX, and XXXI as *notariis*), appear in the Frankish rites, even though they have nothing in particular to do with the organization of Carolingian ecclesial polity. In fact, their function is sometimes assigned to personages more a part of the Frankish church (such as the archdeacon in Ordo XXXA). Nevertheless, the Frankish attempt to be faithful to Rome kept these notaries in the rites until, by the end of the ninth century, they became allegorized figures in the very dramatic Easter vigil baptismal rite of the Pontifical of Poitiers.

Let us recall the actions surrounding the blessing of the candle *(benedictio cerei)* as they came to be performed in the Frankish lands during the ninth century.[19] It appears that by the time of Ordo XXVIII, the practice of blessing the new fire followed by the blessing of the paschal candle was well established. The order of service proceeds as follows: (1) the candle having been lit from the new fire, everyone proceeds from the sacristy with the candle, in silence, singing nothing; and the candle is placed in a candle stand before the altar; (2) one of the deacons, having asked the priest for his prayers, stands up and says, "The Lord be with you," and, after the response, says the prayer from the sacramentary (i.e., the Exultet up to the Sursum Corda); (3) thereafter, the priest sits in his chair as the deacon, still standing, continues the blessing with the Sursum Corda chanted in the manner of the Canon; (4) two candles in two candlesticks are lighted, and from these are lit all the candles in the church that had been extinguished; (5) the vigil proceeds with the reading from Genesis.[20]

This basic pattern that makes specific the general direction of the earlier ordines to "bless the candle" is the one that continues in use, with variations, throughout the Frankish lands.[21] The "rite of the two candles," which was present in the earliest Roman practice, and which we may imagine formed the basis of the blessing of the new fire in the papal liturgy of Holy Saturday, continues to appear during the eighth, ninth, and even tenth centuries, in those Frankish ordines that, like Ordines XXIX, XXXI, and XXXII, include the fully developed rite of the *benedictio cerei* using the Exultet. The bearers of the two candles are still referred to as *notariis* (Ordines XXIX, XXXI), even though this term refers to officials in the papal ecclesial hierarchy, and they continue to stand at the right and left corners of the altar, even as the paschal candle is being blessed. They continue, as in Ordo XXIII, to accompany the celebrant of baptism to the font for the blessing thereof.

A peculiar detail concerning this rite in the Easter vigil contained in the late-ninth-century Pontifical of Poitiers points to a process of liturgical evolution that might be called the Principle of Dramatic Justification. This principle, I believe, developed under the influence of the application of the allegorical method to the interpretation of the liturgy by such writers as Amalarius of Metz (c. 780–850).

If, as Baumstark posits, duplications in liturgical formularies lead finally to the loss of the earlier forms, we might expect the "rite of the two candles" to have disappeared with the advent of the blessing of the paschal candle. Such a disappearance does, in fact, eventually occur. In the interim, however, there seems to be a process whereby disparate elements, especially if they carry the weight of authority, can be melded into an overall meaning attached to the whole rite. This meaning, in the Middle Ages, took the form of dramatic allegory. We see it in Amalarius's interpretation of the paschal candle as "the humanity of Christ assumed by his divinity" and as "the pillar that preceded the children of Israel . . . as our pillar precedes our catechumens."[22] This principle can include even the most disparate historical elements in an imaginative dramatic unity. A case in point is the "drama" of the Easter vigil contained in the Pontifical of Poitiers.

In the lengthy rubrics of this Gallican pontifical, the influence of Amalarius is evident from the beginning of the Holy Saturday rites. The candle in its stand is the "type of the pillar that led the people out of Egypt."[23] But the drama does not stop with simple typology. The action in this book is more elaborate than anything found in previous ordines. The lighting of the candle is done with elaborate signs of the cross, made with a taper; and the candle itself is inscribed with the year. After the completion of the blessing according to that contained in the sacramentary *(sicut in sacramentorum continetur),* two candles are lighted from the paschal candle, which are then carried by two *notariis* to stand at the right and left of the altar. This is what we have seen in earlier ordines. In fact, the *notariis* are straight out of the papal liturgy.

The new element, which I believe acts to "dramatically justify" this "rite of the two candles," comes in their allegorical interpretation. The right-hand candle is embossed with the words "The angel who sits at the head," and the left-hand candle has on it "The angel who sits at the feet."[24] This is explained as the "type of the two angels in the Lord's sepulcher sitting together before it throughout the Lord's Day dressed in white robes." These same "angels," after the lessons of the vigil, lead the procession to the font, where three candles standing before the font are blessed using the *Deus mundi conditor.*

Apparently the font at this cathedral is covered by a wooden "city," complete with turrets, one of which houses the chrism in a carved dove.

To celebrate their arrival at this place, which is now both the tomb of Christ and the heavenly Jerusalem, the hymn *Urbs beata Hierusalem* is sung as the bishop descends to bless the water. What is striking here is the incorporation of so many diverse elements into a unified, though polysemous, drama that reveals baptism to be flight from Egypt, burial in the Lord's tomb, and entrance into the new city, Heavenly Jerusalem. That the two Roman *notariis* have been incorporated into this scenario is indicative of the power of tradition and of the Principle of Dramatic Justification.

This drive toward the dramatic was not, however, taking place in a vacuum, especially in the Aquitaine. It seems to me no accident that the earliest extant manuscript of the *Quem quaeritis* trope, dating from the early tenth century, was written at the monastery of St. Martial at Limoges, not far south of Poitiers.[25] This trope on the Introit of the Easter Mass was in use during the ninth century.

As we have seen, by the tenth century St. Ethelwold, in his *Regularis concordia,* had already recorded the custom of having this trope acted by monks dressed in copes at the third nocturn of matins on Easter morning.[26] If such was the temperament of the monastic churches, it is not surprising to find a cathedral involving the people in the divine drama. It is, further, an indication of the way in which the Frankish Church adapted the rites of Rome, even those that made no liturgical sense, to its own increasingly dramatic liturgy, a liturgy that, by the end of the next century, would be well on its way toward a piety of seeing, and in which the dramatic element would become more and more the primary mode of lay participation.

What we have witnessed in this evolution is the process by which a practical act, the illumination of the church for night offices, takes on more and more symbolic meaning as it is interpreted by prayer and gesture. This evolution takes place according to that Principle of Dramatic Justification, by which liturgical actions, retained because of their "authority," are integrated into the rite by being given symbolic and dramatic meaning. We have seen this at work in the transformation of an action as it passes from one ethos to another.

Certainly the papal church in the city of Rome retained the simplest rite of the paschal vigil for centuries. As enamored as the Frankish kingdoms were of the Holy Roman Church, they had their own ethos that, although it might retain the Roman forms, would transmogrify them by a growing search for symbolic and dramatic meaning. That transformed simplicity returned to Rome in the Romano-Germanic Pontifical of the tenth century. The book would be a compendium of all that went before: the blessing of the candle and the new fire using the *Deus mundi conditor,* the setting up of that "great" candle in a stand "before the altar in the midst of the church" where it could be clearly seen by all the clergy and people; the *benedictio cerei;* the Exultet, sung by the archdeacon; and the lighting, from the "great" candle, of two other candles, held by two "men" (no longer *notarii*), from which were illuminated the lights of the whole church.

As for our two *notarii,* they appear again as the bearers of the two candles that were lit from the paschal candle. It is they who lead the bishop and the people to the font and who continue to precede the bishop "until everything has been accomplished."[27] It is, perhaps, Amalarius who lends the interpretation to these rites that will endure into the High Middle Ages. The paschal candle for him is Christ's humanity set aflame with the light of Christ's doctrine, which is "the fount of all wisdom, by which the catechumens' darkness is expelled." The other candles, the ones carried by the two *notarii,* become Christ himself and the apostles, to whom Christ said, "You are the light of the world." These two stand together in the church and together "lead our catechumens to baptism."[28]

The complex interchange and borrowing of verbal and gestural events that we have discovered in the enactment of the Easter vigil represent a process both of *traditio,* the passing on of authoritative material, and of *construction.* Words and actions may remain the same from ordo to ordo to pontifical; but the performance—the way in which they are done and the "meaning" of that doing—undergoes an intentional interpretation by a sort of dramatic expansion. The action, that is, is the object not only of allegorical interpretation in commentaries and expositions of the Mass *(expositiones missae)* but also of statements within the enactment itself that seek to move it from one sort of performance to another.

Drama as Liturgical Commentary: The Late Middle Ages

The period of European history beginning in the eleventh century and culminating in the Fourth Lateran Council of 1215 witnessed a major semiotic shift [29] in Western culture. This shift can be seen in the rise of a new way of expanding and commenting upon the intricate structure of symbols that constituted medieval Christianity, a change that Robert Schreiter characterizes as one from an analogical methodology to a more rigorous and scientific system based in the use of dialectic, metonymy, and, more specifically, the newly discovered philosophy of Aristotle.[30]

Until the rise of scholasticism, the "text" of Christianity could be contextualized by a process that used the same tools of symbolic expansion used since New Testament times. Just as the New Testament writers could find analogies (Paul's types)[31] between the events to which the early disciples bore witness and those proclaimed in the Scriptures, so the early fathers could continue to expand the literal sense of the biblical text through layers of typological meaning: analogical, tropological, and anagogical.

This kind of imagistic expansion through analogy can be seen as the progenitor of the grammatical analysis that informed Berengar's arguments concerning eucharistic presence in the eleventh century. As R. W. Southern points out, Lanfranc's counterarguments using dialectic and Aristotelian categories represent a shift in what we are referring to as the rules of semiotic expansion. "Increasingly," writes Southern, "scholastic theory sought to clarify the physical events which accompany spiritual changes, whether in the consecration of bishops, or in the processes of penance, or . . . in the Eucharist. The Eucharistic dispute was the first important symptom of this change of emphasis in European thought."[32]

The methodology of the "old semiotic" centered on the collection of analogous texts into the so-called *florilegia,* the "little bouquets" of writings of different authorities from different periods, which provided spiritual interpretation of the central biblical texts. The "semiotic advantage" of this methodology was that it involved a basically intuitive or imaginative expansion of the basic text. Such a process, while not precise enough for what we would call scientific observation, was potentially more open to nonspecialists. In fact, the analogical method is really one involving mental pictures and stories and is rooted in the human imagination.

A prime example of this kind of semiotic methodology can be seen in the numerous versions of the legend of the Holy Rood current in the Middle Ages. In this imaginative tale, a central artifact (or *relic,* to use a more resonant term) of medieval Christianity, the cross, is brought into semiotic juxtaposition with the story of salvation as told through those events of the biblical narrative that medieval commentary found important. Both the narrative and the artifact are symbolically expanded in this process to form part of a larger, more unified whole. The cross is seen as the final utterance of the wood that came from the Tree of Life in the Garden of Eden and endured through the ages first as Moses' staff, then as the roof-beam of Solomon's temple, then as the bridge over which the Queen of Sheba passed into Jerusalem.[33] Such an expansion of the text can be rich in "spiritual" and analogical meaning and accessible to what might be called the "popular" imagination; but it would crumble to pieces under the scientific dialectic of the schoolmen and the legalism of the canon lawyers during the twelfth and thirteenth centuries. It represents the flowering of the method for which Berengar was condemned, the method that would be replaced by Lanfranc's dialectic (to which Berengar would have to submit).

But the new semiology, if indeed scholasticism can be called such, employed a methodology that required training and a specialized vocabulary. It reached conclusions that could be thought but not easily visualized or imagined. Such, to take the most famous example, can be said even of Thomas Aquinas's intricately woven theory of transubstantiation. Who can imagine the central miracle of the event: accidents without substance sustained only by the direct miracle of God?[34] Yet, as Berengar had had to admit, the eucharistic bread is the very flesh of Christ eaten and chewed not mentally but with the teeth.

The subtlety of the formulation still required analogies to be communicated and appropriated by unlearned Christians. The more refined the dialectic, the more real became the need to translate the truth into images that could be grasped, seen, touched. In fact, the attempt by scholasticism to hold together the most subtly expressed doctrines with the most physically confessed presence could only act as a goad to the imagination. How could the truth of the Eucharist be imagined without the use of Aristotelian categories? That is the question that the church in the later Middle Ages would have to solve or else risk becoming a gnosis for theologians.

If there was, indeed, a shift in semiotic expansion during the period prior to Lateran IV, it was not a shift that included everyone. One does not have to accept the myth of total illiteracy during the Middle Ages to realize that not all, not even all those literate, not even all those literate in Latin, would have access to philosophical or scientific theology. The manuals for catechesis and confession modeled on Archbishop Peckam's Lambeth Constitutions of 1281 formed the basis for carrying out the renewed involvement of the laity envisioned by Lateran IV. But this involvement would not take the form of initiating the people into the categories of speculative theology. In fact, the exempla and stories and saints' legends, and the mnemonic devices of the preaching manuals and *Lay Folks' Mass Books*, continued to use the semiotic method of the prescholastic period to present the theology of the schoolmen to the laity. This very sense-oriented method of analogy and imaginative symbolic expansion would always exist in tension with the dialectical, scientific, and essentially nonsensual method of official theology.

It is interesting to note that the drama in the West, a form that grew up in the very bosom of the church, began its tentative life in the tenth century, about the same time that the church was beginning to discover a more rigorous way to do theology (the first skirmish in the battle, that between Ratramnus of Corbie and Paschasius Radbertus, had already taken place in the ninth century). It is of even greater interest to our notion of a semiotic shift that the height of scholasticism in the thirteenth and fourteenth centuries was accompanied by the rise of a vernacular nonliturgical drama based on a semiotic expansion of the basic theological text that, like the exempla and the manuals, was imaginative, narrative, visual, sensual, and analogical. Perhaps this drama—which by the fifteenth century was being written and performed in the vernacular by the laity—is a locus of nonscholastic theology, of a popular religion of the people of Europe during the late Middle Ages before the events of the sixteenth century would put an end to such expressions in favor of a unified, official theology.

One other aspect of the semiotic shift that we have been postulating remains to be examined. It is a commonplace that the eucharistic piety of the later Middle Ages was intensely visual, a "piety of vision." This way of appropriating the Eucharist is often dismissed as merely an unfortunate by-product of the exclusion of the laity from Communion especially after the twelfth century. I would argue that the visual focus of popular medieval piety is also an aspect of the perdurance of the more analogical, imaginative semiotic throughout a period when official theology was increasingly focused on a scientific realism accessible only through the categories of Aristotelian philosophy. How, we might ask, could the official doctrines of real presence, transubstantiation, the sacrifice of the Mass, and concomitance be appropriated in a lively and personal way if not through the analogical imagination expressing itself through images of "bleeding Hosts" and miraculous appearances of Christ in the Sacrament?

The Eucharist, like any public event, inevitably invites a confrontation between (at least) two understandings of its meaning. Even in an age of dogmatically defined sacramental theology, such as obtained during the late Middle Ages, there is no escaping the disparity born in that vast abyss between the act and its perception, between the word and its appropriation. Even if there is no conscious formulation of a "popular" theology in opposition to an "academic" or "official" theology, there remains, as with any performance event, a potential (if not inevitable) difference between the perception of the "theologians" and that of the "people."

In fact, one might argue that the term *popular* refers not only to the products of so-called popular culture in stories or music or art but to a particular way of perceiving informed by different categories from those of the "academy." Thus even an "official" doctrine, promulgated by the theologically educated, can be perceived "popularly" in a way that may contradict the intended meaning of the promulgators.

While the scholastic theological tradition, the "official theology" of the medieval Eucharist, is amply documented in liturgical books, conciliar documents, and theological works, it is more difficult, as in any period, to discover how the vast majority of Christians received those official statements. What, in fact, did a fifteenth-century English merchant or carpenter imagine was happening when he was present at the Sunday (noncommunicating) Mass? What was the nature of the Host that was lifted for his adoration and that had been the focus of such intense theological debate since the battle had first been engaged in the ninth century between the "realism" of Radbertus and the "symbolism" of Ratramnus? And what was the effect on him of all the mystery and wonder that had come to surround this event, this meal, this sacrifice, this sacrament?

Among the various inroads into the medieval popular imagination that could be devised (popular sermons, *Lay Folks' Mass Books*, pictures and sculpture, popular heretical movements), one that includes, perhaps, the most creative input from nonacademics and the broadest popular appeal is the one that leads us to the Passion plays of Holy Week and the mystery or cycle plays produced by the various guilds for the great processions that, by the mid-fourteenth century, marked the feast of Corpus Christi in England. Based ultimately upon the scriptural accounts of the history of the cosmos from Creation to the Last Judgment, with special emphasis on the life and passion of Jesus, these plays nevertheless depart at certain critical points from a mere relating of the biblical story and manifest traces of interpretation and imaginative addition that may be seen to flow from the minds of those usually anonymous guild members who wrote, produced, and acted in these expressions of their faith.

The real transition from liturgical drama produced by the church to a truly popular form awaited two momentous innovations of the fourteenth century. The first was the appearance by the mid-fourteenth century of religious plays in the vernacular. The second was the official promulgation in 1311 of the feast, first sanctioned by Urban IV in 1264, of Corpus Christi. By 1350 this feast had spread throughout Europe and was the occasion for the great cycles of vernacular religious drama that have come down to us.

That these plays should find their place in a feast dedicated to the adoration of the consecrated Host in itself speaks volumes about the place of the Sacrament in the popular imagination. So important was the reality and power of this most concrete product of Christian piety that its worship could become the occasion for processions and pageantry and a dramatic enactment encompassing the entire cosmos from Creation to the Last Judgment. By the fifteenth century, the English cycle plays from York, Chester, and Townley (to name only those that are extant) contained, among others, scenes of the Creation and Fall, Noah and Abraham, the Annunciation and the Nativity, the passion, death, and resurrection of Christ, the harrowing of hell, and the Last Judgment (one of the most popular segments, as it usually included a grotesque "hell-mouth" from which issued smoke and fire and the screams of the damned).

Whereas these dramas, having long left behind the interior of the churches, were played out on mansion stages arranged around the public square in France and Germany, in northern England they seem to have borrowed from the feast of Corpus Christi the idea of a procession. It is generally thought that the individual stages, or pageant wagons, were drawn through the streets, pausing at specific "stations" to enact the drama they housed. In fact, there is evidence that by the sixteenth century the procession of the pageants in some places threatened to eclipse the procession of the Sacrament.

By the fourteenth century the rise of the towns and the guilds of craftsmen and merchants had created a new class in Europe. The age of voluntary associations had dawned. Men of like profession or interest banded together to protect and enhance their power and wealth in the evolving middle class. At the same time, the presence of the laity was beginning to be felt in the church in the growth of the confraternities, especially in France. It was to the guilds in England that the task of producing the Corpus Christi plays fell. Once the provenance of clerks, religious drama was now the responsibility of the laity in their secular associations.

Each guild was responsible for the part of the cycle that best expressed its craft. Thus the shepherds produced the Nativity play, the carpenters the Crucifixion, and the bakers the Last Supper. The plays were part of civic pride and the object of economic concern.[35] In the process of revising the scripts year after year, an occasional person of literary gifts might be employed, such as the so-called "Wakefield Master"; but the plays remained the preserve of the lay guilds and of their vision of the content of the Christian faith.

Let us see if we can find in these dramatic enactments a species of popular commentary on the doctrine of the church and, more specifically, on the parallel enactment of the liturgy. If we wish specifically to discover attitudes toward the Mass, we could certainly look at many of the episodes of the Passion and cycle plays for evidences of a theological mind-set. But it would seem most efficient at least to begin with the plays that present the story of the Last Supper or other events that contain eucharistic resonances. Three plays in particular, one from a Corpus Christi cycle, one from a Passion play, and one noncycle play, can serve as models for such a method: *The Last Supper* from the Chester cycle, *The First Passion Play* from the N. Towne plays, and the noncycle *Play of the Blessed Sacrament*.

The Last Supper *from the Chester Cycle*

The mid-fifteenth-century Chester cycle presents a fairly straightforward account of the Last Supper that is derived primarily from Scripture. Unlike the York and Townley plays, it shows no influence of the *Northern Passion*.[36] Yet if we remove the obviously biblical parts we are left with an interpretation of the events that is very much in keeping with late medieval theology. Here is the scene of the Last Supper:

JESUS

> Now, brethren, go to your seat,
> this paschal lamb now let us eat,
> and then we shall of other things entreat
> that be of great effect.
> For know ye now, the time is come
> that signs and shadows be all done.
> Therefore make haste, that we may soon
> all figures clean reject.
>
> For now a new Law I will begin
> to help Mankind out of his sin
> so that he may Heaven win,
> the which for sin he lost.
> And here, in presence of you all,
> another sacrifice begin I shall,
> to bring Mankind out of his thrall,
> for help him need I most.

Then Jesus shall recline, and John shall sleep in his bosom.

> Brethren, I tell you, by and by
> with great desire desired have I
> this Passover to eat with you, truly,
> before my Passion.
> For I say to you sickerly,
> my Father's will Almighty
> I must fulfill meekly
> and ever to be boun.

Then Jesus shall take bread, break it, and give it to his disciples, saying:

> This bread I give here my blessing.
> Take, eat, brethren, at my bidding,
> for, lieve you well, without leasing,
> this is my body
> that shall die for all Mankind
> in remission of their sin.

This give I you, on me to min,
ay after evermore.

Then he shall take the chalice in his hands, with eyes turned to heaven saying:

Father of Heaven, I thank thee
for all that ever thou dost to me.
Brethren, take this with heart free;
that is my blood
that shall be shed on tree.
For more together drink not we
in Heaven-bliss till that we be
to taste that ghostly food.[37]

This account relies heavily upon Luke 22 with some dependence on John 13, especially in the mention of the "new Law," the *mandatum novum* from which would derive the English "Maundy Thursday."[38] What differentiates this scene from the biblical account is the very medieval emphasis on the "reality" of the Sacrament and its character as a sacrifice "to bring Mankind out of his sin."

We must remember that the pattern of worship for the vast majority of laypeople at least since Lateran IV (1215) had become weekly attendance at Mass with Communion once a year. The seeing of the Host as it was raised at the elevation was the climax of a time spent in private devotions as the clergy and choir performed the liturgy. Because the Canon of the Mass was said quietly, few laypeople had even heard the words, and the church had long forbidden any publication of the text. Nevertheless, the church had affirmed ever more clearly, since Berengar's forced submission in 1059, the physical presence of Christ in the eucharistic species.

By the fourteenth century the "realist" approach had won out over other interpretations that took a more symbolic stance, and Aquinas's formulation of transubstantiation remained a solid expression of this doctrine despite challenges from ultrarealists such as Duns Scotus, who had taught the annihilation of the bread during the consecration. It was this "sacramental realism" that the church labored to pass on to the people.[39]

What did *transubstantiation* mean to the laypersons who produced these plays? One echo of the doctrine appears in what, perhaps, is an image derived

from a popular hymn attributed to Thomas Aquinas. In the play, Jesus tells
his disciples, "For know ye now, the time is come / that signs and shadows be
all done." Although there is some relation to the theology of the book of He-
brews in this thought, a more clear resonance is with Aquinas's hymn *Pange
lingua,* a hymn that extols the consecrated bread and was, in fact, used as a
processional hymn during the outdoor procession of the Sacrament on the
feast of Corpus Christi.[40] A modern translation of verse 5 indicates both the
adoration and mystery of the Sacrament and its reality beyond types:

> Therefore we, before him bending,
> this great Sacrament revere;
> *types and shadows have their ending,*
> *for the newer rite is here;*
> faith, our outward sight befriending,
> makes our inward vision clear.[41]

The play presents Jesus as consciously entering into a work of creating
a new reality in instituting this sacrament: "Therefore make haste, that we
may soon / all figures clean reject." This work will be, in keeping with the
view of the medieval church, a "sacrifice" that Christ begins "in presence of
you all" for the purpose of bringing "Mankind out of his thrall." The development of the doctrine of the sacrificial nature of the Eucharist is beyond
the scope of this work. Important for our present argument is the fact that
much of the impetus behind the "realist" presentation of the Sacrament was
the desire to preserve the efficacy of that sacrifice offered each day on the
altars of Christendom.

If this sacrifice were to be efficacious for the remission of sins, then
it could be no less than the sacrifice of the One who had sacrificed himself for the world.[42] What a layperson saw at the altar of the Mass was this
sacrifice, the very "lifting up" of the Christ whose immolation redounded
to their benefit and to the benefit of the dead. In the words of Jungmann:
"That the Mass not only offers God due honor but also redounds to the
welfare of the living and dead was already the conviction of Christian an-
tiquity. But now this side of the sacrifice comes to the fore. In the declin-
ing Middle Ages it becomes the main theme of sermons on the Mass. Formal enumerations of the fruits of the Mass are compiled, especially of those
fruits which derive from a devout hearing of Holy Mass."[43] *The Last Supper,*

then, presents the Jesus known to the people, the one who instituted a new reality, glimpsed in the Sacred Host, begun and continued in his sacrifice by which humankind is given the fruits of redemption.

The First Passion Play *from N. Towne*

The cycle of plays contained in the British Library MS Cotton Vespasian D VIII comes apparently from northern England (Craig argues for Lincoln, Meredith for southwest Norfolk) in the mid–fifteenth century.[44] The play that deals with the Last Supper in this cycle is listed as "Passion I: Maundy III" and is much more complex both in its imagery and in its dramatic action than the *Last Supper* we have just examined. The action of this play goes to great lengths to present the supplanting of the Old Law by the New by using the dramatic device of having the "curtain rise" on Jesus and the disciples having just completed the eating of the paschal lamb as directed in the Old Testament.

Meredith notes that both Ludolf of Saxony in his *Vita Christi* (mid–fourteenth century) and the *Legenda aurea* (mid–thirteenth century) employ this sort of spiritual interpretation of the Last Supper as the fulfilling of the Old Law so that the New might be begun. This play, however, is the first instance of a dramatic presentation of such an allegorical interpretation of the Passover meal.[45] As in the Chester *Last Supper* Jesus defines a new sacrifice to replace the figure of the Paschal Lamb:

> This figure shall cease. Another shall follow thereby,
> Which shall be my body, that am your head,
> Which shall be showed you by a mystery
> Of my flesh and blood in form of bread.
> * * *
> And as the paschal lamb eaten have we
> In the old law was used for sacrifice,
> So the new lamb, that shall be sacred by me,
> Shall be used for a sacrifice most of price.[46]

We may glimpse in the ensuing monologue the kind of instruction that, at least since the time of Amalarius of Metz (c. 780–850), had formed the

meat of preaching and instruction of the laity. Jesus makes a "ghostly interpretation" of the entire account of the directions for eating the Passover
lamb (Exod. 12). One suspects that the source of this interpretation is some
popular sermon or collection of exempla, such as the two books mentioned
above.[47]

Beyond this point, the play continues according to the order of the
Exodus account, with each direction allegorized as a spiritual preparation
for reception of the Host. Thus the "bitter suckling" means "bitter contrition" for sins; "the head with the feet" indicates the Godhead and humanity of Jesus; the leaving of nothing uneaten reminds the disciples that
"if thou understand not all this, put thy faith in God"; the "girdle" is the
"girdle of cleanness and chastity," and so on. All of this, which moves Peter
to make a confession ("Wherefore what I have trespassed in word, thought
or deed, with bitter contrition, Lord, I ask thee mercy"), is a prelude to Jesus'
giving to the disciples "his body." What the disciples have heard is what the
laypeople of the late Middle Ages would have experienced: instruction, confession, and (once a year) Communion.

Alan Fletcher, in an essay on the N-Town plays, understands this sort
of dramatized exegesis to be a clue to the motivation behind the making of
these plays, a motivation that is in keeping with our view of the plays as a
continuance of the analogical and imaginative method of doing theology.
The playwrights, he says,

> were making exegesis into a game, and this not only where the exege-
> sis is explicitly enacted in the drama's narrative, as happens in Passion
> Play I. In a more general sense too, the polysemous play of signs . . .
> could be regarded as drama's counterpart to exegesis, as an extension
> into dramatic terms of exegetical awareness: the literal sense *(sensus lit-
> teralis)* of the narrative is glossed and re-glossed into multivalence by a
> drama which, like exegesis itself, liberates audiences from the necessity
> of limiting apprehension of meaning to single possibilities.[48]

However, whereas Fletcher sees in this a process of playful refraction
of the official sermonic sources into "something rich and strange," I would
suggest that the very liberation from the necessity of a single official meaning (which he mentions) might indicate a deeper and more engaging motivation for retaining this sort of imaginative expansion of the "text." This

imaginative expansion does not have to be subversive in content to remain, nevertheless, a means of retaining the power to do lay and popular theology while still abiding within the fold of official theology. This symbiosis between official and lay theology is at the heart of the success and popularity of these plays and their "piety of vision." Let us examine more closely the image of the eucharistic action presented in the N-Town play.

The consecration in this play is addressed to the Father and does not include the words of institution (which would have been inaudible to the people). Jesus does make clear, however, that, just as the priest's words at Mass are instrumental in the moment of transubstantiation, so "by virtue of these wordes that rehearsed be, / this that showeth as bread to your appearance / is made the very flesh and blood of me." He later declares: "this is my precious body. / Now I will feed you all with angeles meat: / Wherefore to receive it come forth seriatly."[49] That is, the disciples, like parishioners in a medieval church, are to come forward in a line to receive the very body of Christ, made physically present by the prayer of the priest. Except for the self-reference, the late medieval priest could have spoken the words placed in the mouth of Jesus: "And thus through thy might, Father, and blessing of me, / of this that was bread is made my [Christ's] body."[50]

If the transubstantiation of the physical elements of the Eucharist formed one focus of the teaching and devotion of the Middle Ages, the other central debate raged around the concept of concomitance. As the Eucharist became, from the twelfth century on, more and more the preserve of the clergy, and as the elements became more and more looked upon as the physical flesh and blood of Christ, the cup was withdrawn from the laity and from the range of possible accidents that could happen to the "precious Blood" during the course of reception. This, coupled with the desire, in Vorgrimler's words, "to be able to see and receive the *whole* Christ, in his divinity and his humanity,"[51] prompted theologians to develop the notion of concomitance. Drawn via Avicenna from the philosophy of Aristotle, "*concomitance* was a link between a reality and something outside its essence, but inseparable from it."[52]

Using this idea, it could be held not only that the whole Christ *(totus Christus)* is present in the elements of the Eucharist but that the whole Christ is present in each species. "He does not show himself to believe well who when he gives the flesh dips it in the blood; as if the flesh lacks the blood, or the blood exists outside the flesh."[53] Thus the pattern for the laity was Communion in one kind only, but much teaching was expended on educating them to this doctrine, especially after 1415, when the Council of Constance forbade the cup to the laity. This action was occasioned by the *utraquism* (Communion in both kinds by the laity) practiced by the followers of John Hus, who was condemned at this council.

The Cotton Vespasian Passion play shows the strong influence of the doctrine of concomitance in every part. After the long allegorical teaching, when Jesus gives his disciples Communion, he says: "*This is my body, flesh and blood, / that for thee shall die upon the rood.*"[54] As if to make clear the other aspect of the doctrine, he later adds, "Whoso eateth my body and drinketh my blood, / *whole God and man he shall me take.*"[55] This most orthodox Jesus gives to the disciples *totus Christus,* the whole Christ, flesh and blood, divinity and humanity. But this play contains a further detail, found in no other medieval cycle play,[56] that even more reflects the belief of the time.

The disciples, like the laity of the Middle Ages, receive the bread that is sufficient for their communion *toto Christo.* Even Judas is included: "My body to thee I will not deny. / Sithin thou wilt presume thereupon, / it shall be thy damnation verily, / I give thee warning now beforn."[57] The place of Judas in the scheme of salvation had been a matter of debate since the New Testament itself. It was generally assumed that Judas had been one who, having eaten unworthily, had eaten to his damnation.

The Demon in the play, after Judas has gone out, gloats over him: "Ah! Ah! Judas, darling mine! / Thou art the best to me that ever was bore. / Thou shalt be crowned in hell pain, / and therefore thou shalt be secure for evermore. / *Thou hast sold thy master and eaten him also.*"[58] Thus Judas. But his leaving, unlike that in any other play, takes place *before* Jesus gives the cup. It is as if the playwright cannot bring himself to allow to Judas that which is withheld even from the lesser sinners of his own day, namely the cup.

Moreover, the cup, given now to the faithful disciples, takes on the special signification that we may imagine it had for the people of the Middle Ages. Jesus says to the remaining disciples: "To be partable with me in my reign above, / you shall drink my blood with great devotion."[59] The whole Christ is given to all, some for their salvation, some to their damnation, in the Host. To the inner circle, the "clergy," is given the cup by which they are included in Christ's reign. These disciples are then to do Christ's bidding on earth:

Wherefore, Peter, and you everyone,
If you love me, feed my sheep.
That for fault of teaching they go not wrong,
But ever to them taketh good keep.
Giveth them my body as I have to you,
Which shall be sacred by my word.[60]

There lies, at its best, the medieval lay image of the clergy as pastor, teacher, and purveyor of the Body of Christ, set apart by intimate contact with the real source of power. Such an uncritical stance would almost convince one of clerical authorship. But it is necessary to look no farther than the sermons and teaching of the clergy for the source of this piety. Moreover, as we shall see, those who opposed such an image of the clergy were invariably the heretics who also opposed the performance of these plays.

One final play will complete this chapter and introduce us to "material designed, quite self-consciously, to capture the 'popular mind,'" namely the exempla. These collections of miracles, illustrative of Christian virtue and the power of the Sacrament, were provided to the clergy, especially from the thirteenth century onward as sermon aids for the friars who preached, converted, and confessed. According to Rubin: "The sources used by the composers of the tales and compilers of these collections were those which could be found in any library of a monastery or cathedral school: Gregory the Great's *Dialogues*, Bede's *Ecclesiastical History*. A convenient collection of eucharistic tales was Paschasius Radbert's *De corpore et sanguine Christi* of c.831, where miracles were used to substantiate his physical interpretation of the eucharist."[61]

This "pool of miraculous lore" became the main tool for popular instruction, and Rubin quotes Berlioz and David in claiming that the exempla are "lieu privilégié de la rencontre entre la culture savante et la culture populaire ou folklorique."[62] Our contact with this genre is through a play that is both *not* part of a larger cycle and also "the only thing of its kind in Medieval English."[63] I refer to the Croxton *Play of the Sacrament* (late fifteenth century).[64]

It is the plot of this play rather than particular details of text that gives insight into the medieval vision of the Sacrament. The play, based on a story that appears in Italy as early as Villani's *Cronaca* (before 1348),[65] tells of a

Christian merchant who, for a hundred pounds of gold, procures for a Jewish merchant, one Jonathas, a consecrated Host from the church. Jonathas takes the bread to his house and lays it on a table, delivering these lines, which reveal the Christian view of the nonbeliever's understanding of the Eucharist:[66]

> Sirs, I pray you all, harken to my saw!
> These Christian men carp of a marvelous case;
> They say that this is Jesus that was attainted in our law
> And that this is he that crucified was.
>
> On these words their law grounded hath he
> That he said on Shere Thursday at his supper:
> He brake the brede and said *Accipite,*
> And gave his disciples them for to cheer:
> And more he said to them there,
> While they were all together and sum,
> Sitting at the table so clere,
> *Comidite Corpus meum.*

Jonathas and his colleagues Jasdon, Malchus, and Masphat continue to rehearse the story of the Gospel until, speaking of the Crucifixion, they decide to test the Host to see "if he have any blood." With dagger strokes accompanied by cries of "Have at it! Have at it, with all my might!"[67] they hack the bread into four quarters. So far, we have what would appear to be a late medieval piece of xenophobia and anti-Semitism. However, it is important to remember that there had been no Jewish community in England since the expulsion in 1290. Swanson believes that

> in the absence of Jews the stereotype might change its function. "Jews" might become merely archetypes of the opponents of Christ, transferable by analogy to other more immediately perceived threats. That would apply most obviously with plays centering on host desecrations, like that of Croxton (written after 1461), where the play's defence of the doctrine of transubstantiation could be turned mentally against other detractors of the true faith; in the context of late medieval England these would be the Lollards.[68]

In fact, at this point in the play the stage direction reads: "Here the Host must bleed." This detail places this play squarely in the genre of those eucharistic exempla that Rubin describes as "the appearance of eucharistic properties, usually flesh, blood or the Man of Sorrows, to a knowing abuser—a Jew, a witch, a thief, a negligent priest—and the ensuing punishment."[69] Such a story only confirms our picture of the belief in a palpable, real, and physical presence in the Host of the body and blood of Christ. There is no sense here of the subtleties of transubstantiation or of sacramental reality. One is led to believe that if Aquinas was vindicated in the schools, Duns Scotus and his annihilation had prevailed in popular teaching and belief.

However, the purpose of this sort of tale was not merely to reinforce a realist view of the Eucharist. It is the power of God revealed in the sacred species that is the teaching of this play. The tormentors try to cast the pieces of the Host into four gallons of boiling oil; but when Jonathas picks it up, a piece adheres to his hand: "Out! Out! it worketh me wrake! / I may not avoid it out of my hand."[70] His cohorts are forced to bind him, nail his hand to a post, and pluck it from his body.

When they throw the hand with its clinging Host into the cauldron, they are again astonished to find that the cauldron begins to overflow with blood. Jason "with his pincers" extracts the Host and throws it into a fiery oven that proceeds to "bleed out at the crannies."[71] Then the quintessential miracle occurs, the miracle of the Mass of St. Gregory, the miracle hoped for by the people in every elevation of the Host, the miracle that they were taught to see by faith at every Mass: "an image appere owt with woundys bledyng" who speaks to the tormentors:

JHESUS

> *O mirabiles Judei, attendite et videte*
> *Si est dolor sicut dolor meus.*[72]

"Behold and see if there be any sorrow like unto my sorrow." The visual proof of the physical reality of the presence of the Crucified One, sacrificed at each Mass for the sins of the world, is given to the unbelievers. Where other similar stories end with horrible punishments inflicted upon the blasphemers, this play, perhaps because it is so strikingly visual in its presentation, ends with their repentance and conversion.

It is by seeing the wounded Jesus in the bread that the unbeliever is converted and the sinner is made penitent. Doubt is removed. Note that I use the most concrete of nouns to describe this popular understanding. The play presents no theory of signs or sacraments beyond that the bread *is* Jesus, objectively, whether to believer or unbeliever; and that he/it suffers and bleeds out of love.

The action is completed by a further act of mercy. Jesus bids Jonathas thrust his mangled arm into the cauldron. When he does so, his hand is miraculously restored. When the bishop is fetched, so that confession can be made, he too sees the vision and himself repents:

> How this painful passion wrencheth my heart!
> Lord, I crie to thee, *miserere mei,*
> From this rueful sight thou wilt revert.
> Lord, we are all with sorrows smert,
> For this unlawful work we live in languor;
> Now, good Lord, in thy grace let us be girt,
> And of thy sovereign mercy send us thy succour;
> And for thy holy grace forgive us our error.
> Now let thy pity spring and spread;
> Though we have been unrightful, forgive us our rigor,
> And of our lamentable hearts, good Lord, take heed.[73]

The proper and expected response of the creature before the Crucified One is penitence and amendment. This having been accomplished in the play, "here shall the image change agayn into brede." The denouement includes the baptism of the converts and the penance of the merchant, but not before a procession, recognizable to those who have seen the processions of Corpus Christi, is made with the Host to the church:

> Now will I take this Holy Sacrament
> With humble heart and great devotion,
> And all we will go with one consent
> And bear it to the church with solemn procession;
>
> Now follow me, all and some,
> And all those that have been here, both more and less,

This holy song, *O sacrum Convivium,*
Let us sing all with great sweetness.[74]

Certainly this play holds a storehouse of piety and popular devotion that is, in Western culture, a piety and devotion about the physical world, the world in which "seeing is believing." If the unseen world can be imagined, it is only because it can be imagined visually. If it can be believed in, it is only because it is made visible to the eyes of faith, even if that faith, like that of the unbelievers, tests and assaults and attacks the physical world to tease out its hiddenness. It was to this very physicality that the reformers, from Hus and Wycliffe to the figures of the high Reformation, objected. It was from these academics, moreover, that most objections to medieval drama sprang.[75]

Thus official religion would resist the ultrarealism of bleeding Hosts that, while an image perfectly suited to the imaginative semiotic of the plays and exempla, would seem absurd to Aquinas (and even to Duns Scotus). Likewise, there seem to be no plays that present the Last Supper as anything other than a Mass or the reality of the Sacrament as any other than absolutely physical, powerful, and visually miraculous. The images do not contradict official teaching, but neither do they present the problems of scholastic debate. The influence of the Corpus Christi Office seems more in evidence than the entire *Summa.* The popular and the official, at least until the end of the fifteenth century, are poles dynamically unified in a semiotic dialectic.

The borders were to ossify, however, and the poles tear apart into opposition at the very end of the history of the medieval drama. It was when they began to be suppressed by a politically powerful Protestant establishment that they revealed how deeply they expressed the piety of the people. Craig remarks:

> The records of the suppression of the medieval religious plays indicate that people in many English provincial cities were much attached to them and gave them up with reluctance, indeed were persistent in their efforts to keep them alive. Ordinary people were of course not sufficiently learned to be aware of doctrinal issues. The mystery plays were not theological or propagandistic; they were religious. They sought from the beginning to give instruction in the means of salvation. . . . Their offence was that they formed a rallying-point for those

who not only preferred the old customs but the church that had fostered them.[76]

Most of the cycle plays, along with the feast of Corpus Christi, were done away with in England. Those plays that survived were altered in accordance with the prevailing doctrine, especially plays that tended "to the maintenaunce of superstition and idolatrie or which be contrarie to the lawes of God or of the realme."[77] Because of their vast popular appeal, an appeal that derived from the physical portrayal of a very physical reality, the religious drama of the Middle Ages would be too literal for the subtleties of the Reformation debate. The Western world would continue for a while to believe what it saw, but never again would that seeing lead so directly to salvation.

Likewise, drama would cease to be an acceptable hermeneutical tool for the exposition of the liturgy because, after all, dramatic performance requires a concrete enactment and a kind of visual symbol unsuited to dialectic. The drama, from the Renaissance forward, would develop its own life as worship became more and more word centered in the Protestant churches and more matter centered in Roman Catholic eucharistic piety. "Performance" was left to be the sole provenance of the theater.

◆ 3 ◆

Performing Drama, Liturgy, and Being-as-Event

İn January of 1969 an audience entered the auditorium of the Brooklyn Academy of Music to take their seats for a performance of the Living Theatre's *Frankenstein*. On the apron of the stage about a dozen people, dressed in blue jeans and T-shirts (presumably the actors), sat in the lotus position, eyes closed, apparently deep in meditation. Periodically a voice from a loudspeaker announced, "Ten minutes to levitation . . . Seven minutes to levitation," and so on. No curtain had gone up; no lights had dimmed; no other announcement had been made to "start the play." Rather, the audience found themselves in the midst of an event that was as yet undefined. It appeared reasonable to expect that the people on the stage would indeed levitate, such was their concentration and such was the insistence of the voice from the speaker. Whatever would happen, this was not the accustomed signal for the beginning of a play. This event was not clearly a play, although it was, clearly, a performance of some sort. In fact, it made use of the kind of rising suspense and anticipation that is the very essence of dramatic structure. But the audience was prepared for something different because the usual cues, the usual social conventions that marked a theatrical production in the mid-twentieth century, were strangely missing.

Since the 1960s, critics have been examining theatrical events using a set of critical tools that can be grouped under the heading of "performance theory." This approach, which draws on prior work by anthropologists, sociologists, semioticians, linguists, and dramatic critics, can be considered a response to the sometimes radical experimentation with theatrical form that began early in the twentieth century and that is exemplified by the work of such performers as the Living Theatre, the Polish Laboratory Theatre, and the Performance Group. These groups had in common a departure from the conventions that had set the standard for theatrical production in Europe and America since the nineteenth century (if not since the Renaissance). Specifically, the boundaries between actor and audience, stage and auditorium, text and performance, and even theater and "everyday life" were targeted for reorientation or even demolition.

These boundaries, of course, had been permeable throughout the history of the theater. What was perhaps new in the approach of these experimental companies was the self-conscious and intentional transgression of theatrical convention as it had been inherited from the realist playwrights and directors of the late nineteenth century. The theatrical "frame," to use Goffman's term, which had taken the form of the proscenium arch and the box set in the theaters of Ibsen and of Stanislavsky, and which divided the theatrical experience into performers and spectators, would be radically redefined and redelineated in such a way that the audience, at times, found themselves at the center of the dramatic action while the erstwhile performers looked on.

Whatever effects these experiments in dramatic form may have had on theatrical performance in the late twentieth century (and they have been considerable), they have served to cast a bright light on the ambiguities inherent in all the possible definitions of *theater* or *drama* or *performance* or *ritual*. The audience attending the 1853 production of *A Midsummer Night's Dream* at Sadler's Wells in London, like the actors who performed the play and the stagehands who manipulated the wing-and-drop scenery, quite probably believed that they knew what *theater* and *drama* meant. Certainly they saw no similarity between what transpired at Sadler's Wells on Saturday night and what would take place on Sunday morning at St. Paul's Cathedral or even at Notre Dame de Paris. Theater was theater, whatever its genre; and religion was religion, whatever its denomination.

Matters had not been so clear on Easter Even in 952 for the newly baptized experiencing the *Quem quaeritis* at Winchester, nor at the feast of Corpus Christi in 1450 for the guild members performing *The Last Supper* at Chester, nor would they be again in 1968 for the participants ("audience" and "company") in the world premiere of the Living Theatre's *Paradise Now* at the Festival d'Avignon. In all of these instances the definitional lines separating "theater" from "performance" from "ritual" or even from "liturgy" were either unconsciously or intentionally blurred. If the *Quem quaeritis* was an expansion of part of the liturgy into something resembling "drama," and the Chester *Last Supper* was a "commentary" on the liturgy in the form of a festival processional play, *Paradise Now* was to be nothing less than a series of "Rites" that were "physical/spiritual rituals/ceremonies . . . accompanied by Actions . . . performed by the public with the help of the actors . . . to lead to a state of being in which non-violent revolutionary action is possible."[1]

Even less conformable to inherited notions of theater and drama were those "happenings" and "performance art" pieces that usually employed nontheatrical spaces and either made the audience into performers or focused on a single performer who did not necessarily assume a traditional "character." The average theatergoing audience was (and perhaps still is) accustomed to sitting in an auditorium facing a proscenium stage on which actors play dramatic characters involved in a structured action called a plot. The description and analysis of such a theater could assume certain conventions: the actors were not the characters of the play but rather "played" the characters; the audience knew that they were seeing a "play" that was not the same as "real life" (despite certain stories from the American West of overzealous cowboys shooting the "villains" in traveling melodramas); audience and actor usually occupied separate spaces and had different functions in the theatrical experience—the actor performed *for* the audience. The implication of this set of conventions was that the theatrical event, as a work of art, was separate from those who experienced the event as art. Like a painting, though less durable, a play was an "object" made *by* artists *for* an audience. It could be understood by understanding its structure and the craft of those who wrote, directed, costumed, staged, and acted it. But this understanding ran into serious difficulties when confronted with "audiences" asked to carry out "instructions passed out to them when they entered" the gallery for Allan Kaprow's *18 Happenings in 6 Parts* (1959)[2] or with Chris Burden's *Shooting Piece* (1971), in which Burden had a collaborator actually shoot him in front of an audience.[3]

Clearly, something more is at stake here than a simple disjunction between the theory of the drama and its practice. Theatrical performance in the twentieth century, like the other art forms, is begging a far more fundamental question. Colin Counsell draws on the work of Jean-François Lyotard to define that question: "[T]he postmodern work forces us to recognize that reality is something other than our formulations of it, and that those formulations are therefore constructs; in Lyotard's terms, it is to recognize 'the incommensurability of thought with the world.'"[4] Nevertheless, postmodern critiques have not, as a result, ceased to attempt to make an account of the nature of "performance." If anything, the deconstruction of the nineteenth-century theatrical tradition has opened the way for a theory, or for *theories,* of performance that comprehend its engagement in far larger spheres than those of "entertainment and teaching" or even of "art for art's sake." Postmodern performance has more in common with the theater of fifth-century B.C.E. Athens or of medieval Europe than with the plays of Scribe and Sardou. To make an account of such theatrical events, critics have had to look to disciplines that possess the language structures to speak about words, social structures, play, human psychology, and the nature of action itself. That is, they have found it necessary to remove performance from its isolated aesthetic function and to recognize a fundamental performance quality not only to much of social reality as we know it but to the very act of criticism that attempts to perform an understanding of that reality.

Marvin Carlson, in his *Performance: A Critical Introduction,* outlines the approaches that have been most influential in recent years in the development of the broad range of disciplines for which "performance" has become a governing metaphor. I will mention here only those that I believe have some bearing on the application of performance theory to the performance of the liturgy.

Carlson groups the contributors to performance theory under three headings according to the methodology used: "anthropological and ethnographic approaches," typified by the theories of Victor Turner; "sociological and psychological approaches," particularly represented by those of Erving Goffman; and "linguistic approaches," of which the speech act theories of J. L. Austin and J. R. Searle are the most influential. All of the theories Carlson examines have in common their diverse attempts to make a place for performance, even for theatrical or dramatic metaphors, in the "real world" of social interaction among people. To make a place for performance in culture, they perforce must at least hint at what differentiates theatrical performance from cultural performance. They must, that is, confront the very questions raised by the sort of theatrical performance that tries to break down that differentiation. In doing so, they may offer clues to the nature of the performance we have seen in the shifting boundaries between the drama and the liturgy in the Middle Ages. This, in turn, might offer insight into the unexamined performative aspects of the liturgy at any period of history.

The anthropological theories examined by Carlson all attempt both to use the metaphor of performance to understand human behavior and at the same time to differentiate what is called "performance" from human behavior in general. Dell Hymes, for example, contrasts *performance* with *behavior* and *conduct*. "Conduct is a certain subset of behavior, and performance Hymes defines as a further subset within conduct, in which one or more persons 'assume responsibility to an audience and to tradition as they understand it.'"[5] Carlson notes that this "responsibility to tradition" plays a central part in performance theory "that sees all performance as based upon some pre-existing model, script, or pattern of action." Thus we might list as an initial differentiator between performance and other human behavior the quality of patterning or scripting, what Richard Schechner will call "restored behavior."[6] Such a "pre-existing model" can certainly be seen in the literal script of a play, but it is also there, this approach would say, in the courtroom and legislature, in business transactions and national holidays, and in the patterned conduct of the liturgy. What may be of use in such an insight, moreover, is that this patterning is a patterning of *behavior,* something en-acted, and not merely repeated words. Such a model encourages us to look not to the script but to the script's repetition as the significant factor in performance. Further, this repetitive performance within culture may serve either to reinforce cultural assumptions or, on the contrary, to provide a "possible site of alternative assumptions."[7] Mikhail Bakhtin, for example, sees "carnival" as "the place for working out, in concretely sensuous, half-real and half-play-acted form, a *new mode of interrelationship between individuals,* counterposed to the all-powerful socio-hierarchical relationships of noncarnival life."[8] We shall see more of this aspect of performance when we examine the work of Victor Turner. Let us first discover if anthropological theories offer any other insights into a definition of performance.

If the material of performance is some kind of "restored behavior," that behavior must be performed by someone. A second differentiator of performance naturally centers on who performs (and for whom). Carlson discusses how the work of William H. Jansen suggests "a classification model with performance and participation as two ends of a spectrum, based primarily upon the degree of involvement of the 'audience' of the event."[9] As we have seen, the permeability of the boundary between audience and actor has been one of the principal characteristics of nontraditional twentieth-century theater. This same permeability certainly obtained in the liturgical dramas and cycle plays of the Middle Ages. In fact, this "confusion" is perhaps the chief cause of inadequate differentiation between "drama" and "liturgy" among scholars who limit the difference to this audience-performer dichotomy. As Jansen points out, participation and performance lie on a continuum. We are again indebted to Schechner for drawing out this anthropological insight for performance studies. It is necessary to reiterate that the bipartite model of actor/audience may have become skewed and rigidified in early-twentieth-century thought due to the absolute bifurcation inherited with the proscenium stage and "well-made" play.

It is precisely *not* such a dichotomy that informs Milton Singer's concept of "cultural performance." In his *Traditional India: Structure and Change* he argues that South Asians, and perhaps all peoples, "thought of their culture as encapsulated in discrete events, 'cultural performances,' which could be exhibited to themselves and others and provided the 'most concrete observable units of the cultural structure.'" These performances all possessed certain features: "a definitely limited time span, a beginning and an end, an organized program of activity, a set of performers, an audience, and a place and occasion of performance."[10] Singer moves closer to an inclusive definition using all of the elements of dramatic performance by adding to the organization of the event (what we have called patterning or scripting) and the audience/performer relationship the further dimension of "time span"—having a definite beginning and ending—and "place and occasion." These terms serve further to delimit or differentiate performed events from everyday events. They do not, in these anthropological concepts, necessarily differentiate what we would call "theater" from "ritual," whether religious or social. Nonetheless, in gathering up *differentia* for distinguishing performed action from ordinary action, these qualities of specialized time and space are essential. The nature of "cultural performance," like that of the medieval Western drama, confirms that drama and liturgy cannot be differentiated using a single factor such as "costuming" or "characterization," not only because these terms themselves can be ambiguous but also because performance itself overlaps with other cultural phenomena.

One of the most widely discussed (among anthropologists) of these other cultural phenomena has been that whole complex of actions called "play." Perhaps best known from Johan Huizinga's *Homo Ludens* (1950), so-called play theory represents another attempt to discover what distinguishes certain types of human action from the "everyday." Huizinga's characterization of play as "voluntary activity" that is "set apart from ordinary life" underwent an expansion in Roger Callois's *Man, Play, and Games* (1961) to include six qualities of playing, described as (1) not obligatory, (2) circumscribed in time and space, (3) undetermined, (4) materially unproductive, (5) rule bound, and (6) concerned with an alternate reality.[11] This set of *differentia* differs from the one we have been compiling in *not* being concerned with the audience/performer dichotomy. "Play," in this sense, is the play in which all are involved rather than the "spectator sport" in which one group performs for another.

What this definition adds, however, is the category of the end or purpose for which the act is intended. Thus play, as opposed to other activities, is "materially unproductive" and "concerned with an alternate reality." This would seem to be another important category in any definition of a performance, whether of play or drama or liturgy: To what end is the act being performed? Thus, to take an example entirely from the history of the liturgy, there is a difference between an act of public worship that sees its end as the education and edification of the people (as in certain Reformation theories) and one that intends the confection of the Body of Christ and its "immolation" (as in certain medieval Western theories). It may further be said that the various characteristics of any performance are related in such a way that the ends will help determine the other characteristics. We may discover that the patterning, the performer-audience relationship, and the circumscribing of time and space will be handled very differently to achieve these very different ends. Moreover, these differences may be "hidden" behind apparently theological arguments that do not directly address any of these *differentia*. Witness, to continue the above example, the rearranging of "furniture" that occurred throughout the Reformation to bring the Mass into line with the changing theology. Altars were reoriented, pews were added, worshippers sat rather than knelt. Such theological enactments did, in fact, become self-conscious in the Anglican debate over the "black rubric," but how many other theological changes throughout the centuries have been reflected unintentionally in liturgical practice? How many theological changes have been the results of changes in liturgical practice?

The fact is that definitions of drama and play and liturgy are difficult because they require a degree of abstraction from powerful, often unconscious, patterns of behavior. Like the practitioner of yoga becoming aware of breathing or of the movement of thought, whoever would define play or liturgy must do so against the background of actions accepted as either "natural" or beyond analysis. How, that is, does one know that one is playing? How would one *not* know? Such questions lead us into the realm of language, which we will examine more fully below. More specifically, they force us to confront the question of how actions communicate. Gregory Bateson uses the concept (borrowed from Richard Bauman) of performance as "marked" in order to be interpreted in a particular way. His "A Theory of Play and Fantasy" (1954) is concerned with "how living organisms distinguish between 'seriousness' and 'play.' In order for play to exist . . . the 'playing' organisms must be 'capable of some degree of metacommunication,' to signal to each other that their mutual interactions are not to be taken 'seriously.'"[12] Such metacommunication hints at the fact that in the process of performance something is "happening" in the act itself beyond what the participants may think they are doing and beyond the meaning of whatever words or gestures may be called for by the "script." The action is framed in some way so as to differentiate it from what can be called the "everyday." The performance itself "says" something about the possibility of human action. It is in the content of the metacommunication that we shall discover, in the semiotic analysis of Umberto Eco, another essential *differentium* between theater and ordinary life and, by extension, liturgy.

In theatrical performance such metacommunication may be a function not only of the cultural frame or "markings" of the performance but of the organization of the very body of the performer. Eugenio Barba, whom Carlson sees as the performance theorist most closely allied with the anthropological approach that we have been examining, divides potential bodily activity into three types. "The purpose of the body's daily techniques is communication. The techniques of virtuosity aim for amazement and the transformation of the body. The purpose of extra-daily techniques, on the other hand, is information: they literally *put the body in-form*."[13] This set of extra-daily techniques is employed by the performer at the "pre-expressive" level, causing the spectator "to recognize behavior as performance."[14] For theatrical performance this involves such things as "balance, opposition, and energy." Thus Barba's *Dictionary of Theatre Anthropology: The Secret Art of the Performer* presents an elaborate analysis of the precise kinds of movement, especially those that keep the body off balance, used by traditional theater forms, both Eastern and Western, to make the metacommunicative "statement" that what is happening is *other than* an everyday action. Again, as we saw with the differing theological purposes of different liturgical styles, the cues given by different liturgical gestural styles can be seen as metastatements about the nature of the liturgical act. Something quite different is perhaps being "said" by the elaborate, highly structured movement and "manual acts" of the medieval Solemn High Mass than is being "said" by a celebration in which the participants try as hard as possible to use only "daily" technique in movement and gesture. The manner of performance, that is, constitutes a further *differentium* that must be taken into account not only in differentiating performance from nonperformance and dramatic performance from liturgy but also in accounting for the different effects of liturgies performed in different manners.

In all of these attempts to differentiate between one kind of act and another there exists the inherent problem of privileging one term or the other (seriousness over play, everyday behavior over performance) by grounding the second term in the first. Jacques Ehrmann has attempted to expose in these theories the "strategy of creating a false 'grounding' of a binary by making one of its terms the axiomatic base of the other. . . . Ehrmann, like Derrida, resists the model that derives play from a fixed, stable reality that proceeds and grounds it."[15] This represents the basic postmodern critique of unexamined "metaphysical" assumptions. We shall have to take such a critique into account as we examine the liturgy, which itself makes claims upon a privileged reality. Moreover, it is perhaps the privileging of liturgy over any other sort of performance in the post-Reformation period that has blinded liturgical theologians to the performative aspect of the liturgy and, indeed, to the performative nature of sacramental reality. This problem will engage us at the end of the present chapter.

To conclude our examination of what Carlson calls "anthropological and ethnographic approaches" to performance theory, let us look more closely at the suitability for liturgical analysis of perhaps the most widely applied recent anthropological model, that of Victor Turner. Turner's model

of "social drama" is of particular interest to performance theory both because of its use of a dramatic analogy for social change and because it was
developed, in part, in consultation with Richard Schechner and his work as
a practicing theater artist and theorist.

  Turner's model, developed especially in *Dramas, Fields, and Metaphors*
(1974) and *From Ritual to Theater* (1982), derives from Arnold van Gennep's
early-twentieth-century work on rites of passage.[16] Van Gennep had identified three "rites" used by societies to negotiate transitions between "two
states of more settled or more conventional cultural activity": *rites de sépa-
ration* (separation rites), *rites de marge* or *limen* (transition rites), and *rites de
agrégation* (incorporation rites).[17] Turner expanded this schema into a four-
part process *(breach, crisis, redressive action, reintegration or schism)* that he called
"social drama." Describing social life in Ndembu villages, he writes: "[Con-
flict] manifested itself in public episodes of tensional irruption which I
called 'social dramas.' Social dramas took place in what Kurt Lewin might
have called 'aharmonic' phases of the ongoing social process. When the in-
terests and attitudes of groups and individuals stood in obvious opposition,
social dramas did seem to me to constitute isolable and minutely describable
units of social process. Not every social drama reached a clear resolution, but
enough did so to make it possible to state what I called the 'processional
form' of the drama."[18]

  Carlson notes that, unlike the other anthropological theories we have
been examining, which define performance by its frame or marking or other
social dynamics, Turner's looks to the structure or form of these "pro-
cessual units," which he calls "social drama" to differentiate them from the
"steady state" of ordinary social life. This interest in structure, it seems to
me, represents a further refinement of the *differentia* we have already noted
whereby performance is defined in terms of its patterning/scripting. That
is, this approach begins to take seriously the form or structure of an event
as the locus of the event's purpose or "meaning." This interest in the dramatic shape of an event has made Turner's model of particular interest
to performance theory. Because it forms the basis of many of Schechner's
theories and because it takes seriously the relation of performance to social reality, it seems good to examine this model in more detail as a tool, however incomplete, for analysis of the enacted liturgy.

  To begin with, Turner is very much aware that he is engaged in a process of using metaphor. In fact, he specifically wishes to avoid the misun-

derstanding that the kind of process of "becoming" that he sees in culture has anything to do with the "ancient metaphor of organic growth and decay." Rather, he says, "[M]y metaphor here was a human esthetic form, a product of *culture* not of nature."[19] This locates the kind of performance he is describing squarely in the realm of "made things," even if those things are made not by individuals (as in the modern concept of "art") but by human collectives (as may be more the case with liturgies and "social dramas" themselves).

"Social dramas" begin when there is a "*breach* of regular, norm-governed social relations . . . signalized by the public, overt breach or deliberate non-fullfillment of some crucial norm regulating the intercourse of the parties."[20] This breach may be enacted as the flouting of a norm by an individual, but it always represents a "symbolic trigger of confrontation or encounter" between groups over a long-standing societal condition. Next a " phase of mounting *crisis* supervenes, during which, unless the breach can be sealed off quickly within a limited area of social interaction, there is a tendency for the breach to widen and extend until it becomes coextensive with some dominant cleavage in the widest set of relevant social relations to which the conflicting or antagonistic parties belong."[21] This is the stage described as *liminal*, "since it is a threshold between more or less stable phases of the social process."[22] "This brings us to the third phase, *redressive action*. To limit the spread of crisis, certain adjustive and redressive "mechanisms, . . . informal or formal, institutionalized or ad hoc, are swiftly brought into operation by leading or structurally representative members of the disturbed social system."[23] Such action can range from personal advice to juridical procedures to the performance of public ritual. Finally, what results is either "the *reintegration* of the disturbed social group or . . . the recognition and legitimization of irreparable schism among the contesting parties."[24]

During this entire process, but especially in the liminal period, a "new" kind of social relationship and cohesion grows among the antagonists, an "antistructure" that Turner calls "communitas." Being liminal, such relationships often border on the sacred and are especially in evidence in pilgrimages.[25]

As interesting as such a model may be for the analysis of social change and even of history (Turner himself applies it to the events surrounding the murder of Thomas Beckett in 1170), Richard Schechner's use of Turner's work has most affected performance studies and is of most value in the

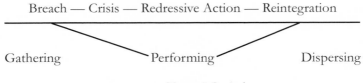

Breach — Crisis — Redressive Action — Reintegration

Gathering   Performing   Dispersing

FIGURE 3.1   Turner's Sociodrama

application of these theories to the liturgy. In a 1975 paper delivered at the
Ethnopoetics Symposium in Milwaukee and later published as "Selective
Inattention" in the *Performing Arts Journal,* Schechner "borrows back" the
dramatic metaphor from Turner and develops a model for theatrical performance based on "social drama." He does this by "framing" the Turnerian
phases of breach, conflict, redress, and reintegration with the acts of "gathering" and "dispersing." These actions, indeed, form an aspect of the metacommunication by means of time and place that "sets off" the theatrical
event in the ways we have been describing. That is, the performance is defined or framed by the participants' own actions of "gathering" before it and
"dispersing" afterward. Moreover, this entire set of actions (diagrammed in
Figure 3.1) fulfills a particular end. "The 'theatrical frame' allows spectators
to enjoy deep feelings without being compelled either to intervene or to
avoid witnessing the actions that arouse those feelings."[26]

The end to which this is done is a certain transformation of the participants. Schechner comments:

> Turner locates the essential drama in conflict and conflict resolution. I
> locate it in *transformation*—in how people use theater as a way to experi-
> ment with, act out, and ratify change. Transformations in the theatre
> occur in three different places, and at three different levels: 1) in the
> drama, that is, in the story; 2) in the performers whose special task it is
> to undergo a temporary *rearrangement* of their body/mind, what I call a
> "transportation" . . . ; 3) in the audience where changes may be tempo-
> rary (entertainment) or permanent (ritual).[27]

That performance can effect transformation (and how this takes place)
will be of central importance when we examine the liturgical theologies
of several modern writers and when we confront the Aristotelian notion
of catharsis in the next chapter. For now, I would like to concentrate on

Turner's and Schechner's examination of the *structure* of theatrical performance and its analogue, social performance. Schechner is careful to differentiate between what he calls "social and aesthetic dramas." The key difference between them is "the performance of the transformations effected."
Social dramas tend to bring about more or less permanent change in the
participants. These include the results of "feuds, trials, and wars" as well
as the permanent changes in status effected by rites of passage and political ceremonies. Aesthetic drama, on the other hand, begets no "permanent
body change." "A gap is intentionally opened between what happens to the
figures in the story and what happens to the performers playing that story."
Because this distinction between aesthetic and social drama raises important considerations for applying performance theory to the liturgy it is necessary to quote here Schechner's complete definition:

> Aesthetic drama works its transformations on the audience. In aes-
> thetic drama the audience is separated both actually and conceptually
> from the performers. This separateness of the audience is the hall-
> mark of aesthetic drama. In social drama all present are participants,
> though some are more decisively involved than others. In aesthetic
> drama everyone in the theater is a participant in the *performance* while
> only those playing roles in the drama are participants in the *drama* nested
> within the performance. . . . The performance as distinct from the drama
> is social, and it is at the level of performance that aesthetic and social
> drama converge. The function of aesthetic drama is *to do for the conscious-
> ness of the audience what social drama does for its participants:* providing a place
> for, and means of, transformation. Rituals carry participants across
> limens, transforming them into different persons.[28]

The structure of the Turnerian social drama is thus nested within the
performance that is itself nested within ongoing social reality. It is differentiated from the everyday by being "marked" or "framed" by the actions of
gathering and dispersing, actions that include both audience and performers.
This framing, Schechner would say, changes the effect upon the participants
from what they would experience in a pure social drama. As in "play," the
very real structure of social reality is reduplicated in a nonthreatening manner that nonetheless becomes a means of transformation. There are, moreover, three categories of performance: "1) aesthetic, where the audience

changes consciousness while the performer 'rolls over' [metaphorically speaking, the performer rolls over the audience like a circular printing press and makes an impression on it]; 2) ritual, where the subject of the ceremony is transformed while the officiating performer 'rolls over'; 3) social drama, where all involved change."[29]

This schema raises questions about the nature of liturgical performance in different periods of its development. Not only do all three categories of performance seem applicable to the liturgy at any one time, but each could be argued to have been dominant in one historical epoch or another. Thus it might be argued that the medieval and baroque Masses appeared to fulfill more of the "aesthetic" definition of performance, while the patristic and modern strive more for something akin to the "social drama." In fact, this model sheds light on the tendency of any sort of "ritual" or "social drama" to eventuate in "aesthetic" performance. Structurally, these categories have a very similar shape and are, as we shall see, affected by the shape of the social structures that frame them.

What would a liturgy, for instance the Holy Eucharist, look like when viewed through the lens of Schechner's model? Are there evidences of the "social drama" structure in the enactment—evidences, that is, of a structure that would lend itself to the kind of "dramatic" commentary found in Amalarius and in the medieval drama?

Certainly, to begin with, liturgies are framed by the gathering and dispersing that Schechner sees as the "nest" supporting the conflict inherent in social drama. The *synaxis* or "coming together" of the early church even gave its name to what would become the Liturgy of the Word. In like manner, the dispersal of the Mass is formalized in a liturgical dismissal *(Ite, missa est!)*. Thus, even during the first eight or nine centuries of the church's life, when clerical dress did not differ substantially from that of the people, and even during the first three centuries, when the gathering place may have been indistinguishable from an ordinary house, the event of liturgical enactment could be marked or framed by this act of gathering and dispersal.

Any public event, of course, is framed by gathering and dispersing. That is what constitutes it as "public." This in itself, however, may be the first characteristic of liturgy that needs to be accounted for. Its synactic nature places it in a position to be confused with other public events (including theater) and defines it as essentially "corporate"; liturgy is a gathered, public event. That is, gathering may be essential to its "meaning" and enactment. Private prayer may be possible, but it may be an entirely different act from liturgy. As such, we would expect to see different forms, different structures, used in the constituent acts of liturgical and individual prayer.

Is there any evidence, once the community has gathered, that the structure of the liturgy has any of the characteristics of a transformative social drama in the sense that Schechner and Turner use the term? To begin with, the shape of the liturgy has changed drastically at several points in its development. Specifically, the place of the intercessions, the homily, and the dismissal of various subgroups (catechumens, penitents) has undergone major alterations even within the Western liturgy, not to mention the divergence of the Western liturgy from the Eastern. These changes have been accompanied by changes in the various Eucharistic Prayers—for example, by the addition of certain intercessions into the Great Thanksgiving itself. Moreover, the advent of the "silent Canon" would have greatly affected the perception of the overall action of the Eucharist because the words, being inaudible to many of the people, would have ceased to have any perceived meaning. The acts of the celebrant, on the other hand, would have still been part of the action and thus part of the perceived meaning. One would seem justified in postulating, then, that the enacted shape of the Eucharist would be different at different times and different places. The question remains whether any of those varying shapes present anything like the breach-crisis-redress-reintegration structure of social drama framed by the community's gathering and dispersal.

I would like to present at this point a tentative sketch of such a model to be critiqued and expanded later when we engage a more neo-Aristotelian structural analysis in chapter 5. What we are seeking is evidence of an enactment within the liturgy of a pattern that is like the pattern of social drama and that, in Schechner's words, "compels the transformation of the spectators' view of the world by rubbing their senses against enactments of extreme events, much more extreme than they would usually witness."[30] This, at any rate, is what Schechner sees as the function of the drama; the liturgy may perform the same sort of transformation but with different means.

The worshippers gather for the Eucharist divided by class and race and gender ("slaves and free, Jew and Greek, male and female"). The *breach* that is inherent in this diversity is brought to a head by the confrontation with the readings from Scripture and especially (for as long as it was a part of the liturgy) with the sermon. Before the sixth century (in most of the

West), this division was enacted, was brought to *crisis,* by the dismissal of the catechumens at the conclusion of this Liturgy of the Word. They, and later also those who were separated because of their sins, were literally excluded from the rest of the enactment until another but related liturgy, holy baptism, would enact their reintegration into the eucharistic community. But that is another story, another liturgy. The dismissal does, however, shed some light on a moment in the social dramatic action of the Eucharist that was to become obscured when the catechumenate (and the "order of penitents") was no longer practiced. It was a moment in the history of this liturgy when the unity of the community was visibly and dramatically enacted, when the prayers and the meal (all of which followed the "expulsion") were a literal sign of membership in a redeemed and thus transformed community.

The Eucharistic Prayer, in its earliest forms, seems to have looked toward the enactment of this reintegration into the "kingdom" through its acts of remembering, offering, and communion. Even such an early proto-anaphora as that found in chapter 9 of *Didache* expresses this desire: "As this broken bread was scattered over the mountains, and when brought together became one, so let your Church be brought together from the ends of the earth into your kingdom."[31] The redressive action that would constitute this new community would come to be seen as nothing less than the remembrance (anamnesis) and offering of the passion, death, and resurrection of Jesus.

This bloody sacrifice always lay behind the "unbloody sacrifice" of the Eucharist. Here the Eucharist comes very close to "rubbing [the people's] senses against enactments of extreme events" in a way redolent of Schechner's definition of aesthetic drama. It is little wonder, then, that the Eucharist began to be interpreted in dramatic metaphors as early as the fifth century (Theodore of Mopsuestia) given that its structure is designed to remember the events of Christ's passion by enacting an event that calls upon that passion to constitute a new and redeemed humanity.

Of further interest, the curtailing of the Liturgy of the Word (beginning in the fifth and sixth centuries with the loss of the dismissal of the catechumens and the prayers of the people and continuing in the eleventh century with the general loss of the homily during Mass) leads to an expansion of the role of the Canon of the Mass in enacting the social drama structure. Thus even as early as Amalarius (ninth century) the Liturgy of the Word is largely allegorized as *preparatio euangelii,* while the Canon bears the full weight of enacting the passion, death, and resurrection of Jesus. Moreover, as is well known, the loss of regular communion of the people (complete by the thirteenth century in the West but reaching back in some places to the fifth and sixth) led to greater emphasis on the transformation of the eucharistic elements as opposed to the eucharistic community. The Schechner-Turner model would explain this as keeping the basic shape of the enacted social drama but translating the moments of the drama to different elements of the Eucharist.

With the return, in modern liturgies, to the more complete early shape (minus the dismissal of the catechumens), the sermon can be seen to enact the function of the break that brings about a crisis in the gathered community, which must understand itself in confrontation with the word of Scripture. The prayers of the people (and confession in the rites that place one at this point) begin the redressive action by the community, offering itself for the needs of the world in communion with Christ, whose ultimate redress is remembered in the Eucharistic Prayer. Finally, reintegration is enacted as a new community is formed of those who enter into communion with one another through their communion with Christ. It is this new community that disperses into the world.

This model, though not exhaustive, is at least suggestive of the need to discover structural analogues to the actual social process in the liturgy. The liturgy, like the drama in Schechner's view, is not merely a theological show. Rather, it has something in common with other social performances; it attempts (to use the scholastic formula) to accomplish what it represents. We will return to this aspect of the liturgy, but first we must continue our overview of other possible performance theories.

Carlson arranges his second group of theories under the heading "performance in society; sociological and psychological approaches." He notes that "more recent performance theory has been much more directly influenced by the sociological model, particularly as represented by the work of Erving Goffman, whose writings in this area have exerted an influence at least equal to, and perhaps greater than, Turner's in the anthropological study of performance."[32] Goffman, in *The Presentation of Self in Everyday Life* (1959), defines performance as "all the activity of an individual which occurs during a period marked by his continuous presence before a particular set of observers and which has some influence on the observers."[33] Note here the set of parameters similar to those developed by the anthropological writers. Here, again, are the performer-observer dyad, the marking off of time and place (presence), and the "end" or purpose to which the performance is done (influence). What is missing is any sense of the structure of the event as in any way different from everyday events. In fact, in Goffman's model, any action may be called performance if it is performed for an audience, even unconsciously. As Carlson rightly notes, the essential quality of performance defined by Goffman is "that it is based upon a relationship between a performer and an audience."[34] Because performance has no particular shape or form, Goffman relies heavily on the notion of framing to differentiate it from the everyday. His *Frame Analysis* (1974) explores this concept, borrowed from a 1954 essay by Gregory Bateson entitled "A Theory of Play and Fantasy." According to Bateson's theory, "[W]ithin the 'play frame,' all messages and signals are recognized as 'in a certain sense not true,' while 'that which is denoted by these signals is recognized as nonexistent.'"[35] This particular use of the concept of the "frame" raises the issue of the place of "reality" or "truth" in performance. Heretofore we have been examining ways to differentiate play or other sorts of performance from the "everyday;" but little has been said (except, perhaps, in Ehrmann's critique) concerning the relationship of performance to reality. Certainly Goffman's definition, because it deals with "play," strongly locates performance in the realm of fantasy or fiction. This framing would serve well to differentiate a variety of forms that are normally called performance, such as play and traditional Western theater. But it would be of less value when applied as such to the liturgy because the liturgy must lay some claim, indeed a very large claim, to being precisely real and true. This, in fact, may be the chief danger in applying performance theory to the liturgy uncritically. Without discerning the structural analogies between performance and liturgy, we would be left with liturgy as simply another subspecies of performance. As much as this may appear to be the case (especially to the proverbial "outsider"), it fails to make an account of the intended end or purpose of the liturgy to those who perform it. Again, we are struck by the fact that adequate definition requires more than a single *differentium* if we are to avoid reductionism.

What is helpful, however, in the notion of framing, as in the previously examined concept of marking, is the way these terms point to a subtle shifting (a metacommunication) of the agreed-upon reality of all the participants in such an event. Reality, that is, is neither a *unicum* nor necessarily independent of those who participate in it. If there can be "play" and "reality," then there may also be the possibility of other framings, including the different microframes of each individual personal act. Moreover, the framing of play may represent a process of metacommunication similar to the framing of a liturgy but with a different "content," a different social reality participated in by the performers.

Such a dynamic is very much at work in the social constructionism exemplified in Peter Berger's and Thomas Luckman's *Social Construction of Reality* (1967). Carlson enumerates three basic assessments of the place of performance and role playing in the construction of the social self. (1) Goffman represents a neutral position. "The 'responsibility' taken by the performer is one of ease and clarity of communication, and the question of whether the 'self' being represented is the 'true' self or not is a relatively minor concern."[36] (2) Plato, Nietzsche, Santayana, Sartre, and Wilshire point to the negative effects of performance as opposed to existential reality. (3) Robert Park, William James, J. L. Moreno, and Berger and Luckman suggest a more positive and creative function for performance or role playing as providing the means by which the self is actually constituted.[37]

The Platonic suspicion of mimesis, which suggests that role playing (and, in fact, any artistic making) subverts or denies the really real, lies at the heart of much of the church's ancient distrust of the theater.[38] Implicit in this suspicion is the question of ethics raised by the phenomenologist Bruce Wilshire. Wilshire argues that any use of performance or theatrical metaphors for social reality (such as Goffman's) "blurs the distinction between 'on stage' and 'off stage' activity, with an attendant *erosion of ethical responsibility*"[39] (emphasis mine). Such a judgment, as is true with any Platonic schema, once again privileges one term of a binary, in this case "off stage." The implication would have to be that there is a really real (Plato's forms) that exists independently of its imitation or expression in particulars. Ethical responsibility would then be responsibility to this absolute. Any sort of performance could be at best only a copy, an imitation, of these concerns that belong to the "real world." Whereas much of the dramatic repertoire clearly avoids ethical responsibility in its desire to entertain, the kind of performance we are examining is not limited to entertainment. Moreover, we shall have occasion to take to heart Louis-Marie Chauvet's critique of the Platonic view of reality with its metaphysical privileging of the absolute;

and we shall look to Bakhtin for a philosophical grounding that sees performance as the basis not only for ethics but for reality itself. It is important, for now, to note that any application of performance theory to the liturgy will, indeed, have to make an account of not only the performance of ethics but also the place of performance vis-à-vis the "real" and the "true."

Goffman's "neutral position," on the other hand, could easily reduce any sort of performance to an act of communication. Communication may be involved in performance (in fact, it may be a necessary element), but I wish to avoid the implication (again, as with the Platonic view) that something is already there that is complete outside of and unrelated to the act of performance. Again, Bakhtin's understanding of "act" will give us a means to meet this objection. We shall take a line closer to that of social constructionism in advocating that the self (and even more than the self) is actually constituted in the performance of certain acts.

Schechner once again points in this direction in his 1970 essay "Actuals: A Look at Performance Theory," in which he argues that art is not a way of imitating reality or expressing states of mind. Rather, the mystery can only be approached by the "altogether upsetting idea of art as an event—an 'actual.'"[40] "An actual has five basic qualities, and each is found both in our own actuals and those of tribal people: 1) *process,* something happens *here and now;* 2) *consequential, irremediable,* and *irrevocable* acts, exchanges, or situations; 3) *contest,* something is *at stake* for the performers and often for the spectators; 4) *initiation,* a *change in status* for the participants; 5) space is used *concretely* and *organically.*"[41]

This sort of event, far from being mimetic in the limited Platonic sense of the imitation of something else "already there," points to the constitution of a unique present reality. In such a process, "if something has happened here and now, if the actual is made of consequential, irremediable, and irrevocable acts and exchanges, and if these involve risk for the performers (and maybe for the spectators too), then there will be changes, new dimensions of integration and wholeness."[42] I would suggest that this "actualization" has distinct similarities to the anamnesis of Jewish and Christian liturgical prayer, that "re-calling," or "re-membering" that is, at heart, a reactualization of the past or the "other" in the present.[43] Such a reactualization is not a mere mimesis of the past, not an imitation. Neither is it divorced from any connection with something or someone else. Rather, the past is enacted in such a way that the present moment (including the present enactors) is brought into a transformative, consequential relationship with it. This is both "restored behavior" (in that it is an enactment, a repetition, of an act) and also utterly new (in that it is enacted in *this* present by *these* actors in *these* circumstances). Moreover, the intention of an "actual" is the transformation (initiation, change in status) of the participants. This is neither the simple communication of a previous reality nor a lessening of the real through imitation. Rather, actualization and anamnesis point to a reality constituted by performance, or, perhaps to use a word less encumbered by mimetic and purely aesthetic resonances, by *enactment.*

Put another way, the terms *mimesis* and *anamnesis* may be differentiated by mapping them against the *ontological* and the *me-ontological,* the metaphysical and the postmodern in the sense explored by Chauvet. Thus mimesis is the attempt to represent or make present that which is "somewhere else" or "something else" (having a separate ontological reality). This is consistent with metaphysical thinking even insofar as there can be the mimesis of the divine Being. The anamnetic, on the other hand, in its Hebrew sense (prohibiting mimesis in the making of idols), is re-calling, not in the sense of making present that which has a separate existence (i.e., the Exodus event) but in the sense of constituting a new thing in the present of which the re-called event remains a symbol or image but is being constituted in its own power and presence in the present. The past event is a symbol used to re-call the meaning of the present event. Thus the symbol, or rather the enactment, is dynamic and constitutes reality. It is once-occurrent Being made answerable (Bakhtin) by that which has been experienced and is remembered as past.

From this perspective, we may view the liturgy as a process not unlike the social construction of reality. At the very least, modern liturgical theologians posit some sort of transformation of the worshippers and of the liturgy itself in such a way that, in the words of Aidan Kavanagh, "what has happened is an adjustment in the assembly of participants to its having been brought to the brink of chaos in the previous liturgical act. This adjustment causes the next liturgical act to be in some degree different from its predecessor because those who do the next act have been unalterably changed."[44] How this change is effected will engage us in the next chapter. It is important to note here that even in nonliturgical performance more is at stake than the mimesis of some absent or imagined object that may or may not be "more real" than the imitation. Performance theory, drawing on the observations of sociology, points the way to an understanding of performance as the way in which reality (at least social reality) is constructed. It may also be noted that reducing the liturgy to social constructionism may meet with objections from theologians who would argue for a deeper or more unique function of the liturgy. How, that is, can we make an account of the liturgy's claim to a unique mediation of the "presence of the Trinity," or of "sanctifying grace," or of "the real presence of Christ's Body and Blood"? Is there, in other words, a difference between actualization and anamnesis, between an actual and a sacrament? To begin to answer these questions we will need some further tools, some of which are provided in Carlson's last category of approaches to performance theory: "the performance of language."

Perhaps no approach has more historical connection with the liturgy than does that which we might call "the linguistic." Because the liturgy, like the drama, is performed in a specific time and place by a specific group of people, like the drama, it leaves no residue for history outside of chance descriptions by its participants and its written text, its words and rubrics. Add to this the deep Judeo-Christian fascination with the Word and the power of words, and it is not surprising that theo*logy,* Godly discourse, has (certainly since the eleventh-century controversy between Berengar and Lanfranc) carried the weight of liturgical interpretation. Because theology uses words not only to describe other orders of words (i.e., Scripture and tradition) but even to describe its own processes, words have come to play the principal part in any understanding of meaning in Christian thought. In fact, meaning may be characterized as an "order of words" analogous to some other order of words (those that "have" the meaning). Moreover, such an order of words can also be used to describe events, gestures, or even experience. What linguistics has come to recognize is that language is constructed according to structures that both make possible and at the same time limit the potential meanings described by these analogous orders of words and thus set limits to meaning itself.

Carlson rightly traces the advent of performance language in linguistics to Noam Chomsky. Chomsky's transformational grammar envisions language systems based on competence (native speakers' ability to generate correct sentences in their language) and performance (the actual sentences generated). This distinction appears to follow the classic division by Ferdinand de Saussure of language into *langue* (the language system) and *parole* (the individual's use of the social sign system in speech acts and texts).[45] The implications of this model both for semiotics and for performance theory as applied to the liturgy are manifold. To begin with, it points to an understanding of sign, whether linguistic or other, as more complex than a conventional "standing for" some absent signified. That is, it implies that reality is not merely a process of naming or signifying ontologically completed objects. Rather, to signify is to participate in the constitution of reality; to perform is not to create ex nihilo, but neither is it merely to describe what is prior to the performance. There is a quality to reality of what Bakhtin calls "once-occurrent Being-as-event." I shall return to this formulation later in this chapter. It is necessary, for now, to point out that the linguistic and semiotic model speaks to the ability of liturgy as enactment to perform theology, sacrament, and even presence in a way unavailable to words alone. That is, because of its performative, embodied quality, a liturgical act is an instance not only of theological content but of the immediate presence of that which it performs. Moreover, by being reiterative (or "restored," to use Schechner's term), liturgical performance has the potential of making evident the performative quality of symbols so that they do not become univocal over time. To use Chomsky's terms, theological competence, though always made actual in performed symbols, cannot be reduced to any one iteration by any one person in any one time and place. The iteration has a context that must be accounted for. Moreover, the iteration, far from being a mere repetition of "something else" (even something as important as the exodus of the Hebrew people or the Last Supper), is seen as a unique performance of the reality that it signifies.

It is, I hope, clear at this point that we are dealing with words not so much in their discursive, or narrative function but as "performatives." This term was coined by J. L. Austin in his William James Lectures delivered at Harvard in 1955 and subsequently published as *How to Do Things with Words*. "The name is derived, of course, from 'perform,' the usual verb with the noun 'action': it indicates that the issuing of the utterance is the performing of an action—it is not normally thought of as just saying something."[46] Words, according to Austin, can be what he called "speech acts," utterances intended not to give information but to accomplish some end. There are three types of utterances or verbal actions: the *locutionary,* or any meaningful utterance; the *illocutionary,* utterances that call into being, order, promise, inform, affirm, or remark (e.g., "Give me that book"); and the *perlocutionary,* utterances that attempt to affect the hearer by convincing, persuading, deterring, surprising, or misleading (e.g., "Nice people don't do things like that").[47] This approach was continued by John Searle, although Searle calls *illocutionary* any intentional utterance and uses *perlocutionary* to describe the effect on the hearer. In any case, Austin and Searle have made more systematic the practical insight of stage actors trained in the tradition of the great Russian director and teacher Constantin Stanislavsky, namely that every utterance of a character in a play is made with some *intention*. In a play, that is, words spoken by characters are generally not merely descriptive or narrative or discursive. Rather, they are actions of the character in his or her attempt to accomplish some goal. This is the *motivation* of the character; and most Western drama until very recently can be analyzed in terms of the use that the characters make of their words (and certainly of the use to which the playwright has put those words in the structure of the play). Austin and Searle contend that the same sort of use of words takes place in everyday life. A similar approach, though more distinctly structural, is that of Kenneth Burke, who examines human motivation in terms of a dramatic model that he calls, appropriately, *dramatism*.[48] To remember that words can have these functions, that they can be acts, that they are, indeed, performative, is central to an understanding of the liturgy as enactment. What this implies is that the action taking place in a liturgical event is not to be confined to the overt gestures, such as the "manual acts," or to large physical movements, such as processions. Rather, the words themselves must be seen as speech acts, as elements in the accomplishment of the intention of the liturgical action, whatever that may be. In fact, words, though privileged in the discursive disciplines of science and theology, may constitute but one element of the sign system of the liturgy.

That the linguistic model can be applied to sign systems other than language is the argument of the varied proponents of semiotics or semiology. Roland Barthes, for example, has applied a semiology derived from Hjelmslev's reworking of Saussure's model to "other significant systems," including garments, food, furniture, and architecture.[49] The field of semiotics is vast and could form the basis of an entire approach to the liturgy. For our present purposes, however, because we are examining performance theories as models for liturgical study, the analysis of a theatrical event by the Italian semiotician Umberto Eco can serve as a useful entrée into semiotics.

His notion of "ostension" opens the way to perceiving the sign potential of things other than words: of objects and spaces and even human beings.

In "Interpreting Drama,"[50] Eco attempts to answer the question posed by Charles Peirce concerning what kind of sign could have been defined by a drunkard exposed in a public place by the Salvation Army in order to advertise the advantages of temperance. As soon as he has been put on the platform and shown to the audience, the drunkard is no longer merely a real body; he is, rather, a semiotic device, a sign. But he is not the same kind of sign, according to Eco, as a word or picture. These have been produced; he has been picked up and shown, or *ostended*. "Ostension is one of the various ways of signifying, consisting in de-realizing a given object in order to make it stand for an entire class. But ostension is, at the same time, the most basic instance of performance."[51]

What is particularly important about this line of attack is that, for both theater and liturgy, Eco's approach facilitates a discussion of the nonverbal components. Although metalinguistic statements may be made about ostended objects ("This is my Body"), there is a process by which those objects and persons, by their very ostension, become signs outside the influence of any verbalization. Eco calls this a "square semiosis": "With words, a phonic object stands for other objects made with different stuff. In the mise-en-scene, an object, first recognized as a real object, is then assumed as a sign in order to refer to another object (or to a class of objects) whose constitutive stuff is the same as that of the representing object."[52]

It is this process, I believe, that creates the precondition within liturgical enactment for the kind of allegorical or, more accurately, dramatic interpretations engaged in by commentators such as Amalarius. Here the symbolic imagination is sparked not so much by what the words of the text are saying as by the framed movement and gesture of the enactors and by the ostension of the objects and architectural space. Deriving his explication from Goffman's "frame analysis," Eco asserts that it is the framing that ostends and makes significant the object. "The very moment the audience accepts the convention of the mise-en-scene, every element of that portion of the world that has been framed (put on the platform) becomes significant."[53] "So the semiotics of theatrical performance has shown its own proprium, its distinguishing and peculiar features. A human body, along with its conventionally recognizable properties, surrounded by or supplied with a set of objects, inserted within physical space, stands for something else to a reacting audience. In order to do so, it has been framed within a sort of performative situation that establishes that it has to be taken as sign."[54]

This framing, however, has a linguistic, or at least metalinguistic, aspect. Eco sees in the ostended drunkard a locus for all the problems discussed by Austin and Searle concerning speech acts and the crucial antinomy of Western thought seen in the "liar paradox": "Everything I am saying is false." Thus every dramatic performance is composed of two speech acts. "The first is performed by the actor who is making a performative statement— *I am acting*. By this implicit statement the actor tells the truth since he announces that from that moment on he will lie. The second is represented by a pseudo statement where the subject of the statement is already the character, not the actor."[55] Here, then, is the semiotic point of difference between dramatic performance and liturgical. Most liturgical theologians (and most practicing Christians) would not want to frame a liturgy with the metastatement "Everything from here on is a lie." Even if the "lie" invoked by Eco is designed only to signal a "willing suspension of disbelief" so that the dramatic event may work its own particular truth, there is something implied in the corpus of liturgical theology that requires a different name for the frame than that which may apply to the drama. Perhaps this is really a species of the same problem encountered by anthropologists as they struggle with the difference between the insider and outsider perspectives on any cultural phenomenon. For semiotics, however, the problem is not intractable. Prescinding from the debate over the relative truth of drama as opposed to liturgy, it is possible to recognize a similarity in the semiotic process of the framing of the event while allowing for the use of a different metastatement to define the frame. In fact, the opening "I am acting" may not be, certainly in the performance events of the late twentieth century, the real frame of performance. Eco himself adverts to this when he declares that the drunkard "says" who he is not in and of himself but in the context of the frame provided by the Salvation Army; and he would signify something quite different if ostended under the standard of a revolutionary movement. Thus the significance of the ostension of the object or person is very much based upon the structure of the event, the enactment, that frames it. It is just as possible for the particular context to make a metastatement such as "Everything I do from this point on is done as if in the presence of God," or "Everything that happens from this point on enacts what it is to be a human being." We shall return to this process when we take up the final cause of the liturgy.

Before turning to the work of liturgical theologians who have approached the liturgy as enactment, it is necessary to find a bridge between the aesthetic theories that we have been examining (however wide-ranging and inclusive) and the truth claims made by traditional theology for the words and acts of the liturgy. If we do not attempt to construct such a bridge, we will be continually hounded by the assumption that the term *performance* and any theories that account for it are "merely" aesthetic events, framed, at best, by suspension of disbelief and, at worst, by outright falsehood and entertaining fantasy. We need, that is, a "middle term" between the "truth" claimed by theological and specifically ethical language and "performance" language, which is so descriptive of human institutions and especially of art. Of the various bridges available (those, for instance, built by Heidegger, or by Habermas), that presented by Mikhail Bakhtin in a recently discovered fragment of his *Toward a Philosophy of the Act* is attractive for several reasons. In the first place, Bakhtin writes from a context of literary and aesthetic theory that is his primary métier. Second, he is concerned not merely with the ethical implications of action but, more in accordance with our present inquiry, with Being itself as act or event or performance. Finally, Bakhtin proposes *aesthetic reason,* which includes emotional and volitional components, to be a valid, if not *the* most valid, means to experience the true. Certainly a theory of liturgy would need to involve these dimensions in order to do justice to the liturgy's performative aspects.

We need to begin with an outline of the theory developed by Bakhtin in *Toward a Philosophy of the Act.* This essay is only the introduction to a larger (not extant) work in four parts that was to encompass "fundamental moments in the architectonic of the actual world of the performed act or deed; . . . aesthetic activity as an actually performed act or deed"; the ethics of politics; and religion.[56] Nevertheless, even this brief introduction contains a systematic and provocative approach to the performance not only of the "social self" but of the "world-as-event." It attempts the same sort of paradigm shift (a turn from what Bakhtin calls the "fatal theoreticism" of Kant) as that which we shall see in Louis-Marie Chauvet's turn, in liturgical theology, from ontology to *meontology.*

Central to Bakhtin's argument is the notion of *act.* "My entire life as a whole can be considered as a single complex act or deed that I perform:

I act, i.e., perform acts, with my whole life, and every particular act and lived-experience is a constituent moment of my life—of the continuous performing of acts."[57] This is the starting point; for Bakhtin the concrete human being in its "once-occurrent uniqueness or singularity," rather than anything that can be abstracted from that singularity, is the locus of any further speculation. This once-occurrent uniqueness cannot be thought of; "it can only be participatively experienced or lived through." Such a living through is a moral orientation within the event of once-occurrent Being-as-event. "This Being cannot be determined in the categories of non-participant theoretical consciousness—it can be determined only in the categories of actual communion, i.e., of an actually performed act, in the categories of participative-effective experiencing of the concrete uniqueness or singularity of the world."[58]

The process of participative-effective experiencing is essentially aesthetic and consists of movement of empathizing, objectification, and return to self similar to that outlined by Hegel. The subject, in aesthetic contemplation, empathizes into an individual object of seeing in such a way that the object is seen "from inside its own essence." This moment is always followed by the moment of objectification—placing the object so understood outside oneself, which is a return to oneself. "And only this return-into-itself consciousness gives form, from its own place, to the individuality grasped from inside, that is, shapes it aesthetically as a unitary, whole, and qualitatively distinctive individuality."[59]

But this aesthetic process, although a species of contemplation, is neither the loss of the subject in Being nor a mere apprehending of Being. Rather, "empathizing actualizes something that did not exist either in the object of empathizing or in myself prior to the act of empathizing, and through this actualized something Being-as-event is enriched (that is, it does not remain equal to itself)."[60] Pure empathizing would be impossible because loss of self in the other would actually lead to an impoverishment of Being—one participant rather than two. Rather, the act of empathizing is what Bakhtin calls the *answerable act,* a deed of self-abstracting or self-renunciation in which "I actualize with utmost activeness and in full the uniqueness of my place in Being . . . : self-renunciation is a performance or accomplishment that encompasses Being-as-event."[61] That is, not only can Being be understood only through my unique enacted participation in it, but it is constituted only in its once-occurrent Being-as-eventness by that enactment.

Being-as-event comes about not by my being absorbed by Being or my absorbing Being but by my doing the answerable act of self-renunciation into the other, recognizing that the other is, in fact, "other," a separate unique other that is now in a specific and unique relationship with my self. The moment of that relationship becomes something new in Being, reducible neither to one nor the other, but enacted in the unique relationship. This is an aesthetic event: "The entire aesthetic world as a whole is but a moment of Being-as-event, brought rightfully into communion with Being-as-event through an answerable consciousness—through an answerable deed by a participant. Aesthetic reason is a moment in *practical* reason."[62]

Such aesthetic reason, or *seeing,* replaces the "fatal theoreticism" of Kantian formal ethics that reduces ethical action to the "possible generation of already performed acts in a theoretical transcription of them."[63] Bakhtin wishes to confront the uniqueness of actually performed acts. "It is only from within the actually performed act, which is once-occurrent, integral, and unitary in its answerability, that we can find an approach to unitary and once-occurrent Being in its concrete actuality. . . . The actually performed act—not from the aspect of its content, but in its very performance—somehow knows, somehow possesses the unitary and once-occurrent being of life."[64]

There is, then, according to Bakhtin, "more" Being in performance than there is in any abstraction from or generalization about Being. Performance is the only action that adds to Being rather than subtracting from it. The implication for theology is that a performed theology would contemplate Being more actually than a theology built only on abstraction and generalization. The Word must be made flesh; and it must be made unique flesh. Because the answerable act is the "actualization of a decision," "the performed act constitutes a going out *once and for all* from within possibility as such into *what is once-occurrent.*"[65]

This performance of once-occurrent Being-as-event has value, what Bakhtin calls *emotional-volitional tone.*

> Everything that is actually experienced is experienced as something given and as something-yet-to-be-determined, is intonated, has an emotional-volitional tone, and enters into an effective relationship to me within the unity of the ongoing event encompassing us. . . . [The] function of the object within the unity of the actual event encompassing us is *its actual,*

affirmed value, i.e., is *its emotional-volitional tone.* . . . No content would be actualized, no thought would be actually thought, if an essential inter-connection were not established between a content and its emotional-volitional tone, i.e., its actually affirmed value for the one thinking. . . . The emotional-volitional tone *circumfuses the whole content/sense of a thought in the actually performed act and relates it to once-occurrent Being-as-event.*[66]

The *emotional-volitional tone* designates the moment of experiencing an experience as *mine*. It is the active appropriation of event as it really concerns me. My relation to lived experience has "a sensuous-valuational—performative—character" that is the attitudinal component of my *answerable act.* Performance has as its "content" this emotional-volitional tone. In fact, Bakhtin calls this sensuous or valuational characteristic of relating *performative*—"the moment constituted by the performance of thoughts, feelings, words, practical deeds is an actively answerable attitude that I myself assume—an emotional-volitional attitude toward a state of affairs in its entirety, in the context of actual unitary and once-occurrent life."[67] This, again, constitutes performance as more than abstraction because performance includes the emotional-volitional tone; and it implies that such a component would be a necessary part of any performed theology.

Morality, in this schema, is action that assumes the stance of *my non-alibi in Being*—my acceptance of the individual concrete uniqueness of my own performed act, not as something designed beforehand according to some abstraction, but as the answerable act of choice and response to the object at that moment. In this act I realize the value not only of self but of other. "In cognizing it, I universalize it: *everyone* occupies a unique and never-repeatable place, *any* being is once-occurrent."[68] Because of the act of going out from self, one realizes that there are many once-occurrent beings and one enters into the performance of Being.

An answerable act or deed is precisely that act which is performed on the basis of an acknowledgment of my obligative (ought-to-be) unique-ness. It is this affirmation of my non-alibi in Being that constitutes the basis of my life being actually and compellently given *as well as* its being actually and compellently projected as something-yet-to-be-achieved. It is only my non-alibi in Being that transforms an empty possibility into an actual answerable act or deed (through an emotional-volitional referral to myself as the one who is active). This is the living fact of a primordial act or deed which produces for the first time the answerably performed act—produces its actual heaviness; it is the foundation of my life as deed-performing, for to *be* in life, to be *actually,* is to *act,* is to be unindifferent toward the once-occurrent whole.[69]

It is this performance of one's unique answerable act in the world that Bakhtin will later define as love, because the basis of aesthetic seeing is to see lovingly. To see lovingly imparts goodness to the other thus seen, as opposed to finding some abstract goodness as the basis for subsequent love. "In aesthetic seeing you love a human being not because he is good, but, rather, a human being is good because you love him. This is what constitutes the specific character of *aesthetic seeing.*"[70] Aesthetic seeing, that is, is no mere passive receptivity to some external value. Rather, it is the active involvement of the seer in enacting the architectonic of the world as valued.

> [T]he center of value in the event-architectonic of aesthetic seeing is man as a lovingly affirmed concrete actuality, and not as a something with self-identical content. Moreover, aesthetic seeing does not abstract in any way from the possible standpoint of various values; it does not erase the boundary between good and evil, beauty and ugliness, truth and falsehood. Aesthetic seeing knows all these distinctions and finds them in the world contemplated, but these distinctions are not drawn out of it and placed above it as ultimate criteria, as the principle of viewing and forming what is seeing; they remain within that world as constituent moments of its architectonic and are all equally encompassed by an all-accepting loving affirmation of the human being.[71]

In fact, the actual world as performed is based on this dichotomy of *I* and the *other* as two value centers "that are fundamentally and essentially different, yet are correlated with each other: myself and the other; and it is around these centers that all of the concrete moments of Being are distributed and arranged."[72] Goodness, that is, derives from act; it is not prior to act. Rather, goodness is constituted by the very act of the loving going-forth from oneself and realizing the other center of unique once-occurrent value.

There are implications of this theory for the performance of liturgy. Liturgy is an act performed by a number of subjects who must find a means of performance that absolutely enables their unique enactedness, that insists upon acts that have no alibi. There can be no place to hide in generalities and abstractions. This is a mandate for the liturgy to be the locus of something more than individual or privately practiced piety. It makes liturgy the enactment of what Kavanagh will call *theologia prima*.

Moreover, it implies that value is not reducible to abstractions; it must be enacted by unique centers of value valuing others and by that act bringing value into concrete enactment. The word, that is, cannot only be heard; it must be enacted or it is less than Being. This implies a relationship between aesthetics and ethics similar to that suggested by Hans Urs von Balthasar in *The Glory of the Lord*. It is the aesthetic, Bakhtin's "lovingly interested attention," that enacts value in the world: "only lovingly interested attention is capable of generating a sufficiently intent power to encompass and retain the concrete manifoldness of Being, without impoverishing and schematizing it."[73]

All schematizing, all Kantian formalism, inevitably lessens actual Being-as-event. The genius of sacramental reality, we might say, is that, because it is enacted, even though that enactment has a definite structure (or because it has a definite structure based upon the unique answerability of a particular people), it does not diminish Being by the presentation of abstraction. Rather, it enacts what we would call presence, the actual once-occurrent Being-as-event that is the locus of actual value. In the liturgy, the participants, the performers, presumably enter into a relationship with once-occurrent Being-as-event in the real present, providing that they do so answerably, with no alibi in Being. Faith, from this perspective, is answerability, what the enactors bring to the enactment that constitutes the real present that the theologians call God.

Before gathering up the insights into liturgical performance that we have derived from these various inroads into performance theory, we must recognize that such a critique has already entered into the formulations of contemporary liturgical theologians. Though usually employing models derived from linguistics, several writers from different denominations have attempted to move beyond theological discourse about the liturgy into an examination of the theology enacted by the liturgy.

Contemporary liturgical theology requires that we distinguish among three basic intentions in the works of those who engage in this discipline.

Any one of these approaches can claim the privileged place of *theologia prima,* depending upon the viewpoint of the particular theologian.

Although various contemporary writers would differ as to which might claim historical primacy, liturgical worship or theological reflection, it is clear that the twentieth century has inherited a long tradition, codified by the Scholastics, of understanding the liturgy through the lens of the treatise *De sacramentis.* This, the first intention, understands the liturgical theology as *theology of the liturgy,* a systematic analysis of the sacraments derived from prior systematic reflection on (e.g., for Aquinas) the Incarnation and/or Christology.[74] From this perspective, the liturgy is an expression of the doctrine of the church, although this does not preclude discovering support for this doctrine in the actual liturgical tradition. Nevertheless, for theology of the liturgy, the final critique of the rite is its fidelity to right doctrine (orthodoxy).

For the second intention informing liturgical theology the liturgy itself is conceived as *theologia prima.* In what might be termed *theology from the liturgy,* actual Christian worship, as enfleshed in the rites of the church, is the primary way in which Christians *do* theology. Such an approach often takes as its standard the *lex orandi legem statuat credendi* of Prosper of Aquitaine.[75] In its most extreme form, this approach sees the actual locus of theology to be the liturgy as performed by the people. Reflection on such worship can be verbal and even systematic, but liturgical theology achieves its proper modality only in the transformation of the lives of the worshippers and/or in the performance of the next liturgy.[76]

A third approach, exemplified by Louis-Marie Chauvet's monumental *Symbol and Sacrament,* goes even further to develop a theology that is, in method and content, liturgical. Such *theology as liturgy* discovers in the symbolic action of liturgical rites the very structure of theology. The liturgy, in this intention, reveals not merely elements of doctrine to be systematized, or even expressions of doctrine to be developed in subsequent liturgies, but rather the very symbolic, dialogical, and intersubjective nature of reality, which, for Chauvet, can be encountered only in a concrete sacramental mode. Because he makes a definitive break with the entire onto-theological tradition of Western theology in favor of adopting an entirely symbolic model, Chauvet accomplishes a move into a whole new liturgical theology hinted at by others but impossible as long as something "more real" than the liturgy was seen to be hidden "behind" the liturgy.

Although several liturgical theologians (Kavanagh, Power, and Chauvet, for example) hint at a silencing of interpretation, at a purely liturgical or ethical expression of liturgical meaning, none has ceased to reflect on the liturgy using other verbal structures as tools of analogy. It seems that we cannot transcend words without using words (perhaps the ultimate demonstration of the primacy and givenness of language). Nevertheless, it would appear that great caution must be exercised when reflecting on the liturgy so that verbal analysis does not reduce the liturgy to a verbal modality. The basic problem with most current symbolic analysis is that it originates in linguistic theory and assumes that all symbols function on the analogy of language.[77] Thus metaphor and communications theory[78] are used as critical tools for "unpacking" the meaning of Christian liturgical events. Perhaps more useful for discovering the unique character of ritual acts are those approaches (especially Power's and Chauvet's)[79] that draw on the insights of anthropology, ritual studies, and the involvement of the body as the essential locus of liturgical worship. However useful the application of verbal analogies to bodily experience (and Chauvet applies them brilliantly), the body, as the primal experience of space and time through its ability to move (the most primary act) and touch, may be said to embody categories that are a priori even to language. It is in locating both the human being and symbol in act that we will discover both another dimension of the liturgy and the grounding of the creation in the economic Trinity, the acts of the One who proclaims, "I will bring to pass what I will bring to pass" (Exod. 3:14).[80]

The critique leveled against Western metaphysics both by Heidegger *(Being and Time)* and by Whitehead *(Process and Reality),* in the simplest terms, identifies a preoccupation in philosophy with Being as an objective, and therefore ultimately static, a priori in which beings somehow participate. Such a system (which Chauvet characterizes as onto-theology in its religious manifestation, or, simply as metaphysics) leads inevitably to a cosmos spoken about as objects (material or spiritual, visible or invisible) arranged (or not) in (more-or-less empty) space. Action, in such a cosmos, can consist only of action by objects on objects and requires a "first principle," an "unmoved mover," to be set in motion. Act, at any rate, is understood as secondary only to Being, since only beings act.

The "Copernican revolution" in postmodern philosophy has been the deconstruction of this objectivist cosmos by means of Heideggerian critique, Whitehead's philosophy of organism, and linguistic theory culminating in Derrida's deconstruction. *Process* and *becoming* have replaced *being* as the central metaphor for understanding reality.[81] This shift has led to several radical reorientations in our way of speaking about God (theo-logy) and of being in relationship with God (lit-urgy). In fact, the greatest reorientation made possible is the one implied by the very difference between the notion of *logos* (word and speech to and about God) and the *ergon* (the work, the action of relation with God). Needless to say, the "work of the people" *(leiturgos)* has always had its place in Christian theology. Nevertheless, it is only with the radical deconstruction of the word by the word in the late twentieth century that we can begin to be free of the tyranny of verbal objects that has gone hand in hand with onto-theology. To begin to understand reality as a dynamic, intersubjective realm of occasions (Whitehead), events, acts, is finally to discover a language in which the mystery of the Trinity begins to have some relationship to actual occasions, to *Dasein*. It is to begin to take seriously for theology and life and liturgy the illocutionary potential of language and the insight that the basic structure of our being is acting. Human beings, that is to say, *are* by virtue of their *act*. Being-in-time (Heidegger) is always act because in time there must be process and change and becoming.

Being has been understood by the metaphysical tradition as somehow outside this process. Thus God has been conceived as Unmoved Mover, *Ens suprema,* the first cause who is himself (paradoxically as the subject of prayer and the "author" of creativity) unchanging, unchangeable, unmoved, eternal. It often seems as though the only thing that has kept Western thought from complete ossification has been the impossible, irrational, unspeakable mystery of the Holy Trinity.

Theologia prima, at least as it is defined by Kavanagh and others, since it includes the rites as performed, cannot be the domain of liturgical theology, if by that we mean only systematic reflection on the liturgy. Reflection is, of necessity, a verbal, discursive process, whereas the liturgy is primarily act, event, *dromenon*. Kavanagh and Lathrop recognize that the liturgy can reflect upon itself insofar as any subsequent liturgy is a response in kind to its antecedent. But this process is not theology as such unless there is no difference between theology and praxis. What I am proposing is that *meaning* is a term we use for an order of words that reflects upon and restates another order of words. Thus one might ask, "What does that prayer mean in terms of our theology?" The answer would take the form of an order of words analogous to the words of the prayer. However, the liturgy is composed primarily not of words whose task is to mean, but rather of words that function as acts in a structure that is one of action. Thus liturgical words are, in Austin's term, illocutionary: they function as elements in a structure of action.[82] They are of the nature of verbal gestures and thus cannot be understood outside the context of enacted rite.

This enacted structure of the liturgy does not preclude our reflecting upon it using words. It does, however, mean that these words will be not a description of meaning but rather a description of act, of the shape of the action. Subsequently we will ask, then, not "What does this mean?" but "What are we doing?" The question of meaning is placed a step further away from the rite itself. To answer it requires first a description, an account, of the dramatic structure called liturgy, a structure that is not merely one of meaningful words but rather one of structured action, intentional action, movement in a direction. Until this unified action, in which word, physical gesture, sound, movement, and plot function as an architectonic whole, is discovered, there is nothing upon which to reflect. Rather, we run the risk of reflecting on a part that has an entirely different meaning when taken out of its context in the rite. We become, that is, like the blind men describing the elephant as a wall, a snake, and a large leaf because they do not perceive the wholeness of the beast. We look for moments of consecration; we think to involve people more merely by giving them more words; we explain everything as if liturgy were under the order of meaning and not under the order of act. In Lathrop's incisive insight, we remove the tension of the juxtapositions that make the liturgy, like the Trinity that they incarnate, irreducible to univocal verbal structures. A similar reductionism can be seen in those forms of literary and dramatic criticism that try to reduce theatrical plays to a theme. *Theme* is a *meaning* word, a description of some verbal scheme supposedly analogous to something in the drama.

The issues raised by the performance theories we have examined point to a structure in any enactment that is not entirely reducible to such verbal analogies. We may summarize these issues, issues that raise questions about the liturgy as performed act, under six headings. Each of these has been considered by one or more of the theorists to be essential to the definition of performance: (1) patterning or scripting, what Schechner would call *restored behavior;* (2) the relationship of actor to audience, performer to spectator; (3) time and place; (4) the purpose or end for which the performance is enacted; (5) the "framing" of the performance by some means of metacommunication; and (6) the relationship of performed act to ethical action and of both of these to what might be called reality or, in Bakhtin's term, Being-as-event. The next chapter will attempt to gather up these elements into a working definition of liturgy and to answer some of the questions raised by their application to liturgical enactment.

✦ 4 ✦

Constructing Sacrament
Poetics of the Liturgy

From our survey of performance theories in the previous chapter it is apparent that "performance," especially when viewed in all its historical and anthropological variety, cannot be defined by just one of its characteristics. It is not simply the presence of costumes or dialogue or a stage that enables us clearly to differentiate among theater and liturgy and the performance of civic ritual. Only by making an account of a variety of elements, and of the differences among these elements in such forms as theater, liturgy, and performance art, can these forms be differentiated as well as fruitfully compared.

But there are not, it would appear, an infinite number of elements. Time and again the various theories, whether anthropological, sociological, or semiotic, return to the same categories in their attempts to define performance. There is always *something* (some script or behavior), being performed by someone (often for someone else), using some performative *means* and *manner* (some place and time and action), to accomplish some *end*.

I will argue that these categories are the same as those proposed by Aristotle as necessary for any complete definition of a "made" (as opposed to "natural") thing and that a definition including all of these "causes" can be derived for any sort of performance — theatrical, social, or liturgical. I would contend, furthermore, that only in taking account of all the causes can adequate differentiation be made among the various kinds of performance.

Specifically, I would like to use as a model for this differentiation the famous definition of *tragedy* that Aristotle "gathers up" in book 6 of the *Poetics*. But I will take as my guide the critical posture taken by the Chicago school,[1] whose members used the *Poetics* not merely for the analysis of classical Greek tragedy but as a "handbook" for a systematic program of criticism encompassing all artistic making. Although they would make a case for this having been Aristotle's intention (because *poesis* is a category of practical philosophy that includes all "making"), such an approach to the *Poetics* is recent and has earned the Chicago critics the name of "neo-Aristotelian."

Two seminal essays by Chicago critics, Elder Olson's "An Outline of Poetic Theory" and Richard McKeon's "The Philosophical Bases of Art and Criticism,"[2] set forth a method for employing the basic structure of Aristotle's argument for understanding not only the structure of the various arts but also the way in which the various critical tools used to examine those arts are related to each other. Central to this enterprise is a rediscovery of the aptness for critical theory of Aristotle's four-cause analysis.

The basis for such an analysis, as becomes evident in the various attempts to define *performance,* is found in the very process of trying to describe or account for artifacts, non-natural occurrences, of any kind—art objects, institutions, performances, liturgies, or even the critical tools that try to account for these. Adequate differentiation requires that any made thing be defined by all four of these causes: the formal (the object), the material (the means), the efficient (the manner), and the final (the end). Any made thing (whether a tragedy, a painting, or a liturgy), that is, is made somehow (whether in language or in colors or in acts) in some medium (whether speech or paint or gestures) to some end (whether to move or to teach or to please or to transform). Form is imposed somehow upon some matter for some purpose.

Although there are many critical approaches to a single art form, criticism that follows this "neo-Aristotelian" model focuses primarily on the structure of the particular work and the way the four causes define it. Specifically, the Chicago critics were interested in how the structure of the work itself produces its particular end, what Aristotle called the "powers and effects" of the work.

I would suggest that the liturgy, like art, is not "natural." That is, it does not, like the oak tree, grow from something else; rather, it is form imposed upon some matter. As such, whatever it does, or purports to do, or intends to do (whatever its "peculiar effects"), it does because of the particular way its parts are synthesized.

Aristotle's *Poetics* begins by deriving the particular *parts* out of which tragedy (as well as, to some extent, comedy or epic) is constructed. To differentiate between liturgy and other constructs using this model, we would have to determine the number and nature of the parts out of which it is constructed and how they are arranged to achieve the effects of the liturgy (whatever they may be). The model for such a definition can be derived from the one that Aristotle gathers up for tragedy in the sixth chapter of the *Poetics*. In Olson's words, "[P]oetics is a science concerned with differentiation and analysis of poetic forms or species in terms of all the causes which converge to produce their respective emotional effects."[3]

The important caveat here is that I am not arguing that the liturgy *is* tragedy or even a species of drama. Rather, I am proposing that it is possible to make a more complete definition of the structure and function of the liturgy by using an analytical model that takes into account all the parts of the liturgy and that can be used to define other made things, including drama and other kinds of performance, for purposes of comparison.

Each of the performance theories that we have examined approaches performance from the point of view of one or more of the "causes"—the *object,* such as Turner's social drama or Schechner's restored behavior or Huizinga's "play"; the *means,* exemplified in all the discussions of the *ostension* of the person as sign and the use of bodily technique; the *manner,* explored in discussions of time and place and performer and audience; and the *end,* implicit in all the discussions of play and the function of social drama and the transformation of the audience. What, we might ask, would be the shape of a definition that included all these causes? How would such a definition of liturgy compare to that of tragedy or comedy or a court trial or a football game?

In chapter 6 of the *Poetics*, Aristotle presents his famous definition of tragedy: "A tragedy, then, is the imitation of an action that is serious and also, as having magnitude, complete in itself; in language with pleasurable accessories, each kind brought in separately in the parts of the work; in a dramatic not in a narrative form; with incidents arousing pity and fear, wherewith to accomplish its catharsis of such emotions."[4] Debates have raged for centuries over this definition, especially over the nature of "imitation" and "catharsis."[5] For our purposes, however (as for the Chicago critics), the way the definition is *constructed* rather than the specific elements of tragedy will become our model.

Certainly there would be real historical reasons to see a purely fortuitous sequence of events in the liturgy. No one composed its structure in the same way that Shakespeare composed Hamlet. However, the crafting of the liturgy can be seen as a process of selection and pruning of already existing material according to the prevailing will of an individual (e.g., Gregory the Great or Benedict of Aniane) or of a culture (the "Gallicanization" of the Roman liturgy). In either case, some form has been imposed upon the inherited material (or merely accepted as given) by someone for some end. The problem is to discover the end for which certain structures and practices are retained while others are excluded.

Returning to Aristotle's definition of tragedy, we discover that it is indeed derived from all four causes; and from these causes Aristotle derives the "six parts" of tragedy. Because the stories are acted, says Aristotle, "it follows that in the first place the Spectacle (or stage-appearance of the actors) must be some part of the whole."[6] This is the *dramatic manner,* the efficient cause of tragedy.

The "language with pleasurable accessories" comprises the *means* of tragedy, which Aristotle further describes as melody (or music) and diction. These represent the material cause of tragedy. The *object* of imitation in tragedy is "an action," but not just any action. Rather, tragedy presents a "serious action, complete in itself . . . with incidents arousing pity and fear." This is the formal cause; and Aristotle goes on to say that the governing or architectonic part is the plot, the form of the action, which is itself caused or motivated by character and thought.

Finally, the *end* to which tragic action is imitated is the whole, completed work of art, which is seen to be complete because it accomplishes, in its wholeness, the catharsis (the purgation, purification, or clarification) of the pity and fear aroused by the incidents. Plot, according to Heffner, is the end, the purpose of tragedy, and as such has the other five parts as means. From a complementary point of view, plot as the form of tragedy has the other parts as its matter.[7]

These well-known "six parts" of tragedy are specific to tragedy and are logically derived from the nature of tragedy when looked at according to causal analysis. Thus epic, or what we would call narrative, shares with tragedy the linguistic means and can even share the object of presenting actions through characters and their motivations. What clearly differentiates the two forms is that tragedy employs the dramatic or enacted manner whereas narrative employs a purely linguistic manner.[8]

Dramatic manner is, in fact, the part that most clearly relates the text of the drama to theater, the enactment of drama. The "manner" is, therefore, an important starting point for any definition of liturgy because it represents the locus of the most confusion between liturgical and other enacted forms. That is, failure to find a specific liturgical manner (as opposed to the dramatic manner) is what leads to confusion of liturgy with drama and reduction of the difference between the forms to "costuming" or "impersonation." Moreover, failure to make an account of liturgical manner is what leads to a reduction of the liturgy to a narrative or purely linguistic form in the work of many liturgical theologians.

Aristotle's *Poetics* presents a critical tool that recognizes in the drama a primary organization around action rather than words. The key to this structural approach to the drama is based on Aristotle's insight that the drama is an architectonic whole, the parts of which are related to each other, not as in the random grouping of the logs in a cord of wood, but as in the functional unity of the parts of a shoe or of a chair. Thus plot, character, thought, diction, music, and spectacle are arranged in a causal hierarchy, each acting as the *formal cause* of the part below it in the order and as the *material cause* of the one above.

Thought, which is the idea content of a work, its organizing meaning, is thus emphatically not the organizing principle of enacted drama. Rather, the plot, by which Aristotle means the structured action of the play, the carefully crafted revelation of the characters through what they do and suffer and the production of the powers and effects of the drama through the movement of *discovery* and *reversal,* is *the* architectonic part upon which any discussion of meaning depends.

One cannot, that is, confront an enacted work, whether of drama or of liturgy, without confronting the structure of the action, the effect of the plot, on the participants. Any reflection that limits itself to what is said in a play or in an enacted rite will discover only the literary meaning of the event—the thought.

In other words, the way a drama engages those who experience it (the much-debated process of the arousal of fear and pity and their catharsis), is directly related to the structure of the play as crafted by the playwright. Whatever psychological effect a drama might have upon an audience, that effect is mediated not by words and ideas alone but by the unfolding of the action of the play.[9]

I am not suggesting that the sort of crafted manipulation of the "audience" that makes for good drama has any place in the liturgy of the church (however often, in fact, such manipulation may have been employed throughout history). What I wish to extrapolate from Aristotle's theory is the realization that *any* enacted form operates on the level of something analogous to plot structure and that in ignoring that structure we run the risk of missing—remaining unconscious of—the real organizing principle of the enactment. In the case of the liturgy, this is not only to remain ignorant of the vision of the church and of God mediated by the structure of the rite but to ignore the *effects* that this structure will have, inevitably, on the participants.[10]

I am not implying that the liturgy of the church is reducible to some sort of ritual drama, even one as serious *(saxios)* and effective as the Greek tragedy of Aristotle's analysis.[11] What I wish to borrow from Aristotle is the point of view that looks for a principle of organization for the liturgy in the structure of the liturgical act rather than merely in the thought content of its diction (prayers, readings, canons, hymns, tropes, and even rubrics).

That one would look to something analogous to dramatic structure for such a point of view is not surprising given the history of ancient religion and its offspring, the drama. A case could be made for the notion that the allegorization of the liturgy during the Middle Ages was an attempt, given the tools at hand, to recognize this deeper (dramatic) structure in the rites of the church.[12]

Karl Young's differentiation of liturgy and drama on the basis of the presence in the latter of "impersonation" is thus too simple and applies only to the actors rather than to the structure itself.[13] O. B. Hardison is more correct in claiming that those who described the liturgy allegorically in the Middle Ages were not so much looking at it in terms of levels of personification or of character as interpreting the structure of the liturgy as drama. None would have said that the priest was "playing Christ" (even if standing *in persona Christi*). That is, the difference between drama and liturgy is more complex than just saying that in *Hamlet* the actor is pretending to be Hamlet whereas in the liturgy the celebrant is not pretending to be Christ.

All of the medieval allegorical commentaries on the Mass concentrate almost exclusively on what can be seen or heard rather than on the content of the prayers or their theological meaning. Thus both Amalarius and Honorius derive their "dramatic" sequence from the enacted rite. The prayers, even the Canon of the Mass, are interpreted as something that Jesus or someone else is *doing*. The interpreters have no particular regard for the text of the prayer (which would, at any rate, have been unheard by the worshippers). Even such liturgical texts as the people would have heard, such as the proper preface, are interpreted (for example, in Honorius) not according to their content but rather as an enacted moment, in this case "the cry of Christ hanging on the Cross."[14]

What sort of act, then, is the liturgy? What are its parts, its architectonic part? What are its effects, and how does the ordering of the parts produce those effects? What elements would be included in the modern liturgy as opposed to, for example, the liturgy described in the *Ordines Romani* as used in the Middle Ages? Was the intention the same? How does the method of enactment bring about different ends? And what are the effects of liturgical enactments that do not include "sacramental acts" in the traditional sense—worship services, preaching services, revivals, hymn singing, and so on?

To answer these questions we must consider not only the object of the liturgy (what it is) but also the liturgical manner (how it is performed).[15] It was the structure of Aristotle's analysis that the Chicago critics found useful and not merely his analysis of Greek dramatic forms. Just as Aristotle hints at the application of his model to the analysis of narrative or comedy, so it can be applied to other art forms, including those organized around actual temporal and spatial enactment—what we have been referring to as *performance*.

In the liturgy, as in the theater, this performance may need to include texts or scripts as elements of the whole. However, the principle of organization for performance does not necessarily have to be the "imitation of an action" that is the very definition of the dramatic plot. Certainly we would be hard pressed to believe that a liturgical form such as the Eucharist is unified around the presentation of a dramatic action in the same way that, for example, *Oedipus Tyrannus* is. Even the most avid of the medieval allegorical commentators did not simply map the "story of Jesus' life" onto the Mass.

The action of a liturgy, that is, may have a unity, a shape, a completeness, that produces an effect; but we shall perhaps have to discover the organizational principle of that unity, that shape, in something other than the unfolding of a story. It may, indeed, be something more akin to the development of the kind of social drama posited by Schechner and Turner. It may be closer to the process of transformation or incorporation or embodiment spoken of by sacramental theologians in this century or to the confecting and offering of the Body of Christ looked for in the late medieval Mass. In any case, if we proceed, like Aristotle, to examine the logic of enactment in order to derive a definition of the liturgy as enactment, we cannot escape the liturgy's procession through time, its movement from beginning to end, its signs of change and transformation.

Enactment: The Liturgical Manner

To define the specifically liturgical manner, we must bear in mind that liturgy can be approached both as a structure of performed acts (like the theater) and as a structure of language (like the drama or narrative). In fact, individual performances of a liturgy might be said to bear the same relationship to the liturgical texts (sacramentaries, ordines, prayer books) as theatrical performances do to dramatic scripts. The texts serve as the (perhaps) central reiterated element in the restored behavior of the theatrical or liturgical performance.

In this discussion of the liturgy, although I must borrow (for the present) terms that Aristotle uses in his definition of the drama, I am using them with a difference. The action around which these liturgical events are unified is not the imitation of an action—the representation of a story that one expects in art. Rather, the unifying principle of the Eucharist would seem to be the unfolding of an action of reconciliation or offering or praise or thanksgiving performed by the people involved in the liturgy.

It is a present action that is framed by certain marks by which it is set apart from the ordinary actions of everyday life but that nonetheless depends for its meaning on a past story that informs it and shapes it at every turn. It is not the imitation of the biblical narrative either as a whole or in part, but it does invoke that narrative, and it does enact in the present what that narrative proclaims as its ultimate import.

This enactment in present symbolic action of the argument (not the episodes) of the biblical narrative would seem to conform to the definition presented in chapter 3 of the term *anamnesis*. It is clear, once again, that this process does not imply a representation or imitation (mimesis) of the narrative. Rather, it implies the performance of an action that accomplishes in the present the end for which the narrative is remembered and of which the narrative is the shape and meaning. The unity and completeness of this anamnetic plot, then, would be not the imitation of the whole biblical narrative but the making present and accomplishing of what is proclaimed in the biblical narrative.

An examination of the structure and words of the Eucharist, for example, would reveal what the church understands as the nature of that presence and that proclamation in any particular historical period. Liturgical action, that is, focuses the historical unfolding of God's "mighty acts" into an enactment that is repeatable (restored) and that includes the present participants, the enactors of the sacrament.

Such an act differs from that imitated by tragedy in that its shape, its plot, is governed not by such dramatic elements as discovery and reversal, or probability and necessity—principles essential for producing the tragic powers and effects—but by conformity to the way God acts in human community. Because that act is understood by Christians to be revealed in Holy Scripture and, above all, in the life, passion, death, and resurrection of Jesus Christ, the shape of that narrative informs the liturgical manner in many ways but above all in requiring that the God who acts be remembered and worshipped in anamnetic enactment.

Let us, then, call the manner of realizing this anamnetic plot, this present performance of what is proclaimed in the Gospel, by the word *enactment*. *Enactment* in this definition, however, denotes not a thing or even a specific act but rather a manner of performance, the liturgical manner that is analogous to the dramatic manner of Aristotle's definition of tragedy in that it occupies the same place in the structure of the definition. Just as the manner, the efficient cause, of tragedy is dramatic, so the manner of the liturgy is enacted (Figure 4.1). As we have seen, this implies not the mimesis of an action but the anamnesis of an act—specifically, an act that includes human beings and God as enactors.

The enacted or liturgical manner (like its analogue, the dramatic) takes embodied action in time and space to be the only adequate locus for

Aristotle's Cause	Definition of Tragedy	Part of Tragedy	Definition of Liturgy	Part of Liturgy
Efficient (manner)	In dramatic form	Spectacle	In enacted form	Time/ space

FIGURE 4.1   Efficient Cause

confronting the reality of human life in time and space and thus the only adequate locus in which to meet the God whose Word is made flesh to dwell among us. This is why *lex orandi legem statuit credendi*—not because of some legal grounding of belief in practice but because any reduction to mere de-scriptive words of the act of prayer by human beings in time at some real place, is, as Bakhtin would argue, something less than the reality of the act of prayer itself—an impoverishment of belief.

The manner in which the liturgy is performed, we must remember at the outset, is always one of an actual action or series of actions done in ac-tual time and an actual place. To examine the liturgy in this way it will be necessary to discover the shape of these actions *done* in the liturgy. But this itself necessitates an understanding of the relationship within the liturgy of acts, words, and material things. It requires, in other words, a concept of symbol that includes more than a conventional assigning of some secondary verbal meaning to a word or object.

Rather, we will define *symbol* as the relationship that holds together par-ticular concrete occasions (matter, words, persons) and the act that is their being-through-time. The implication here is that material things are mo-ments or concrescences (to use Whitehead's term in *Process and Reality*) of their histories and that these histories are dynamic unfoldings of action (ei-ther acting or being acted upon) that include the particular object (occasion) in a whole matrix ("plot") of relationships with other occasions. Thus act becomes word by means of symbol.

In the liturgy, words are almost always illocutionary in that they are symbolic occasions for acts of praying, offering, remembering, receiving. Moreover, the things (matter) and people of the liturgy are themselves both enacted and acted upon as their actual histories unfold in the "plot" (the structured movement) of the liturgy. Act, as intentional event, is shaped gesture, gesture that is formed by meaning or, simply, by language. It has a syntax and a grammar that, like those of language, are contextual. Like the verb *to act* there is something repeatable, something intentional in the liturgical act. But it is realized only in the unrepeatable present of the verb *to do.* The "text" of the action must be done in concrete gestures and words in a particular time and place, in an appropriate context.[16]

What mediates act and doing is what we have been calling the "manner." Performance is adverbial; it "is the answer to how in distinction to what."[17] Variations in the liturgical manner will account for many of the differences in liturgical enactment throughout the centuries and among various Christian groups. They will account for the "texture" of the actually performed rites.

Enactment (as manner), that is, far from being peripheral to liturgy, is of its very essence. It accounts for the relationship between the repeatable, intentional, named act of the liturgy and that act's realization in the unrepeatable, actual present of the worshippers. It is the way in which gesture, word, and material presence are brought into relationship, are "thrown together" *(symbolein).*

The shape of that sacramental act, the form of what the sacramental manner enacts, will be the architectonic part of the liturgy — the analogue of the dramatic plot. The manner in which that "plot" is realized is "enactment," and the material of that manner is *symbol* — gesture and matter shaped as word.

Symbol: The Liturgical Means

If the liturgy is realized in an enacted manner, then the means of that enactment, the form of the symbol, are, as we have seen, language, gesture, and matter (Figure 4.2).

Heffner speculated that Aristotle had ordered the six parts of tragedy hierarchically, each part being the formal cause of the one below in the sequence and the material cause of the one above. Likewise, we may view the words, gestures, and matter of the liturgy as the form of the liturgical enactment. The reality of each of these parts, that is, is contextualized by its place in the liturgical enactment. The words and gestures, as well as material things themselves, have no meaning outside their meaning in the symbolic relationship by which they become the form of the act of worship.

Aristotle's Cause	Definition of Tragedy	Part of Tragedy	Definition of Liturgy	Part of Liturgy
Material (means)	In language with pleasurable accessories	Diction Music	In symbol	Word Gesture Matter

FIGURE 4.2. Material Cause

They are not made up primarily of denotative references to absent objects or concepts real or imagined. Rather, words and gestures and matter form, in liturgical enactment, a single symbol, a language, that is apprehended only in the enactment itself.

Thus, to take an example from the Eucharist, the material "bread" is not merely described denotatively as the "Body of Christ" and then eaten as such. Rather, a complex symbolic (i.e., liturgical) enactment is made in which bread and other elements are taken, blessed, broken, and eaten in thanksgiving, remembrance, offering, petitioning, and invocation carried out by means of word and gesture.

Neither word, nor gesture, nor matter alone would constitute the form of sacramental enactment. Such a symbol, such an act, can be formed only by the mutual contextualization of word, gesture, and matter. To use the linguistic analogy, gesture and matter become word and thus become meaning. But equally, word and matter become gesture, become illocutionary speech acts, just as gesture and word are "materialized" in objects and "take flesh" in persons.

Because the enactment of the liturgy uses for its means symbols that are not merely signs but performances of word, gesture, and matter, even material things are redefined through their sacramental use. The function of the actions of the people and the clergy together has to do with the conferring or expression or enacting of value or reverence or respect or meaning on an object by the way one reacts to it.

For example, the reverence for the consecrated Host has been misunderstood in a number of ways: (1) like uranium or fire, it must be handled carefully because of its innate ability to cause weal or woe; or (2) because it is very precious, rare, delicate, or valued like some rare butterfly, it is protected because of its extrinsic or economic value. Both of these forms of reverence are different from an enactment of reverence or respect or devotion or adoration that is a symbolic action. In such an action the object itself becomes a partner or subject in an enactment of the attitude or the appropriate response to the presence of the holy. In the language of scholastic sacramental theology this is called *ex opere operato.* The very enactment of the sacrament is what enables the individual and the community to have, to do, to express, and to participate in such an attitude.

Outside of the biblical narrative or the mystical experiences in which such an emotion or attitude is a spontaneous event, most people do not have the opportunity to experience it—except as it is enacted in the place of the liturgy. This presents an important means of enabling people to experience such respect and carefulness without having to *pretend* that the object— the book, for example—has become something else. Rather, the object is part of a sacramental symbol (the liturgical means) of which it is the focus: it is holy in the enactment of holiness (the manner).

In that enactment, the church is given a chance to experience an attitude that can inform daily experience, including the experience that we have of other people. We act toward bread and wine and other persons in the liturgical context as if they were the presence of Christ, the presence of the divine. We act as if there were a place in which there was devotion and adoration so that we may become respectful and devoted and enact that respect and devotion in the world.

Anamnesis of Trinity: The Object of Liturgy

So far, we have used the parts of Aristotle's definition of tragedy to derive the means and manner of the liturgy. If Aristotle would understand tragedy to be made "in language with pleasurable accessories" (diction and music being the means) "in dramatic form" (implying the manner employing spectacle), then liturgy can be said to be realized in symbol (i.e., using words, gestures, and matter as means) in enacted form (in the frame of time and space). What remains to be discovered is the object of liturgy—what it enacts liturgically—and its end—what it accomplishes.

Perhaps one of the most important insights into the enactment of the liturgy from this perspective has to do with what Aristotle calls *unity*. The central message of the *Poetics* is that the entire action of a play, the plot, needs to have a unifying principle in order to avoid being merely episodic. Episodic plots have no necessary sequence of events; the individual actions have no necessary relationship to each other through either probability or necessity.[18]

Now, there is no doubt that the liturgy grew by a process of accretion, borrowing (often of inappropriate parts, such as the Gallican use of the stational liturgies of the Roman urban rite), and local custom. It is not, that is, the sort of "made thing" of which Aristotle speaks. Nevertheless, beyond the recitation of historical data, would it not be possible to reflect theologically about the shape of the rite as it has been accepted in much the same way as we reflect on the canon of Scripture as it has been accepted?[19] Is this not, again, the impetus behind the allegorizing of the Mass and, indeed, behind all theology *from* the liturgy? Would such reflection, moreover, not allow us to discover where, in any act of worship, the worshippers might be falling short of what they intend to be doing?

Let us take, as a concrete example of such a critique based upon the unity of the plot of the Eucharist, the position of the General Confession in the Holy Eucharist contained in the Episcopal *Book of Common Prayer*. This act of corporate confession of sin derives ultimately from a similar act (done in English) as a preparation for receiving Communion inserted into the Latin Use of Sarum some years before the promulgation of the First Prayer Book (1549). It formed, in that use, a separate service of confession placed in close proximity to the Communion rite to which it was a sort of prologue.[20] In the 1979 book, such a prayer of confession usually follows the Prayers of the People and immediately precedes the Peace. What the prayer intends to do as an illocutionary act is fairly obvious. It is a petition for forgiveness couched in the second-person plural. Its connection with the Peace, which immediately follows it (after the Absolution), shows it to be the enacting of reconciliation among the members of the church—their willingness and empowerment to enter into the table fellowship that follows. This much of the structure reveals a movement from confession through reconciliation to communion. But what of the structural juxtaposition of the confession with the action that precedes it?

The act immediately preceding the confession in the Episcopal book is the Prayers of the People, the intercessions for the church and the world. This act can be seen as a response to the entire Liturgy of the Word, an action of intercession on the part of those who have heard the good news in

Scripture and homily and creed and who bring that Word into creative dialogue with the needs of their world. The question we may ask of the liturgy is: What is the act symbolized in the movement from the Liturgy of the Word (which has reached its climax in the prayers of intercession) to the act of confession-reconciliation (which leads to the offering and the table)?

It may certainly be said that one of the New Testament responses to the Word is repentance; but does that repentance *follow* intercession and prayer for the world? Historically, rather, did not the community of the faithful (the baptized) offer its prayers in these intercessions; and were not the catechumens and penitents in the early church specifically excluded from participation? The point is that the placement of the act of confession at this point in the liturgy, while perfectly understandable from the point of view of late medieval revisions, is not related to the "plot" structure of the Liturgy of the Word. It intrudes as a sort of afterthought or rebeginning expressing an essentially medieval structure of sacramental piety. How, that is, does one get from intercession to confession as the unfolding of a unified action?

The alternate position for confession at the beginning of the Liturgy of the Word (the place also occupied as an alternative in the English *Alternative Service Book* and as the only location in the Roman Sacramentary) would seem to say that we come before God penitently both to hear and respond to the Word and to offer and partake in the Communion. This is essentially the action of a community that is on the journey, one that is renewing its life and entering together into Word and Sacrament. What is lost, in this structure, is a symbol of the conversion and reconciliation occasioned by our response to the Word proclaimed in our midst and of the sharing of the Peace as a sign of that reconciliation. The Roman rite, it might be added, places the Peace in even closer proximity to the act of receiving Communion, thus linking it to the transformation of our lives occasioned by the anamnesis and oblation of the Eucharistic Prayer, and making it a sign of the communion possible among a redeemed humanity. It seems, in that rite, to be more an eschatological sign, a proleptic act, than an act of reconciliation. In fact, the prayer preceding the Peace in the sacramentary, although it asks Christ not to regard our sins, places the Peace firmly in the context of the gift of Christ to the apostolic church for which that peace is a sign of the unity of the kingdom.[21]

Certainly the oldest position for the Peace is after the prayers and before the offering.[22] This position seems to link it dramatically (i.e., through its symbolic act) with constituting the assembly of the faithful who are invited to the supper. This assembly has already heard the Word and prayed for the world. It enters into the Great Thanksgiving together as an act of the church. From this perspective, the Episcopal insertion of the confession, no less than the frequent interruption of the Eucharist after the Peace for announcements, represents a disruption in the unity of the act that confuses the movement of the liturgy. Likewise the Roman placement of the Peace after the Eucharistic Prayer seems to exclude the people from the eucharistic offering and make of Communion a (perhaps too realized) eschatological event.

These examples serve to illustrate that the varying placement of acts within the movement of the structure of the liturgy creates, first, a very different shape for that "plot" and, second, a consequently very different constellation of meanings. Note that we have not even considered the words used in these acts. "The peace of the Lord be always with you" is an illocutionary act that functions differently according to its position in the (potentially) unified action.[23] Such an analysis could, when applied to historical liturgical forms, reveal theological positions "hidden" within the structure of the liturgy. When applied to contemporary forms it could enable us to do in fact what we intend to be doing in our acts of liturgical worship. At the very least, it might offer clues as to why certain things just "do not seem to be working."

It was argued above that the mode of enactment involved in the liturgical manner is anamnesis as opposed to the mimesis of Aristotelian tragedy. It was further argued that anamnetic performance is shaped not by the kind of arrangement of incidents appropriate to the effects of tragedy but rather by the accomplishment of whatever it is that is proclaimed by the biblical narrative. The narrative itself, that is, does not determine the unfolding of the liturgy, the arrangement of its "incidents."

The commentaries of Honorius of Autun and Amalarius of Metz appear to have attempted to discover such an ordering. However, Amalarius, at least, never reduces the Mass to a dramatization of a unified biblical action in the same way that Sophocles, for example, dramatizes the story of Oedipus of Thebes. As Paul Jacobson points out, "Amalar never presents an interpretation of the liturgy as an unswerving, linear imitation of Christ's earthly life. Rather, Amalar furnishes an elliptical view of salvation history, with an array of overlapping images designed to symbolize, and thus make present, the mighty works of God in Christ."[24]

I would suggest that "the mighty acts of God" is the object of the anamnesis of the liturgy. Insofar as there is a narrative telling of this act in Scripture, the "plot" or shape of the liturgy at times seems to follow the shape of the narrative. Thus the pattern presented in the Acts of the Apostles of preaching-repentance-conversion-baptism can be mirrored in the sequence found in the modern Eucharist of scriptural readings, homily, (prayer and) confession, and the passing of the Peace.

But the liturgy is not primarily such a mimetic enactment. Rather, it is the anamnesis of what might be called the act, or work, of God in the present moment. The shape of that act, the ordering of its constituent parts, would, then, determine the shape of the liturgical enactment. This shape, the architectonic part of the liturgy, certainly has a temporal and spatial dimension, but it is not merely the enactment of the biblical narrative. What, we must ask, is the form or shape of God's act, and how is that act re-called in the liturgy? What sort of God is one who is active in these events?[25] This, in turn, prompts the anthropological question: Who are we who engage in such activities, who thus enact our relatedness to each other and to the One we call God?

The God who reveals Self in history and in the person of Jesus Christ is not an object, even the highest object, even the ground of objects. If reality is, indeed, unfolding act, event, occasion, then the Trinity, in the Trinity's ceaseless relationship of procession and offering, its acts of love, is a more fitting model for reality than any metaphysical absolute (as Chauvet has rightly pointed out).[26] Moreover, the liturgy, as enacted anamnesis of that procession (the economy of creation/salvation) and as enacted offering (the sacrificial movement of our acts in Christ through the Holy Spirit), is a more fitting encounter with that reality than any purely verbal reflection.

If human beings are made in the image of God, our ability to act in time and space, and not some state of being, defines that likeness. Or rather, our being-in-time, our becoming, *is* the only symbol of our being; and it is a real symbol because it reveals the "process-ion" of love that is the act symbolized in every moment, every occasion, every event that we name self and world and other. We do indeed exist in deep relationship with all things because those things are, in fact, moments in a process, in a "plot," and are therefore neither fixed nor immutable nor separated from our subjectivity by some literally spatial gulf ("[M]onads have no windows," as Leibnitz lamented).

The ultimate symbol of such a reality, for the Christian, is the living, undergoing, dying, and rising of Jesus Christ. The overarching movement of this symbol is the economy of creation/salvation of which the doctrine of the Trinity is a picture, an image, and an icon. In fact, the logical consistency and philosophical rigor that we apply to the expounding of this doctrine is itself a symbolic expression of the deeper plot structure by which the act of "Trinitying" unfolds. This act is nothing less than the act of creation that is the continuing process-ion of the Trinity.

The old problem of trying to maintain God's transcendence over creation no longer obtains with this language. Transcendence becomes a matter of continuing creation rather than of external independence. It is the transcendence of the cross, a transcendence that is never prevented by any occasion from further creative act, a transcendence that constantly gives all as potential and redeems all as creative act using the concrete present in all its richness and inevitable mistakenness.

In eucharistic action, human beings enact this creative love by recalling (anamnesis) its symbol and by acting thus (again, at least in symbol) in the act of offering what will feed each other and the world. Offering is, for humans, being-in-time by willing act. The act of sacrifice is the willing assent to action, the not-grasping-at-being.[27] It is the embracing of the constant becoming that ever creates the next moment from the loss of the present. This is the very act by which creation becomes. It is the act that we name Trinity. It is the act that is the dying and rising of Jesus Christ. It is the act that we en-act in the liturgy.

From this perspective creation itself is a symbol, a moment-to-moment concrescence of the process-ion of the Trinity in time and space. The liturgy is the place in which this process becomes conscious and intentional. It is the place of assent, of openness and meeting.

Actions are differentiated by their intention. The intention symbolized by bread is the sum of all potential acts in which bread can be involved. Insofar as it contributes to those acts it can be said to have intention; but this is a very limited (however rich and useful) intention. Human beings, of all known creatures, have the most complex potential for intentionality. In fact, human intentions can include those that run counter to the unfolding of the complex plot that allows for the fullest unfolding of the potential of each occasion involved in the action of that plot. What we call evil and destructiveness, that is, are also potentials.

The liturgy, as the anamnesis of the plot that most perfectly enacts the actual loving process-ion of the Trinity, also involves the participants in an action that is the enacted symbol of that plot. Thus all symbols (bread, wine, water, creation, persons, words) are enacted according to their deepest potential ("what or who they really are" in metaphysical terms) in such a way that the many potentials are realized in the unity of the action of the plot. This is the symbol of the reign of God, proleptically enacted in the liturgy. It is a symbol for the grand improvisation that is the continuing creative act of the Trinity acting in ensemble with the "already" of creation, including the "already" of each human life.

It is this ensemble that is revealed in the liturgy as sacramental reality. Because it only "happens" when there is a sacrifice on the part of each actor, a letting go of the intention to define the plot, it is not what is happening in most of life. The sacramental plot that is enacted in liturgical events is the very self-sacrificial act by which Trinity enacts creation in continual letting go.

Because the sacraments involve us (if we will be involved) in the "plot" that is the "inner life of the Trinity," they "effect what they signify." That is, what we do in the liturgy is an intentional and conscious doing of the ensemble of acts that is the plot of creation/redemption. Insofar as we are able at any one moment, we "become" what we are doing. Needless to say, the implication is that such moments of enactment are themselves moments of the entire process-ion that we live out in everyday life. The intention of the Christian is to discover how to improvise according to the same gracious ensemble action in the less obvious plot structure of the daily world.

As Aristotle realized, the work of art (like the liturgical enactment in our case) needs a proper magnitude lest it be incomprehensible. The thousand-mile-long beast cannot be beautiful because its wholeness, and thus its proportion, can never be seen at once. The plot of creation is in just such a manner beyond us except insofar as it is incarnate in the plot of the liturgy. The liturgy reveals both the deepest reality of creation and the act that creation itself reveals.

If the primary act of God can thus be named Trinity and this act is the form of the ongoing act of creation-redemption, then we may call the object of liturgy—the act of which liturgy enacts the anamnesis—by that same name. The definition that we have been gathering up can then include its formal cause, the object of the enactment: *Liturgy is the anamnesis of the Trinity by means of the symbolic interplay of matter, gesture, and word enacted in time and space.*

The Parts of Anamnesis: Sacrament

Before deriving the final cause, the end to which this anamnesis is enacted, we must ask what parts may be derived from the object of liturgy. For Aristotle, the object defines the architectonic part of tragedy—plot. Plot is quintessentially the "imitation of an action." We need to discover the analogue to the plot of the liturgy, the part that is the ordering of enactment, matter, gesture, and word for the anamnesis of the Trinity.

I am particularly interested not in creating a new liturgical vocabulary but in placing the existing categories in a structural relationship by which each term is defined by its relationship to the others. The overarching structure of this relationship assumes the "enactedness" of liturgy. All the other parts must somehow take account of this enactedness and contribute to it.

For this reason, it would seem unnecessary to invent a word for the architectonic part of liturgical enactment—that which is analogous to the plot of drama as defined by Aristotle. I would suggest that that word, that shaping and informing part, is none other than *sacrament,* especially as the word was understood in the early scholastic writings of Hugh of St. Victor (d. 1142). According to Gary Macy, Hugh "labored to recover the teaching of earlier centuries on the eucharist" and used the word *sacramentum* "to refer to any act which mediated the union between God and humans."[28]

Sacrament would seem to be a fitting name for the architectonic part of the liturgy. This part names an act—one that, as suggested above, is the anamnesis of the act of the Trinity in creation and redemption. Like its counterpart in the drama (plot), *sacrament* names a particular ordering of the other parts of the liturgy as it is enacted in word, gesture, and matter. Unlike plot, sacrament is not organized around discovery and reversal; nor is it, like performance in general, a name for any restored behavior. It is, rather, the shape of the liturgy that enacts the Trinity, by means of word, gesture, and matter, to accomplish the proper end of liturgy. We need to discover what that shape, the shape of sacrament, is.

We have discovered in the anamnetic restored behavior of the liturgy a process by which narrative gives shape and power to the present enactment of the ongoing life of the Trinity in the lives of the enactors. It is relatively easy to recite the narrative — perhaps that is the reason it remains so central in shaping the liturgical enactment. The narrative, the part we have called word, certainly is a necessary component, along with gesture and matter, of any sacramental symbol. In fact, word remains the architectonic part of symbol because it gives form (i.e., meaning) to gesture and matter in their sacramental context.

It is somewhat more difficult to name or describe the structure of enactment that we are calling sacrament because it is necessary not to reduce this structure to a narrative. Sacrament, that is, does not simply, like the plot of tragedy, select and arrange episodes of the narrative (mythos) to achieve the proper effect. As we have seen, the biblical narrative is always implied in the universe of discourse in which the liturgy is enacted; but it does not always, despite the imaginings of Amalarius, shape the actual sequence of events.

What seems clear, however, is that the shape of the liturgy — sacrament — can be described only by verbs. If any particular liturgy cannot be seen merely as the enacting of a particular biblical narrative, nevertheless liturgy is like narrative in that its shape can be described by only verbs — action words. Dom Gregory Dix implies such a method in his classic description of the shape of the Eucharist as "take, bless, break, and distribute."[29]

Antiochene eucharistic prayers, for example, from various ages and traditions follow, in their illocutionary verbal structure, some variation on the pattern *thanking, blessing, remembering (anamnesis), offering, invoking (epiclesis),* and *petitioning.* The shaping of the actual liturgy, that is, is accomplished not only by the juxtaposition of narrative and matter but by the unfolding of a meta-action accomplished by the speech acts of the various prayers and by the gestural acts of the participants. These participants, in the case of the liturgy, we may name church.

The Parts of Anamnesis: Church

However integral to or seemingly disenfranchised from liturgical enactment the various orders of the church have been at any particular historical
period, the sacramentally shaped act has always required the presence of a
defined community to enact that shape. Again, as with the actual shape of
a particular sacramental act in a particular historical period, the form of the
church will vary. The verbal and gestural participation of those present at a
liturgy, that is, is quite different, presumably, in a late medieval Mass when
compared with a modern Holy Eucharist or with noneucharistic worship.
Nevertheless, each act implies some formed community, ordered according
to some notion of boundaries and inclusion, and shaped by the very sacramental act that it performs.

Noting again Aristotle's relationship among the six parts of tragedy
as one of matter and form, I would propose understanding the church to
be in just such a relationship to the architectonic part sacrament. In this relationship, sacrament is the form of church, and church is the material of
sacrament. The shape that informs the enactment of the liturgy, that is, de-
termines the shape or patterning of the community that enacts it. Community is constituted by its enactment of the sacramental pattern. Likewise,
the enduring order of that community is the ground of each successive act
of liturgy, the ordered continuity that expresses in each new act the form of
the act over time.

Following the pattern revealed in the definitions of the other parts of
liturgy, we would have to imagine that the church, too, would have a different
specific form in each historical period and even, perhaps, in each sacramental act according to the shape of the sacrament enacted. Thus, despite the
late medieval church's official recognition of priest, deacon, and subdeacon
(note that the bishop was regarded as a high priest) as the historic orders of
the church, the church enacted itself according to a pattern more accurately
described as clergy (priests), monks, and laity.[30] In this model, the central relationship of laypersons to their spiritual directors (priest or monk) for sacramental penance enacts a church different from that of the official theology.

Likewise, the shape of the sacraments enacted in the late medieval Mass
is a bipartite relationship of clergy and laity constructed by the elaborate
performance of visual piety by the clergy for the people. Late-twentieth-
century attempts to revive the diaconate in the Roman Catholic and Angli-

can traditions have at times been plagued by a lack of functional place for that order within a church defined by the shape of sacrament inherited from the Middle Ages.

If the church is formed by sacrament, then the church clearly has some boundaries. These boundaries could be purely mechanical — for example, if the church were defined solely by presence at a sacramental enactment. However, such a simple framing would take account neither of the exclusion of certain persons (catechumens, penitents) from certain sacramental acts at various times nor of the attitude or subjective stance of those present at liturgical enactments.

Much debate raged during the Reformation, for example, over the relationship between the presence of Christ in the eucharistic bread and wine and the belief in that presence on the part of the receiver. This debate only continued a long medieval disputation on the relationship between the objective substance of sacrament and its subjective appropriation.[31]

The church, that is, is constituted not by enactment per se but by a particular quality of enactment on the part of the enactors. This quality of enactment is the matter of the church, that which expresses its being-through-time. It also has a subjective dimension because, finally, the members of the church are subjects. We may adopt as the name of this part of liturgy the classic name for such an attitude of belief, trust, or willing participation: faith.

Faith in this context, in keeping with the nature of enactment, is understood as an act of will — akin to Bakhtin's non-alibi in Being. It is the subject's conscious (more or less) and willing participation as an actor in the liturgy and, thus, as constitutive of the church. The need on the part of the church to discern and verify such a subjective attitude in its members leads to a critical confrontation between enactment and word. On the one hand, one can "speak falsely" (e.g., the apostasy involved in not confessing one's membership in the church to hostile authorities in the third century). On the other, one can "act falsely" (e.g., receiving Communion without having been shriven in the thirteenth century).

Faith is the form of the symbolic means of the liturgy. That is, such a subjective intention can be made manifest only by word, gesture, and the way in which they are used to define and approach the matter of the sacramental symbol. The Roman emperors who required the burning of incense at their shrines and the sixteenth-century Anglicans who insisted upon receiving the Holy Communion kneeling both understood the potential of symbolic enactment to reveal and construct the subjective act of will that we are calling faith. "Show me your faith apart from works, and I by my works will show you my faith" (James 1:18b, NRSV).

If the analogy to the tragedic six parts holds, then faith is the form of the sacramental symbol, specifically of the word, the narrative or linguistic element of the liturgy that itself shapes and informs gesture. Likewise, the word and the other two parts, gesture and matter, that are involved in the three-part juxtaposition called sacramental symbol are the material out of which faith, as act, is constructed. The symbols of the liturgy, that is, are the material of the act of faith by which individuals consent to be the church. What this church is will be determined by the shape of the particular sacramental act that is performed; but that act always makes anamnesis of the acts of God as Trinity.

Faith has, then, a dimension of making that participation, that enactment, not only intentional and willed but (by necessity) conscious. The enactment of the liturgy foregrounds the particular action of the sacrament from the plethora of daily actions in order both to reveal it and to invite willing and conscious participation in it. This participation, as we have seen, is what we are calling faith. As with any of the parts that we have defined for the liturgy, there is an intentional overlapping of this term with the enactment of faith in the "everyday."

We may conclude from this that the enactment of the liturgy is a foregrounded or marked or meta-enacted instance of action. In fact, it may be said that liturgical action is, in Bakhtin's language, the answerable act of my (and of each enactor's) place in Being-as-event. What I am calling the aspect of "consciousness" in this faith act Bakhtin calls the *emotional-volitional tone*. Thus liturgical enactment is a mode of ethical enactment *if* it is done answerably—that is, consciously, intentionally, and in recognition of one's answerability to the action that is the object of the anamnesis. This conclusion gives us the formal cause or object of the liturgy and its parts (see Figure 4.3).

The Final Cause of Liturgy: Enacting Anamnesis of Trinity

It is, finally, the grace-filled enabling of the willing act of entering into a community shaped by the anamnesis of the Trinity that defines the "final

Aristotle's Cause	Definition of Tragedy	Part of Tragedy	Definition of Liturgy	Part of Liturgy
Formal (object)	Imitation of an action Serious Complete	Plot Character Thought	Anamnesis of act of God (Trinity)	Sacrament Church Faith

FIGURE 4.3. Formal Cause

cause" or end for which liturgy is enacted. As in Aristotle's definition, the final cause really is the accomplishment of the form of the object, the unified whole that, for tragedy, is the effective plot and, for liturgy, is the church enacting Trinity in the world. Such an enactment includes all the moments of the Trinitarian act—creation, redemption, sanctification—and all that is implied by these acts being accomplished in the life of human beings.

Certainly, for Christians, the locus of that accomplishment is the person of Jesus Christ, who enacts the life of the Trinity primarily by the act of self-offering love in the world. Because the whole action of the Trinity is, like Aristotle's "thousand-mile-long beast," incomprehensible, the liturgy enacts the various moments of that one action in a series of enactments that, while part of a whole, focus on specific moments in the constitution of the church. Many of these moments have attained specific repeatable sacramental form and are called "sacraments" (see Figure 4.4).[32]

We can now complete the definition of liturgy and determine if from it we can derive definitions of those specific liturgical acts that have become part of the tradition of the church. *Liturgy is the anamnesis of the act of the Triune God, using symbolic means, to enact that Trinity in the lives of the enactors, transforming them through faith into the church. Liturgy is composed of seven structural parts that are arranged causally, each being the form of the previous and the matter of the next. These parts are time/space, matter, gesture, word, faith, church, and sacrament.*

This definition and its relationship to Aristotle's definition of tragedy are summarized in figure 4.5.

Although liturgy is symbolic act rather than moral praxis, the moral imperative hinted at in this process needs a further note. The word *ensemble,* borrowed from the theory of acting, can be used to indicate the process by which the individual potentials of each occasion involved in an act are realized. This ensemble obtains only through the sacrifice or offering, by each

Aristotle's Cause	Definition of Tragedy	Part of Tragedy	Definition of Liturgy	Part of Liturgy
Final (end)	With incidents arousing pity and fear to accomplish the catharsis of such emotions		With sacramental acts to make anamnesis of the Trinity in the lives of the worshippers, transforming them through faith into the church	

FIGURE 4.4.   Final Cause

Aristotle's Cause	Definition of Tragedy	Part of Tragedy	Definition of Liturgy	Part of Liturgy
Formal (object)	Imitation of an action Serious Complete	Plot Character Thought	Anamnesis of act of God (Trinity)	Sacrament Church Faith
Material (means)	In language with pleasurable accessories	Diction Music	In symbol	Word Gesture Matter
Efficient (manner)	In dramatic form	Spectacle	In enacted form	Time/ space
Final (end)	With incidents arousing pity and fear to accomplish the catharsis of such emotions		With sacramental acts to make anamnesis of the Trinity in the lives of the worshippers, transforming them through faith into the church?	

FIGURE 4.5.   Definition of Liturgy

occasion, of control over the action. The image derives from the actual process of improvisation engaged in by actors and musicians, a process in which they create a unified work of art by reactive attention to each other and to the implications of the musical or dramatic structure at any given moment. Such a process requires much practice, knowledge of the medium, selflessness, and trust.

Such a process is at the heart of the liturgy, even where it is most seemingly fixed in form. The form of the liturgy is analogous to the tonal structure of music or the scenario of a dramatic improvisation. These forms define the ground in which creativity can take place. Likewise, the inherited liturgical forms, when understood as scenarios of actions rather than as scripts to be recited, form the place for such improvisation on the act of creation—what we have called "Trinitying." They become the symbols of ensemble, the place in which the loving process-ion of the Trinity is realized in our own occasions. I believe that the model of the Trinity as a verb rather than as a noun is not only in keeping with the deconstruction of ontotheology undertaken by Chauvet but also closer to the earliest intuitions of this act in the scriptural narrative.

In the next chapter we will apply this general definition of liturgy to a specific sacramental act, namely the Holy Eucharist, in a specific historical period. From what we have discovered, we would expect to find the specific means, object, and manner of the liturgy constructing the specific intention of the liturgy for that rite.

✦ 5 ✦

The Performance of *Ordo Romanus Primus*

İn his essay "The Mass as Sacred Drama," O. B. Hardison draws on the image of the Mass of St. Gregory to illustrate the central attitude toward the performance of the Holy Eucharist that he finds in Amalarius's *Liber officialis.* Specifically, he says, concerning the ninth-century commentator's treatment of the *unde et memores:*

> [T]here are two concurrently developing patterns in the Mass. The first is the ritual, which, in spite of its highly stylized form, is a true and visible sequence of actions and texts. The ritual is timeless. It always occurs in the present and its central features are unchanging. It is not a representation but a re-creation. It is linked indissolubly with a second order of events which occurred in chronological time and which must therefore be re-created in the present by meditation—by an effort of the memory heightened through contact with ritual. The two elements cannot be separated. The ritual is not "pure" ritual (if such a thing can exist) but has explicitly rememorative parts, while the memory of the historical drama is colored and idealized in terms of the images furnished by ritual.[1]

The relationship between what Hardison calls the "ritual" and the "rememorative" recreation of past events is one that is, as we have seen, more in the eye of the commentator than in the structure of the Mass. That

Amalarius and others would map the biblical narrative onto the action of the Mass speaks loudly of the strong performance element that they intuited in the liturgy; but it is not necessarily an indication of what is implied by the words and gestures of the liturgy in themselves. At best, we might say that the allegorical commentaries give voice to a tradition of interpretation (reaching back to biblical typology and the writings of Theodore of Mopsuestia) that sought to account for the unavoidable fact that the liturgy is not merely theo-logy but also the-urgy. It must be addressed as enactment. Using the principles developed in the preceding chapter, I would suggest that this could be accomplished without recourse to a sometimes artificial "dramatization" of the liturgy. The process, however, must begin with a description of the enactment, with an attempt to reconstruct not only the words of the liturgy but the gestures by which those words were enacted in time and space.

The analysis that I will attempt in this chapter, one based on the definition of liturgy derived in chapter 4, differs significantly from the analysis of a dramatic form. In analyzing a drama, especially if that analysis is to eventuate in the actual staging of the play, one must confront primarily the written script. From that script are derived the action and characters of the play, which in turn are the basis for the actors' vocal and gestural delivery, the blocking of the action on the stage, and the design of the setting in which that action takes place. The production values derived from an analysis of the script are further informed by the actual physical site of the production and by the other available means of production—the abilities of the actors themselves, the potential costumes, the lighting, the set design, the musical accompaniment, and a host of other factors influenced by economic and aesthetic constraints.

What I shall be attempting with an early medieval liturgy is, on the contrary, an analysis of the form of the sacrament (the analogue of plot) derived from a reconstruction of the actual performance of the liturgy. That is, I shall reconstruct and describe the performance of a Mass in the eighth century and from that description derive what act of God, what "Trinitying," was being enacted in the sacramental plot and what particular construction of the church this might imply.

Because we are examining the performance of particular liturgies in actual time and space, the experience of such performance would be different for each participating group of worshippers. Thus the experience of the celebrant of the Mass according to the Use of Sarum in the fifteenth century would include more parts than that of the laity outside the rood screen. The very presence of the words of the Canon, much less the intricate dance of the performance, would seem to make his experience far more polysemous than that of the choir or, certainly, of the laity.

But this does not imply that the experience of any group is without meaning. The point of performance is that it allows for a variety of experiences, of *effects,* even in the context of a single, unified act. Even in the theater the experiences of the actors, the audience, and the stagehands are presumably different, yet they are by no means mutually exclusive. In fact, each group participates in unique yet complementary ways. Likewise, the notion of participation in the liturgy cannot be seen as limited to the performance of one set of words or gestures. So-called revisionist historians, such as Eamon Duffy, have begun to point out that, Reformation polemic aside, the late medieval liturgy, for example, was not simply a clerical monopoly dedicated to the disenfranchisement of the laity.[2] Although not the form of participation preferred by the modern church (or, for that matter, by earlier church practice), medieval popular piety, as described in chapter 3, can be seen as a rich and real participation in an enactment that, from the point of view of the people, had its own sacramental form, its own construction of the church, and its own powers and effects. This experience we can discover only by examining the liturgy *as enacted.*

We may discover that this experience is not, in the end, what the church now means by Eucharist, or even what the words of the Canon seem to demand; but the medieval Mass certainly enacted a sacramental plot that constructed a particular church and faith by its use of word, gesture, and matter in the context of actual time and space. This construction, and its powers and effects on actual lives, were not limited to those who read the words or chanted the texts or carried the candles — or even to those few who, at least in the later Middle Ages, ate the bread.

Let us begin by examining the Mass described in *Ordo Romanus I.* This ordo, designed, according to Andrieu, to be used in conjunction with the Gregorian Sacramentary, describes the papal stational liturgy of the city of Rome sometime around the year 700.[3] The setting implied is one of the basilicas used regularly by the pope for the Sunday stational Mass.[4] In fact, if, as some scholars claim, the liturgy described in *Ordo Romanus I* is that of Easter Sunday, then we know that the church in use would have been

St. Mary Major. Whatever the specific setting, however, the ordo attempts to anticipate a variety of seasonal variations in the liturgy and to serve as a general norm for papal stational celebration. Indeed, according to Andrieu, this ordo formed the basis of the rite that Amalarius would allegorize a century and a half later in the setting of the very different world of Carolingian Lotharingia.

To visualize such a performance of the Mass, it is necessary to map out the basic architectural plan of the church that would act as the setting. Because the directions given in *Ordo Romanus I* must be applicable to papal Masses in a variety of stational churches with a variety of architectural layouts, they are, in certain instances, ambiguous and imprecise. Certainly not all churches would include the "confession," the gateway to the martyr's shrine below the altar, before which the pope received the offerings of the chancellor, the secretary, and the chief counselor.[5] But St. Peter's basilica certainly would have included this architectural element. Likewise, references to the pope processing "to the upper part of the choir" *(in caput scola)* could reflect simply the presence of the choir members arranged on either side of the entrance to the *presbyterium,* or it might indicate the ninth-century additions to the basilican architectural plan of a low-walled area (called the *scola* or *solea*) before the altar, as in St. Sabina in Rome. Given this caveat, we may nevertheless hope to reconstruct something of the enactment of the eighth-century papal Mass from the description in the first Roman ordo.

To visualize such a liturgy it may be helpful to bear in mind the layout of the Roman basilicas used as stational churches around the time of the compiling of the ordo (c. 700). Figure 5.1 represents a reconstruction St. Peter's basilica based on the work of Richard Krautheimer and colleagues, as well as that of Jocelyn Toynbee and J. B. Ward-Perkins.[6]

Evident here is the large open space for standing and the altar located in the apse and separated from the standing area by a raised platform with a set of columns. The canopy over the altar is probably not from the earliest period of the building but may well have been in place by the time of our ordo. Looking more closely at the apse, we see the arrangement of the *presbyterium,* the area immediately around the altar and behind the low wall. St. Peter's includes the raised *presbyterium* and altar due to the presence of the shrine of St. Peter, the "confession," located through the small grate in the middle, just below the altar. Access to the altar area is by means of steps rising from either side of this central grate. A mosaic on the apse is located

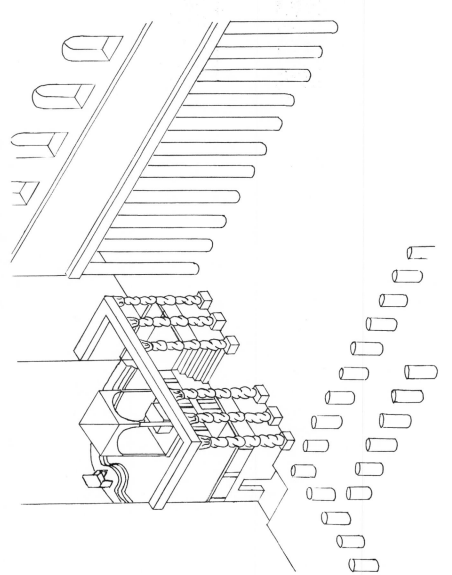

FIGURE 5.1 St. Peter's, Rome, Reconstruction of Seventh-Century Interior

directly above the papal throne that is raised above the seating for the bishops and presbyters.

We note that St. Peter's has the apse in the west end and that the altar is arranged for celebration of the Mass with the pope facing the people (i.e., east). Not all of the stational churches were thus aligned, leading to some confusion as to what the ordo means by "before" and "behind" the altar. In general, these terms seem to indicate positions from the point of view of the presider (the pope) and not from the point of view of the people.

At the opposite end of each of these basilicas, the end that included the doors to the church, was the sacristy, the staging area for the papal entrance into the church proper. This room was usually to the right of the entrance door, that is, in the northeast corner of a building aligned as was St. Peter's.

In its original setting *Ordo Romanus I* envisions an extremely communal pontifical Mass centered on the elaborate enactment of the social ordering of the Roman Church. The preponderance of directions in the ordo deal with the movements and activities of the large number of functionaries—archdeacons, deacons, acolytes, regional notaries, choir, presbyters, bishops, and people—each of whom has specific roles to play in the performance of the liturgy. This wealth of detail is in sharp contrast with the striking (to us who have inherited the late medieval "manual acts") lack of particulars in the treatment of the celebrant's gestures during the Canon.

The enactment of church begins with a great deal of intentionality even before the Introit.[7] The clergy and people gather at the stational church to await the coming of the pope. Clergy take their positions in the *presbyterium*, presbyters in the seats on the right (what will be the pope's left) and bishops on the opposite side; and the rest of the people, by civil rank, gather in the church, except for those whose duty it is to await the pontiff at the door. These dignitaries and acolytes wait, with incense, and bow their heads when the pope arrives on horseback. He then blesses them and dismounts as they form a procession and lead him into the church. Once inside, he goes straight into the sacristy and sits in his chair. Meanwhile, the deacons greet him and go outside the sacristy door to change their clothes and ready the Gospel book. Once the Gospel book is prepared, an acolyte carries it to the altar on which it is placed by a subdeacon-attendant *(subdiaconus sequens)*.[8] While this entrance of the Gospel is taking place, the pope is vesting in the sacristy with the help of subdeacons and other minor clergy.

After it is determined that the choir is ready and that the various readings and chants have been properly assigned, the pope signals the subdeacon to give the command to "light up" *(accendite)*—at which point the processional candles are lit and incense is placed in the thurible. With the permission of the precentor *(priorum scolae),* the ruler of the choir *(quartus scolae)* directs the choir to enter the church two by two, at which time they arrange themselves on either side of the entrance to the *presbyterium.* With everyone in place, the precentor begins the Introit *(antiphonam ad introitum).*

Hearing the Introit, the archdeacon and second deacon enter the sacristy and, after kissing his hands, support the pope in his ceremonial entrance. Preceding them are the thurifer diffusing incense, seven acolytes carrying seven candlesticks, and the remaining deacons. This procession moves toward the altar but stops before arriving so that two acolytes can bring a pyx containing the *Sancta* in order to show it to the pope. This ceremony revolves around the fragment of consecrated bread from the previous Papal Mass sent on ahead of the pope to the current stational church. The subdeacon-attendant takes these fragments in his hand in the mouth of the pyx and shows them to the pope and to the deacon who goes before him. Both the pope and the deacon salute the *Sancta* with bowed heads and determine if there are too many fragments for the later ceremonial addition to the chalice. If there are, some are put in the aumbry.

Presumably the thurifer, candle bearers, and deacons have already arrived in the *presbyterium* because the deacons have removed their *planet*s and given them to acolytes to hold. The pope and his deacon supporters continue until they reach the "choir" (whether architectural or functional), where the candle bearers have divided four on the right and three on the left to allow the pope to pass through to the altar. Here he bows his head to the altar, rises and makes the sign of the cross on his forehead, and then gives the kiss of peace *(dat pacem)* to one of the bishops, to the archpresbyter, and to all of the deacons.

At this point, one of two actions completes the entrance rite, depending upon the season. If the season is one of penitence, during which the Gloria in Excelsis is not sung, then the ruler of the choir brings the faldstool *(oratorium),* whereon the pope kneels and prays until the repetition of the antiphon. Presumably the deacons and others kneel as well. At other times the pope does not kneel but rather signals the precentor to begin the

Gloria Patri that will end the Introit. The deacons now bow two by two to the sides of the altar (where, presumably, they have been waiting either standing or kneeling) and return to the pope, who arises (if he has been kneeling) and kisses the Gospel book and the altar. He proceeds to his throne in the apse and stands facing east. In a church aligned like St. Peter's this would, of course, mean that he faced the people. In an oriented church he, or whatever presider might be using this ordo as the basis for liturgical action, would have to turn and face the throne. It seems significant that these particular directions are given not with reference to the altar or the people but rather with reference to the actual compass direction.

As soon as the Gloria Patri has ended, the choir begins the Kyrie Eleison, which continues for a fixed number of repetitions or until the pope signals the precentor to stop. When it is concluded the pope begins the Gloria in Excelsis. The ordo describes his turning "himself round toward the people" *(dirigens se pontifex contra populum)*. The plain sense of the Latin seems more to be "the pope, standing opposite the people." This would seem to avoid the awkwardness of having him "turn" in those churches in which he was already facing the people. The point would seem to be that, whatever direction he is facing for the Kyrie, he begins the Gloria facing the people. He then directs himself *(regerat se)* to the east after the *incipit* until the end of the chant. At that point, the pope again faces the people for "Peace to you" and "Let us pray" and faces east for the Collect. This completed, he sits on the throne, the district subdeacons place themselves at the right and left of the altar; and the bishops and presbyters, at his signal, seat themselves on the bench that runs around the circumference of the apse.[9]

As soon as the clergy are seated, the rite continues with a series of simple acts devoted to the reading of and response to the lessons appointed for the day. First, the appointed subdeacon goes up to the ambo to read the Epistle. When he finishes, the chorister appointed goes to the same ambo to sing the Gradual. Immediately, another sings the Alleluia or Tract if appointed.

Now begin the actions surrounding the reading of the Gospel. Once again, as in the entrance rite, the enactment takes a turn away from the merely utilitarian. The deacon goes to the pope and kisses his feet, whereupon the pope says to him "in an undertone" *(tacite)*, "The Lord be in your heart and on your lips." The deacon then comes before the altar, kisses the Gospel book, and carries it, preceded by two subdeacons, one carrying the thurible, and two candle bearers, to the ambo. The "choreography" of this series of acts is described in minutest detail. The acolytes part at the steps to the ambo, allowing the subdeacons and deacon to pass between them. The unencumbered subdeacon offers his left arm, on which the deacon rests the Gospel book, and opens the book with his right hand to the place previously marked. Then, "slipping his finger into the place where he has to begin, the deacon goes up to read, while the two subdeacons turn back to stand before the step coming down from the ambo." As practical as these actions are (for the handling of a large book and the reading of the proper pericope), there is nonetheless a clear sense that a visual event is preceding the aural one. Something is being communicated about the nature of the *act* of reading the Gospel by the highly formalized action surrounding its actual reading. After the Gospel has been read, two actions begin simultaneously: the pope says (to the people), "Peace to you" and "The Lord be with you," to which the answer is made, "And with your spirit"; then the pope says, "Let us pray." This is the remnant of the Prayers of the People that have already (by the fifth century) disappeared from this location. The bidding now serves to initiate the complex series of events that comprise the offertory or preparation of the altar. Meanwhile, however, the deacon descends from the ambo and gives the Gospel book to the subdeacon, who gives it to the subdeacon-attendant. The latter carries the book "before his breast, outside his *planet*," to be kissed by "all, who stand in order of their rank" *(omnibus per ordinem graduum qui steterint).* The book is then brought back to the step of the ambo, where it is sealed again in its case to be carried back to the Lateran by an acolyte.

While this act is continuing, a third act begins as the deacon returns to the altar, where an acolyte is standing holding a chalice with a corporal on top. The acolyte lifts the chalice; the deacon takes the corporal and lays it on the right of the altar, throwing the other end over to a second deacon in order to spread it. This preparation initiates what is perhaps the most minutely described act in this ordo, the receiving of the oblations from the various orders of worshippers. Here begins an intricate dance in which relationships among the orders of Roman Christian society are enacted by spatial positioning and by the handling of the offerings of bread and wine that each order brings to the action that will follow.

It would seem reasonable, at this point, to imagine the choir beginning the "offertory" chant that will, according to this ordo, be concluded at a signal from the archdeacon just before the *secreta*. However, there is no indication given for the beginning of this chant, and in later Gallicanized ordines it does not begin until after the handwashing.[10] However, it must be borne in mind that the Gallican rites included an offertory procession of the people and would, in some ways, have been simpler than the elaborate approaches by the pope to the various orders of people envisioned in Ordo I. Whatever one imagines, then, regarding the beginning of the offertory chant, it clearly "covered" at least part of the complex action that follows the reading of the Gospel.

The obvious practical action at this point is the gathering of bread and wine and its placement on the altar. Because of the presumably large number of worshippers, however, and because this action is their offering to God, it takes place in several stages with the pope and the archdeacon playing central roles.

First, various officials (the chancellor, secretary, chief counselors, and district officials and notaries) go up to the pope's throne. The pope then goes down to the place of the notables *(ad senatorium)* and receives the loaves of the princes in order of their authority *(et suscipit oblationes principum in ordinum archium)*.[11] Then the archdeacon receives their flasks of wine, pouring them into the chalice still carried by the district subdeacon (who has been following the archdeacon). When this chalice becomes full, it, in turn, is emptied into a bowl carried by an acolyte. The loaves are handed off to a subdeacon-attendant, who puts them into a cloth held by two acolytes. Having enacted this first part of the symbolic reception of the gifts, the pope moves on while the assisting bishop collects the "rest of the loaves" *(reliquas oblationes)* and puts them in the cloth. Likewise, the archdeacon's task of collecting the wine is taken over by the subdeacon-attendant.

Meanwhile, the pope and the archdeacon have moved over to the women's side (the left, facing the altar) to the "confession" to receive the loaves of the chancellor, secretary, and chief counselor and then those of the women, "in the same manner as detailed above" (including, presumably, the collection of wine by the archdeacon). If need arises (due to large numbers of offerers), the presbyters help collect the bread. This stage of the offertory having been completed, the pope returns to his throne and washes his hands. The archdeacon likewise washes his hands and, at a sign from the pope, approaches the altar.

The subdeacons now carry the collected loaves to either side of the altar; and the archdeacon arranges them. After this, he receives from the subdeacon-oblationer the pope's flask of wine, followed by those offered by the deacons (and from others on festivals [*die festo*]). These he pours through a strainer into the two-handled chalice that has contained (however briefly) all the other wine offered previously before having been poured into the bowl. The subdeacon-attendant then goes to the choir to receive from them a ewer of water. This is poured into the chalice by the archdeacon, who makes the sign of the cross as he does so.

The attending clergy and dignitaries who are so appointed now come down from their ranks and take their places near the altar. When all are in place, the pope rises from his throne and comes down to the altar and salutes it. Although it would appear that the offertory is completed, there is, in fact, a final act of preparation done by the pope himself.

First he receives the loaves chosen from those collected earlier (the ones brought to the altar and arranged by the archdeacon) from the hand of the hebdomadary presbyter and the deacons. Then the archdeacon receives the pope's own offering from the oblationer and gives it to the pope, who, with his own hands, places it on the altar. It is thus the pope himself who "makes the offering" of the bread. Not so with the wine. Now the archdeacon takes the chalice from the hand of the subdeacon and sets it, with the offertory veil twisted about its handles, on the altar to the right of the pope's loaf. He lays the veil on the end of the altar and goes to stand behind the pope. Meanwhile, the subdeacons have gone "behind the altar, facing the pope" (*retro altare, aspicientes pontificum*), and the bishops arrange themselves in a line behind the pope (the senior in the middle), with the archdeacon on the right and the second deacon on the left. Likewise, the rest of the clergy arrange themselves in an ordered line. This accomplished, the pope bows slightly to the altar and signals the choir to stop singing.[12]

In the silence, one more act will cap the enactment of the offertory. Not mentioned in the ordo, but certainly provided in the Gregorian Sacramentary for which it is the plan of enactment, is the *Oratio super oblata*. This prayer is said by the pope, in a low voice, until the words "forever and ever," which are said in a loud voice so that the subdeacons may lead the response, "Amen," from their position of readiness facing him (*ipsi sint parati ad respondendum*).

In the silence of the *Oratio,* which Honorius of Autun would later compare to "Christ as a lamb without voice being led to the sacrifice," the constant movement and complex activity of the preceding enactment have finally coalesced into an image — the church, standing in its hierarchical society, ready to embark on its central constituting act. Given the complexity of gesture that would mark this next act during the later Middle Ages, it is remarkable that it is done so simply in this rite, which is otherwise so rich in movement and visual symbol.

The Sursum Corda and proper preface *(praefatio)* are chanted by the choir and pope; and all bow as the choir continues with the Sanctus. At the end, the pope alone rises to "enter alone into the Canon" *(surgit pontifex solus in canone),* which, in this instance, is presumed to begin with the *Te igitur.*[13] But as he does so, an acolyte comes to the right wearing a linen cloth around his neck and holding the paten before his breast. This paten is large enough to hold the large quantity of leavened bread needed for communion; it would, thus, perhaps be too large, if placed on the altar, to allow the bread to present an adequate symbolic appearance. The acolyte remains standing there until "the middle of the Canon" *(usque medium canonem),* presumably the *Te igitur* or *Nobis quoque.*[14] The bishops, presbyters, deacons, and subdeacons remain bowed down *(permanent inclinati).*

We are accustomed to the practices of the late Middle Ages that survived until recently as the "manual acts" of the Canon of the Mass. These are as yet in the future of Christian worship as we try to imagine the rite of *Ordo Romanus I.* What we see next in this rite is a longer extension of that same ordered hush that previously we imagined surrounding the *Oratio super oblata.* All the participants stand bowed in their appointed places. The pope prays in a speaking voice, standing erect at the altar.[15] No gestures are made, no elevations, no multiple signs of the cross. It is not until almost the end of the Canon, at the words "to us sinners also, your servants, who trust in the multitude of your mercies," that the subdeacons, who have been standing opposite the pope, arise; and the attendant takes the large paten from the acolyte and brings it to the altar to the subdeacon, who takes it and stands behind the archdeacon, who rises at the words "by whom, O Lord, you ever create all these good things . . ."

As this is completed, the pope has reached the final words of the Canon — "by him and with him and in him" — at which point the archdeacon raises the chalice, with the offertory veil through its handles, toward the pope, who touches it with the loaves as the subdeacons respond, "Amen."

The pope then prays the Lord's Prayer up to "and lead us not into temptation," to which the response is made, "but deliver us from evil. Amen." The pope continues with the embolism; and when he reaches the words "and safe from all unquiet," the archdeacon turns to the subdeacon who has been holding the paten, kisses it, takes it, and gives it to the deacon to hold.

The embolism concluded, the pope now takes the *Sancta* (which had been presented for him to see during the entrance rite) and, making the sign of the cross three times over the chalice, drops it in, saying, "The peace of the Lord be always with you." The reply is made, "And also with you." At this point the archdeacon gives the kiss of peace to the chief hebdomadary bishop, then to the rest of the clergy in order, and finally to the people.

Meanwhile, the pope breaks a piece from the right side of one of the loaves and leaves it on the altar. He places the rest of the loaves on the paten held by the deacon. This done, he returns to his throne. Just as the archdeacon had as his particular act the carrying of the peace to the various orders, so now the practical and symbolic act of the fraction will be distributed among the various orders present. The chancellor, secretary, chief counselor, and district officials and notaries take their places in order to the right and left of the altar. Several officials go to the pope to receive the names of those invited to dine at the papal table. They will go down to deliver these invitations at the fraction as the choir begins the Agnus Dei. The Eucharist thus retains a connection (however hierarchical) with the actual meal of which it was once a part.

While this action of invitation is being initiated, the archdeacon has lifted up and given the chalice to the subdeacon to hold near the right corner of the altar. With the chalice safely aside, the attendant with the acolytes brings little sacks *(sacula)* into which the archdeacon puts the loaves from the altar. The acolytes take these to the bishops and by the subdeacons to the presbyters so that they may break the consecrated loaves *(hostias)* for the Communion. The paten, however, with its portion of the consecrated bread, is taken by two district subdeacons to the throne so that the deacons may make the fraction *(diaconibus ad frangendum)*. Once the altar has been cleared of all the loaves (except for the fragment from the pope's own loaf left so that "the altar may never be without a sacrifice"), the archdeacon signals the choir to begin the Agnus Dei. He then joins the deacon at the paten for the fraction that proceeds at a signal from the pope. Thus not only does the task of breaking large quantities of bread get distributed among many hands, but the various orders are again called to enact their function in the liturgy—bishops, priests, and deacons all break the bread that they have offered for themselves and for the people on the altar.

When the fraction is completed, the second deacon brings the paten up to the throne to communicate the pope. At this point, the pope, for a second time, adds a fragment of the consecrated bread to the chalice—this time from the loaf just consecrated. He "bites off" *(mordeo)* a particle from the bread from which he has communicated and, making a cross three times, puts it into the chalice held by the archdeacon. As he does so, he says the words supplied by the ordo: "May this commixture and consecration of the Body and Blood of our Lord Jesus Christ be to us who receive it for everlasting life." The answer is made: "Amen." The pope then says a second time, "Peace be with you," to which is replied, "And with your spirit." Then the archdeacon communicates the pope from the chalice.[16] The archdeacon then goes, with the chalice, to the corner of the altar and announces the location of the next stational Mass.

The Communion of the people follows, as usual, according to rank. Wine is poured from the chalice into a bowl for the laity, while the bishops and presbyters go to the throne to receive Communion—the bread from the pope and the wine from the archdeacon. The chief hebdomadary bishop takes over the chalice from the archdeacon to communicate the remaining orders down to chief counselor. When the clergy have completed their Communion, the remaining wine from the chalice is poured into the bowl for the laity. The archdeacon is given the reed *(pugillarum)* to use in communicating the people, and the chalice is returned to the sacristy. Meanwhile, the pope has come down from his throne and goes to administer the bread to the magnates *(eos qui in senatorio sunt),* to whom the archdeacon then gives the wine to drink through the reed. As soon as this Communion of the people has commenced, the choir begins the Communion anthem *(antiphonam ad communionem),* which continues throughout the Communion.

The rest of the act of Communion contains variations according to circumstances but reflects the same hierarchical ordering as the offertory. The bishops and deacons first, and then the presbyters (apparently if needed), at a sign from the pope, take up the Communion of the remaining men. The pope then apparently moves over to the women's side to communicate the higher-ranking women and returns to his throne as the other clergy come to the women's side to complete the distribution of Communion. Once at the throne, on certain days, the pope communicates the district officials *(regionarios)* and even twelve members of the choir. These otherwise would have been communicated with the other clergy in the *presbyterium*. Presumably, on festival days *(diebus festis),* there is a desire to extend the symbolic contact between the pope and the various orders of the church to include these other orders specifically. The last to be communicated at the throne are the invitationer, the treasurer, and the acolytes who have been holding the paten and the basin and the towel. This having been accomplished, when the pope sees that the Communion of the people is complete, he signs to the district subdeacon to signal the choir to bring the Communion anthem to a close with the Gloria Patri.

Now the pope rises from his throne and comes to the altar for the post-Communion prayer *(orationem ad complendum),* which he says facing eastwards.[17] The action moves now swiftly to a conclusion. At a signal from the pope, the deacon says to the people, "*Ite missa est,*" to which they respond, "*Deo gratias.*" The seven acolytes with their seven candlesticks and the district subdeacon carrying a thurible precede the pope from the throne into the midst of the *presbyterium*. Here, the bishops ask of him a blessing, to which he replies, "*Benedicat nos dominus.*" They answer, "*Amen*"; and the procession moves on to the sacristy, but not before this dialogue of blessing is repeated, by orders, at several stages along the route with the presbyters, monks, choir, banner bearers, porters, candle bearers, acolytes, crucifers, and junior sextons each asking for his own blessing. *Et intrant in secretarium.*

To examine this scenario using the definition of liturgy developed in the previous chapter will entail a degree of imprecision and intuition. The structuralist agenda of scientific analysis of literary forms into absolute correspondences can no longer be assumed in the wake of the work of Derrida and other poststructuralists. Neither would such a method do justice to the many variables and imponderables that form the context of the historical reconstruction of such a performance as we are attempting. We cannot, that is, derive from the actions described in *Ordo Romanus I* a single statement of the meaning of the Mass or even of the Pontifical Mass in the early eighth century in Rome. To do so would be to deny all that we have said about the uniqueness of enacted reality, of "once-occurrent Being-as-event." What we can do is to use the definition and the relationships among its parts to ask questions of this particular liturgical enactment—questions that might help us better to visualize how this rite enacts, in time and space, those specific symbolic relationships among word, gesture, and matter that constitute the faith of the people and how that faith constitutes the church for them. Further, we may be able to discern, in that enactment of church, the form of the sacrament, the specific anamnetic act that, for this rite, is the goal and purpose for the sacramental enactment.

Let us begin with the basic parts of the manner of the enactment, the time and space that serve as the locus of the performance. There would have been some obvious (to those initiated into the community defined by this rite) correspondences between the setting of this act of worship and larger patterns of cultural and religious meaning. We need only remind ourselves that the intended time of the act is Sunday morning to recall the associations with "the first day of the week," which was certainly the earliest locus for eucharistic liturgy. Surrounding the event, then, is a ground of resurrection imagery—however unforegrounded such imagery may be by the eighth century. Nonetheless, the image depicted in the mosaic above the bishop's throne in St. Peter's shows Christ enthroned, an image that carries forward the triumphal theme of resurrection and reign, which is only reinforced by the use of space in this rite.

Spatially, the enactment of the liturgy in *Ordo Romanus I* presents the first metastatement of the social, hierarchical, and ordered nature of this enactment of the urban Christian community.[18] The basilicas, first of all, speak forth the well-documented movement of Christianity out of the house churches at the periphery of Roman society into the very center of the social, political, and economic life of the city. At the center of this life, at the focal point of the long axis of the basilica, elevated above the level of the floor (and even somewhat above that of the altar), sits the throne of the pontiff. This human center to the worship of the church, however, is not an innovation of the post-Constantinian period. Reconstructions of the second-century house church at Dura Europas include a similar seat for the bishop at the end of the long axis of the room presumed to have been used for the celebration of the Eucharist.[19]

Not only does the space have a focus; it is ordered throughout—not so much by architectural elements at this period as by social convention. The implication of the ordo is that the worshippers arrange themselves according to class and gender even without walls or seating to enforce this hierarchy. The only wall alluded to is the one that separates the *presbyterium* from the rest of the basilica. Even the architectural *solea* or *scola* is not part of the building until the ninth century. The men and women know where to stand, as do, presumably, the notables and lesser laity. The arrangement is organized not so much with the altar as point of reference as with the papal throne. Here the clergy and the pontiff continually return, and here even the fraction and Communion originate.

The altar itself forms the second focus. It is the locus of the actions of the offertory and, of course, of the performance of the Canon by the pope. It stands, in the basilicas of Rome, between the papal throne and the people. At St. Peter's it includes the additional element of the burial place of the saint, which is located directly below the altar in the "confession." Thus, as Spiro Kostof points out, in the churches of the West by the seventh century, when all newly dedicated altars housed the relics of a saint, the altar of the church alluded to the altar of heaven in the Revelation of St. John, under which were the souls of those slain for the word of God.[20] The altar, however, seems not to be highly decorated or elaborate. It is "reverenced" and enters into the actions of the offertory and Canon; it is even the place of kneeling at the entrance rite during Lent; but nothing appears to be placed upon it other than the linen cloth, the chalice, and the bread.

The third architectural focus of action is the ambo that is the locus of the readings and of the sung psalm text that became known as the Gradual *(responsum)*. This element varied from church to church and became more elaborate as time went on. What seems to be expected at every location, however, is that the ambo is raised above ground level and is ascended by steps *(gradi)*. Thus papal throne, altar, and ambo are elevated above the people. Certainly the desire for visibility and audibility of the actions that transpire at these locations does not totally reduce the spatial symbolism to mere practicality. What is, practically, the important or focal action is elevated so that all may participate. It is difficult, on the other hand, to separate from that importance the spatial symbol of being "lifted up." The Western Church, according to Kostof, especially in these Roman basilicas used in the stational liturgies, like the Lateran basilica, "fell back on a dated classicizing design, structurally backward and almost revivalist in form. The intention may have been to dissociate the church from most of the public activities of the pagan world which took place in vaulted halls, and to stay close to the basilica form which, with the sole exception of the basilica of Maxentius, had remained faithful to a timber-roofed, columnar look."[21] By contrast, the East, typified by Hagia Sophia in Constantinople, by the fifth century had developed a symbolic use of great heights, a space in the church, created by the high dome, that produced a pure spiritual aesthetic. "The scale is theocratic, god-centered, and therefore diametrically opposed to the humanistic scale of Classical architecture. The user no longer feels the building with his or her body as it were, but instead is taken up by it, in the very least awed, at best uplifted, elevated."[22]

It is emphatically not this use of verticality that we find in the liturgical staging places of *Ordo Romanus I*. Looking again at the reconstructions of Roman basilicas above, we see places that house, however gloriously, an action centered very much on persons, especially on the central figure of the pontiff. Verticality is the necessary setting for important events. It draws the people into the action by making it not remote but accessible to eye and ear. Hierarchy, at least in this instance, is functional and derives from the place of the enactor in the communal act, of which the basilica is, in good classical form, the bodily extension.

Having made these preliminary comments about the *manner* of sacramental performance as revealed in the two parts of enactment—time and space—we must now consider the sacramental *means,* that complex symbol formed by the mutual contextualization of matter, gesture, and word. Matter includes all inanimate objects used within the space and time of the enactment insofar as these enter into relationship with the gestures and words of the enactment to produce the symbolic reality that is the object of the faith of the church. It includes such obvious artifacts as bread, wine, the chalice and paten, the Gospel book, incense, and the processional torches. In a larger sense, however, the space itself, insofar as it is used symbolically, goes beyond being merely the locus for the enacted manner to become part of the means of the sacrament. This use of space is more obvious in buildings such as San Vitale and Hagia Sophia, as stated above, but is present, too, in the Western-style basilica whenever architectural elements such as the throne, the altar, and the ambo take on symbolic meaning through their association with word and gesture.

A fine line can be seen to exist, on the other hand, between manner and means in such architectural elaboration as the canopy over the altar. Is this a mere decorative or aesthetic part of the manner of presentation—

one of those strategies and rhythms for effective utterance that Alice Rayner sees as the rhetorical or "erotic" aspect of performance—or is it a "word" that contextualizes the altar, making it something other than it is without its canopy? For the time being, these questions must be left for a fuller study of the place of architecture in liturgical performance. We will consider most architectural elements as part of the manner of enactment unless they are made symbolic by both word and gesture during the performance of the liturgy.

Gesture, likewise, is any movement, whether of the whole person or only a part, whether with or without an external object, that functions symbolically within the enactment. *Ordo Romanus I* includes such gestures as gathering, processing, bowing, kissing, facing, chanting, kneeling, and handling certain objects. Note that I am including chanting here as a gestural component of the liturgy. Rather than treating music as a separate part of the liturgy, this schema regards it as a form of gesture that functions in a way similar to the manner of the liturgy. That is, this particular way of rendering the words of the liturgy is a matter of style, the manner in which the words are realized in performance. This is not to diminish the effect of such performance in the liturgy. Quite the contrary, the use or nonuse of musical manner and the varieties of musical styles performed throughout history is a major part of the powers and effects of the liturgy. But these effects are always derived from the enacted manner of the liturgy and are open to the same sort of variation as are all gestural elements of the performance. *That* the choir is engaged in chanting during the liturgy is an element of gesture, one of the means of the liturgy. *How* they are chanting (or singing polyphony or speaking in unison) is a question of the manner of enactment—a large part of the performance of the liturgy but not a separate part of every liturgy, as are matter, gesture, and word. Chanting and speaking are, in this model, different gestures for the enactment of text. In like manner, silence may be considered part of gesture, although it has a great affinity with its seeming complement, words.

Finally, word, as a part of liturgical enactment derived from the symbolic means, includes the words of Scripture, the prayers, and other texts proper to the particular Mass. Once again, the way in which these words are rendered, and the silence that forms the necessary ground of that rendering, illustrate that gesture is closely allied with the manner of enactment. The gestures by which the text is enacted are intimately connected with the concept of performance, which, we have seen, includes the most concrete, yet least defined, aspects of the actual present enactment of the liturgy by the actual people involved. Gesture, in a sense, is the defining term for the manner of performance that unites the words and material objects of the liturgy in present concrete symbols in the present time and space of the enactment. Gesture can thus be seen as a style of both movement and vocal rendering that incarnates the words of the text so that they can be joined to the matter of the world. Gesture is the performance of the symbolic means of the liturgy.

Before attempting to discover how these means are built into the faith of the enactors, we need to elucidate the specific symbols that have been constructed through the mutual contextualization of the matter, gesture, and words in this particular rite. Keeping in mind that matter is the least self-significant part of the sacramental means until it is joined by gesture to word, we may organize this preliminary exploration of the sacramental symbols found in *Ordo Romanus I* around the material components found therein. Those components, if we limit them to those involved with both gestures and words, are bread, wine, and the Gospel book. Needless to say, other material is employed in the enactment, but in every case it derives its use and symbolic meaning from one of these. Thus the chalice, paten, pyx, incense, and torches find their significance in their interaction with the basic elements of bread, wine, and book. From the point of view of enactment, it is interesting that the sacramentary and the lectionary, although they contain a good portion of the theologically significant words for the rite, are not mentioned; neither are they the focus of any significant physical gesture. Words in this rite are auditory phenomena, significant visually only in terms of the space where they are rendered or of other materials to which they refer—except in the case of those read from the Gospel book. The latter are treated in a complex manner comparable to that applied to the bread of the Eucharist.

Because the bread is subject to the most complex contextualization, let us examine it first, as a paradigm of the generation of symbol from the joining of matter to word by means of gesture. In the course of the rite described in *Ordo Romanus I,* bread is the object of these gestures: bowing, holding, signing the cross, offering, collecting, praying over, breaking, mixing with wine, distributing, and eating. Further, it is connected by these gestures with the words of various prayers. The words, however, unlike the gestures, are not part of the experience of all the participants in the action. Whereas everyone is able to see the gestures (which are enacted in full view and without any attempt, as in the later Western and Eastern liturgies, to hide them), the words of the prayers will become increasingly inaudible throughout the eighth and ninth centuries. For the most part, and in the presumably most important prayer text, that of the Canon, the words are more and more a part of the presider's symbol complex. For others, the presider's gesture of prayer is far more significant for the context of the symbol than are the thoughts expressed in the words. Gesture is thus the most important element in the contextualization of the bread—in its transformation into symbol for the participants in this liturgy.[23]

Bread is present throughout the Eucharist described in *Ordo Romanus I*—and not simply as the substance of a meal. If this ordo implies a moment in liturgical history during which Communion still included eating the matter of the sacramental action, nevertheless, bread here is connected both gesturally and verbally with much more than the common act of eating. In fact, the bread and, to a lesser extent, the wine are the centers for a complex enactment of church in which the people participate in the eucharistic actions that define this sacrament. The bread, perhaps, is *the* material element that holds together the gestures and words of the community both past and present. As such, it is present not only at the Communion but throughout the rite, beginning at the Introit.

Before even reaching the altar, the pope stops in the midst of the people to engage in a nonverbal enactment that includes not only the various orders of servers but, for those who know the pattern, a sign of continuity with the past of the community. The bread from the previous Mass is contextualized by a solemn meeting with the entering pontiff. It is there prior to his arrival; and it is both carried in a ceremonial vessel, the pyx, and saluted with a bow from the pope and the deacon as the archdeacon holds it in the mouth of the pyx for their view.[24] What is most certainly a practical action to determine the appropriate amount of the *Sancta* to be added later to the chalice is made more than practical by the gestures surrounding it. Although no words are spoken, the pyx and the act of bowing become metastatements saying that this bread, this *Sancta* from the previous Mass, is different from the bread that is even now in the hands of the offerers. This *Sancta* is contextualized by similar gestures as those that will accompany the Gospel book and that will accompany the offered bread at the end of the Canon. At the same time, the subsequent actions of the Mass are contextualized by the presence of this bread. This bread is already here. However central the pontiff's actions will be in the rite that is unfolding, this bread is here *before* the enactment. It is the concrete presence of the previous enactments and thus of the church so constituted. As such, it is also the future of the present community, who know that they will see their offerings made such bread as this already is.

The second major act involving bread is the offertory, perhaps the most complex action described in this ordo. At this point, everyone, always according to social and ecclesiastical rank, makes a gesture with bread. The ordo makes clear that the pontiff himself makes at least a symbolic gesture of receiving the bread offered from representatives of all the orders of the church. Apparently, the magnates serve as representatives of the rest of the laity, whose bread is collected not by the pope but by the assisting bishops.[25]

Again, the practical matter of receiving the offerings of all is contextualized by the ordered gestures of giving and receiving according to rank in the hierarchy of the ecclesial society. The means of exchange in this patterned behavior is the bread (and wine). The handling of the wine, in fact, presents an even clearer metastatement of the nature of offering than does the bread. Whereas the bread is collected by hand and then placed in the linen cloth for transport to the altar, the wine goes through an elaborate series of pourings. All the flasks of wine offered are first poured into the great chalice *(in calice maiore),* which, when full, is poured into bowls. The metastatement is that all of the offerings pass through and are part of the offerings in the chalice that will be placed on the altar for the Canon.

The division of labor among the many clerical functionaries during this offertory bespeaks an attempt to involve the whole church, lay and clerical, in the action of offering the bread and wine. In both instances of the use of bread thus far in the Mass, the verbal part of the symbol has been confined to the words chanted by the choir in the Introit and the offertory. These would have varied with the season and day and would have, in any case, acted as a counterpoint to the repeated action of the offertory. The matter of the bread and wine receive their symbolic context, again, through the gestures of giving and receiving. In fact, no words are spoken in conjunction with these elements until the variable *Oratio super oblata,* which would not have been heard by most participants in the liturgy.

If the pyx contributes to the metastatement made by the *Sancta,* it is the altar that spatially contextualizes the offered bread and wine. Brought by the subdeacons, the collected bread is arranged on the altar by the archdeacon, except for certain loaves (including the pontiff's loaf) that the pontiff himself places there. Again, the pontiff's act of offering is, in this rite, still his own enactment of something done, in the only way practicable for so large a gathering, by all present. The bread (especially) and the wine are the symbolic means for this enactment of community. In the process, however, they become the embodiment of that community over time. The bread, at least, both is contextualized by the enactment and in turn contextualizes subsequent enactment. The process by which this concrescence of matter with gesture and word takes place comes to be particularly associated with the next action in which the bread is involved—the Canon of the Mass.

What follows in *Ordo Romanus I* (as in subsequent Western rites), from the point of view of most of the participants in the Mass, depends more upon the construction of a symbol from gesture and matter than from word and matter. *What* is said in the handling of the bread is of less import than *that* the bread is at hand and *that* the pontiff says something. The enactment of prayer, that is, is of more consequence than the content of that prayer— for the simple reason that the prayer is understood to be the prayer of the pontiff, who "enters alone" into it even when it is still audible.[26] Moreover, there are no overt gestures in this rite to surround the handling of the bread. The act of prayer and the ordered arrangement of the participants carry the weight of symbol, giving flesh to the words of the Canon as understood by this enactment of church.

The gesture of all the participants (except the pontiff himself) during this central action is to bow, a gesture that, as we have seen, is also used for saluting the *Sancta*—the embodiment of the eucharistic action. The involvement of the whole church in the constructing of the bread as symbol thus takes place in their common gesture of bowing while the pontiff enacts the prayer.

What the Canon articulates, however, is the transcendence of the symbol. In the words of the prayer is the faith of the community, which understands this enactment to be not theirs alone but that of the Holy Trinity engaging them in the enactment. This transcendent dimension of the symbol is constructed through the particular role of the pontiff (and of the hierarchized ordering of the community) in the action. He, as custodian of the words, stands for the transcendence and "otherness" that are finally the context of the bread of this enactment. He himself, by his performance of the words of the Canon, becomes a symbol of the involvement of God in this event. It is this contextualization of the presider by the act of praying the Canon, more than his recitation of the words of institution, which constructs him as a type of the Father and/or the Son in subsequent allegorical speculation. He is the symbol of the transcendent dimension of the community's enactment, of its ultimate construction by the divine Word.

The primary text, from the point of view of the entire community envisioned in *Ordo Romanus I,* is the text of Holy Scripture. Variable according to the liturgical season, the words of Scripture are heard at the reading of the lesson and the Gospel. Moreover, during liturgically important seasons, these readings determine the texts of the propers, the chants at the Introit, Gradual, Alleluia, and Communion. Nonetheless, these texts serve more to create the "ground" of the liturgy, the context of the enactment, than to inform the use of gesture and matter. The principal instance of gestures being altered by season (and thus by text) in this ordo occurs at the Introit. There, the pope kneels only during those times when the Gloria is not sung and when the texts tell of penitence or judgment.

Having examined the sacramental manner and means of this ordo, we must now address the *object* of enactment: What anamnesis of the Holy Trinity is accomplished through the enactment of these symbols? According to our definition, the parts of the sacramental object are faith, church, and sacrament. Sacrament is the architectonic part, giving form to the others and revealing the intended purpose or end of the enactment. Faith is the part most closely related to the symbolic means, as it is, indeed, formed from them. Moreover, faith is the part that mediates between the subjectivity of the participants and their (willing) enactment of the more objective and visible structuring of church. This visible church, then, takes the form of its enactment from the sacramental "plot," the act of the Holy Trinity that incarnates in the performance of the enactment.

Faith is, perhaps, the most difficult part to derive from an examination of the enacted rite. The metalanguage of gesture depends for its context upon the gestural universe of discourse of a particular epoch. What the act of bowing to the *Sancta* or to the pope implied to the performer of this gesture in the eighth century may not be what it implies today or at any other period. After all, such a gesture made in the eighth century would not have been contextualized by the controversies over eucharistic presence that began in the ninth century, nor would it have partaken of the eleventh- and sixteenth-century struggles over the nature of the papacy. To make a complete investigation of the complex matter-gesture-word symbols that are the material of faith in this ordo, or of any other, would require an account of the contemporary use of these parts drawn from historical sources. Such an analysis is beyond the scope of the present enterprise, which seeks to define the parameters for such an endeavor and to demonstrate how the various detailed historical accounts can be organized into a comprehensive definition.

Nevertheless, it is important to reiterate that the faith of the participants in a liturgical act is constructed not only of words taken to heart but of an attitude enacted through gesture toward material things as well as people. The basic material of the sacramental enactment, that is, is the way the participants speak and act in the context of the time and space of the liturgy. This faith encompasses, for example, not only a subjective appropriation of the words heard at the reading of the Gospel but the symbolic attitude expressed in the act of reading, in the handling of the book, in the stance of the reader and hearers, in the place that frames the reading, and in the design of the book down to and including the delineation of the letters of the text. The text, too, has been "performed" by the artisans who copied the words and made the elaborate cover for the Gospel book.

Likewise, the words of the Canon hold a privileged place in liturgical theology as bearers of the content of faith; but this content, to reiterate, is appropriated "indirectly" by all but a few participants through the performance of the liturgy. The crucial question that will arise again and again in the subsequent history of the liturgy is one of the perception of disparity between the faith implied by the words of the Canon (or of Scripture) and that implied by the performance of the liturgy.

What certainly comes to the fore in the performance of the liturgy described in *Ordo Romanus I* is a faith that is communal, hierarchical in terms of its organization around the orders of church and society, personal in terms of the central place afforded the pontiff in the enactment of that faith community, and participative in terms of the involvement of all in the actions of gathering, hearing, offering, and communing. Other elements of faith would have to include an examination of the liturgical seasons and their various readings, the homiletical and catechetical environment, and the understanding of the Canon in contemporary theology. Certainly one of the elements of this faith, which becomes clear in the enactment, concerns the intimate relationship between the community and the eucharistic bread. As mentioned above, the bread of the *Sancta* can be understood as a sort of perdurance of the community's act of offering through time and space. As such, it is also the perdurance of the divine in the midst of the community. The community, that is, in its right ordering and right offering, becomes the locus of the divine. But this transformation seems to involve the individual less than it does the community. In the gathering and the enactment of the sacrament the individual finds his or her place in that community, which, like the bread, is the meeting place of God and humanity. Thus the presence of Christ in the eucharistic bread, during this period, is by all means affirmed; but the enactment of that presence as yet does not include gestures to mark off the moment of transformation. Nor does the enactment of that presence seem possible without the gestural involvement of the ordered society that it invokes.

The "picture" we have of the Canon, with all bowed in their ranks toward the altar where the pontiff prays over the bread and wine, speaks of an assembly centered both in and beyond itself—beyond itself in the One to whom the prayer is addressed. Such an image, however, also suggests a society that would seek not to arrange itself for others but rather to bring others into its order, an order that cannot help but be identified with the divine.

The church thus enacted can be defined by its acts in the sacramental plot. That these are acts of faith can only be inferred from the participation of the worshippers. Faith thus always remains the crux of the later debates over the "reality" of what happens in the enactment of sacrament. The more faith is defined in terms of individual assent, the more the ostensibly communal presence of Christ in the enactment is qualified by that assent. By the late Middle Ages, as we know, the questions of reception of the host by sinners (e.g., Judas) and even by animals *(Quid mus sumit?)* have revealed the cracks in the ordered mosaic of the church.

Insofar as we may attribute some degree of congruence between the individual act and the form of the enactment, we may describe the church, in this ordo, in terms similar to those by which we described faith. The church enacted here is an ordered social structure with three centers: the person of the pontiff, the reading and hearing of the Word (proclamation), and the offering and receiving of the eucharistic bread and wine. The three centers attain a sort of congruence in that they are all, at one time or another, patient of the same gestures and spatial position vis-à-vis the community—they all stand in for the center that is them but not them. Thus, at his arrival and exit, as well as at other times, the pontiff receives the same bows from the people, the same accompaniment of candles and incense, as are directed toward the Gospel book at its reading and the eucharistic species at the Canon. Whereas the kiss of peace is offered and received among the pontiff and the people, the Gospel book is itself kissed; and the bread and wine are not kissed but eaten and drunk. This is an enactment of church that includes all of the symbolic means: matter, word, and, in the person of the pontiff, the gestural center of a gesturing community. On the other hand, all symbolism aside, part of the pontiff's role is to preside—to do those acts that can only, for the sake of order, be done by a single person. Thus, when the ordo directs the pontiff to nod for the conclusion of a chant, this gesture certainly enacts his hierarchical role; but it also, and more practically, constructs him as director of the flow and movement of the action.

The individuals in this church are not, however, mere passive observers. Certainly there are differences among the orders in the degree to which words and gestures are engaged. Only the reader reads the lesson; only the deacon reads the Gospel, only the acolyte holds the paten during the first part of the canon. However, at every point, every participant is given something to do to enact his or her participation in the action. This ranges from handing bread and wine to the clergy to receiving Communion to hearing the readings to bowing toward the altar at the Canon. Even the act of gathering for the Eucharist is given shape by the stational procession or by the act of waiting for the arrival of the pontiff.

What we cannot find in this enactment is anything that would salve our post-Enlightenment consciences looking for a democratic ordering of society. This church reflects an order that hierarchizes according to class and gender. What is remarkable is how it enacts within that order a common life and a common action of gathering, hearing Scripture, offering, praying, and eating and drinking together. It is clear, especially in the descriptions of the offertory and the Communion, that there are to be certain symbolic acts that *all* perform in their own societal/ecclesial order. The church is differentiated according to class and gender; but it is one in its enactment of the sacrament.

What, then, does such a church enact—of what does it make anamnesis? What, that is, is the shape of the sacrament that shapes the church in this ordo? Later commentators, such as Amalarius of Metz, would approach this question (asked of a somewhat Gallicanized enactment of this ordo) by finding scriptural narratives that were topological analogues to the sacramental plot. As Jacobson points out, "[F]or Amalar, the eucharistic act is not simply a memorial of the passion, but a making present of the entire history of salvation revealed in Christ."[27] Such an interpretation included the prophecies of the Hebrew Scripture, their fulfillment in Christ, and their realization in the act of the liturgy.[28] Moreover, the entire life of Christ, from his coming upon earth at the Introit, to his acclamation by the crowds of Jerusalem at the Sanctus, to his resurrection at the commingling of the bread and wine, is mapped onto the enacted rite in an attempt to make a case for the anamnetic reality of the Sacrament.[29]

Perhaps some clues to what is being done in this liturgy can be found in the words of the Roman Canon. I would suggest that the large number of commemorations made in this particular Canon reflect the construction of church that we have already discovered in the actions of *Ordo Romanus I.* Throughout the Canon, and especially at those Gelasian additions, the *Communicantes* and the *Nobis quoque,* the present community is contextualized by the larger community of apostles, martyrs, and pontiffs whose names are remembered as even now in fellowship with "all who stand around . . . who offer this sacrifice of praise for themselves and for all their own, for the redemption of their souls, for the hope of their salvation and safety, and pay their vows to you, the living and true God."[30] It is this community that is so vividly enacted in the ordo. Could we say, then, that the image of Trinity being enacted in this liturgy is that procession of God into creation in the act of incarnation by which a redeemed humanity is constituted by the Holy Spirit as the continuing locus of the resurrection of Christ? This "event" seems to follow the ongoing acts of gathering, waiting, welcoming (at least of the pontiff) into its midst, hearing, and, especially, offering together in order to be constituted as a new society in the receiving of Communion. It is not surprising that commentators on the Mass would find in this "plot" an image of the incarnation, life, passion, death, and resurrection of Christ because in that paschal mystery unfolds the narrative of the revelation of God through time and, particularly, in the present moment.

Nevertheless, what is specific to this ordo (and quite different from the enactment of the same rite in the late medieval Use of Sarum, for example) is the enacting of this salvific "plot" by a community that is both hierarchi-

cal and operative throughout its strata. What is also specific to this enactment is the metastatement that the salvation sought, the vows to be paid, the
fellowship prayed for, are always and only enacted in the community so
constituted. What we see is nothing less than an image of the "divine society" of the Holy Trinity enacted in anamnesis of that heavenly society of
the saints with whom the enactment seeks communion. If the means of this
salvific communion is Christ's sacrificial death on the cross, still this event
does not dominate the enactment as described in the ordo. Nowhere is there
any performance of immolation or even recreation of the Last Supper (although Amalarius will find the latter in the actions of the canon in the Gallicanized ordo a century or so later). Rather, the offering of the community's
gifts, accepted by God as were those of Abel, Abraham, and Melchizedek,
are asked to be carried "by the hands of your holy angel to your heavenly
altar in the sight of your divine Majesty, that as many of us as from this altar
of participation shall receive the most holy body and blood of your Son,
may be filled with all heavenly benediction and grace"[31] The gifts are offered
to the Father as "your own gifts and presents, a pure sacrifice, a holy sacrifice, a spotless sacrifice, the holy bread of eternal life and the chalice of everlasting salvation." The offering is not, it would appear, any sort of mimetic
reimmolation of Christ's Body except insofar as the community (empow-
ered by the Holy Spirit) enacts that risen Body in its offering of God's own
gifts. It would seem that *Ordo Romanus I* more closely weds enactment to the
words of the Roman Canon than will later ordines that foreground the confection and immolation of Christ's Body in the Host.

As would be expected from our definition of liturgy, the accomplishment of the object, the sacramental plot, accomplishes the end of the sacrament. In other words, the constitution of the church through the anamnesis
of the divine society of the Trinity, imaged in the heavenly society of the
saints and angels with the risen Christ, in its very enactment constitutes the
salvation that is sought. This salvation *is* membership in the society thus enacted and fellowship with the "angels and archangels and all the company
of heaven." This society is even more effective in that the ordo essentially
celebrates the ordering of Roman society in which the participants will live
their lives outside the liturgy. Put differently, Roman society becomes the
ongoing liturgy of which the sacrament is the image and performance.

What we do not see in either the text of the sacramentary or the ordo
are the fault lines in such a seemingly benign construction of the world.

Such fault lines only show up in comparisons. The subsequent redactions of *Ordo Romanus I* in the Frankish kingdoms with their different social structures will yield incongruities between actions and words. (We have already seen the strange evolution of the "notaries" into the angels of Easter.) Certainly the performance of such an enactment today would raise the central issue of how our current understanding of society can be enacted in the liturgy and whether that model can be understood as in any way making anamnesis of the Holy Trinity. Our age has, perhaps, not yet found an enactment that adequately incarnates its faith or its own lack of transcendence. For, in the end, the liturgy is a response to something larger than itself, something to which it must offer itself, to which the enactors can only give themselves over. Such an event, to be both true and good, requires a constant dialectic between acts and words, the constant making conscious that only that dialectic enables. One without the other—act without word, word without act—inevitably, throughout the course of history, has led to something less than the fullness of sacramentally enacted reality.

That the paschal mystery is enacted in the sacramental plot would appear to mean more than merely the representation of the events of Holy Week and more even than the recollection of the economy of salvation. The enactment of *Ordo Romanus I* points to a performance that is also an enactment, a remembrance that is also a construction. The Mass enacts a world that is both the world of the everyday, insofar as it is constructed according to the same class and gender model as everyday society, and the new world of church constructed by its gathering, praying, hearing, offering, feeding, and worshipping. It does these things according to a pattern, a "plot" that is a construction in time and space of the act that is named Trinity and that, for this ordo, is most clearly revealed in the mutual loving society of the Persons of the Trinity. That society, revealed in its economy as the incarnation, passion, death, and resurrection of the Second Person, is enacted sacramentally in the construction of a society that performs in symbol the acts that its economy enacts. Thus far could any sociological analysis concur. For the enactor, however, for one of faith, this performance is understood to be a participation in the enactment of that economy, to be the construction of a "new thing" made known even as it springs forth—once-occurrent Being-as-event.

Appendix

Ordo Romanus I Integrated with the Text of the Easter Mass
from the Gregorian Sacramentary, with Additional Rubrics from the
Ordo of St. Amand (after the Translation by E. G. Cuthbert F. Atchley)

Gregorian Sacramentary with Ordo Romanus Primus Plain numbers from Atchley's translation; numbers in brackets [ ] from Andrieu, *Les Ordines Romani,* vol. 2	Description
4. [24] At break of day on festivals all the clergy go on ahead of the pope to the appointed station (that is, to the church at which it was previously announced that the stational mass would be celebrated), excepting those whose duty it is to accompany him, as we said above, and await the pontiff in the church, with the papal almoner and the bearers and the rest who carry crosses, sitting in the presbytery—the bishops, that is, on the left hand as they enter, the presbyters on the other hand on the right, so that when the pontiff sits down and looks toward them, he may see the bishops on his right hand and the presbyters on his left.	Clergy gather in presbytery to await pope.
[25] Now when the pontiff draws near to the church, the collets and counselors belonging to the district that is responsible for duty on that day stand humbly awaiting him at the appointed spot, before he comes to the place	Acolytes and counselors and presbyter of title, etc., with incense

where he will dismount; [26] in like manner also the presbyter of the title or church at which the station is going to be held, together with the majordomos of the Roman Church, or the father of the hostelry (should that church happen to have one), with the presbyter subordinate to him [i.e., to the presbyter of the title], and the sexton, carrying a censer out of respect to the pope; and they all bow their heads when he arrives.

await pope outside, bowing head when he arrives.

[27] First the collets with the counselors, then the presbyters with their [curates?], having sought a blessing, separate into groups on either side, as their service requires, and go before the pontiff to the church.

Pope blesses them, and they lead him into church.

[28] But the advocates of the church, although they stand with the majordomos, do not go in front with them but merely follow the pontiff's palfrey, together with the collet who carries the handwashing basins, who must always follow the pontiff until the time when he goes up to the altar and be ready at his elbow in the presbytery when he is called upon by the district subdeacon to offer water.

5. [29] Now when the pontiff enters the church, he does not go straight up to the altar but first enters the sacristy, supported by the deacons who received him when he dismounted from his palfrey; and when he is gone therein he sits in his sedan-chair; and the deacons, after saluting the pontiff, go out of the sacristy and change their clothes before the doors;

Pope enters sacristy.

[30] and he who is going to read the Gospel makes ready the Gospel book (the seal of which has been unlocked by order of the archdeacon), which a collet holds for him outside his *planet*. If it should be necessary, on account of the size and weight of the larger Gospel book, two collets hold it outside their *planet*s while he makes it ready.

Deacons change clothes before door of sacristy and make ready Gospel book.

[31] Which done, the collet carries the Gospel book into the presbytery before the altar, the subdeacon-attendant leading the way, who, taking it, carries it outside his

Acolyte carries Gospel book to presbytery, following

planet and places it honorably on the altar with his own hands.

subdeacon, who places book on altar.

[32] Meanwhile, after the deacons go out of the sacristy, there remain with the pontiff the chancellor, the secretary, the chief counselor, the district notaries, and the subdeacon-attendant, who bears the pontiff's pall with its pins on his left arm outside his *planet.*

6. [33] Now the pontiff changes his vestments, with the assistance of the district subdeacons, in the following manner.

Pope vests . . .

The clerical chamberlain brings them, all folded up, after having received them from the door-warden.

[34] Near the head of the bench the district subdeacons take the vestments to put on the pontiff according to their order, one the linen, another the girdle, a third the amice, a fourth the linen dalmatic, a fifth the larger dalmatic, and another the *planet;* and thus they vest the pontiff in order.

. . . assisted by subdeacons and others.

[35] The chancellor and the secretary arrange his vestments so that they may hang well.

[36] Then, last of all, one of the deacons whom the lord pontiff may choose, or one of the subdeacons whom he may command, takes the pall from the hand of the subdeacon-attendant and sets it about the pontiff's shoulders, fastening it to the *planet* behind, in front, and on his left shoulder by means of the pins.

Then he salutes the lord pontiff, saying, *Bid a blessing, my lord.*

He answers, *May the Lord save us;* and the deacon (or subdeacon) replies, *Amen.*

7. [37] Then a district subdeacon, holding the pontiff's napkin on his left arm over his unrolled *planet,* goes out to the gate of the sacristy and says, *The choir.*

Subdeacon checks in with choir to determine . . .

They answer, *I am present.*

. . . that they are present and . . .

Then he asks, *Who is going to sing the psalm?* and they answer, *So-and-so, and so-and-so.*

. . . who will sing the Gradual . .

[38] Then the subdeacon returns to the pontiff, offers him the napkin, bowing himself to the pope's knees, and says, *My lord's servants, so-and-so the district subdeacon will read the epistle, and so-and-so of the choir will sing.*

. . . and informs pope who will read the epistle and who will chant the Gradual.

[39] And after this no change may be made in either reader or singer, but if this should be done, the ruler of the choir (i.e., the fourth of the choir, who always informs the pontiff on matters that relate to the singers) shall be excommunicated by the pontiff.

[40] When this has been announced, the subdeacon-attendant stands before the pontiff until such time as the latter shall sign to him that they may sing the psalm.

As soon as the signal is given, he immediately goes out before the doors of the sacristy, and says, *Light up!*

Subdeacon, at signal from pope, goes out of sacristy and says, *Light up!* Candles are lit.

[41] And as soon as they have lit their candles, the subdeacon-attendant takes the golden censer and puts incense in it in front of the sacristy doors, so that he may walk before the pontiff.

Incense is put into thurible.

[42] And the ruler of the choir passes through the presbytery to the precentor or the succentor or vice-succentor, and bowing his head to him says, *Sir, command!*

Ruler of choir asks precentor to direct choir to enter.

8. [43] Then they rise up and pass in order before the altar, and the two rows arrange themselves in this manner: the men-singers on either side without the doors [of the presbytery] and the children on each side within.

Choir enters church two by two and goes to appointed area near presbytery.

[44] Immediately the precentor begins the anthem for the entry; and when the deacons hear his voice they at once go to the pontiff in the sacristy.

Precentor begins Introit.

[45] Then the pontiff, rising, gives his right hand to the archdeacon and his left to the second [deacon] or whomever may be appointed, and they, after kissing his hands, walk with him as his supporters.

Pope enters supported by two archdeacon and another deacon . . .

[46] Then the subdeacon-attendant goes before him with the censer, diffusing the perfume of incense;

. . . preceded by censer and . . .

and the seven collets of the district that is responsible for that day, carrying seven lighted candlesticks, go before the pontiff to the altar.

. . . seven acolytes carrying candlesticks [and by remaining deacons].

[47] But before they arrive at the altar, the deacons put off their *planet*s in the presbytery, and the district deacon takes them and gives each severally to a collet of the district to which each deacon belongs.

Deacons remove chasubles and give them to acolytes.

[48] Then two collets approach, holding open pixes containing the Holy Element; and the subdeacon-attendant, taking them, with his hand in the mouth of the pix, shows the Holy Element to the pontiff and the deacon who goes before him.

Before altar acolytes bring pix with *Sancta,* which archdeacon shows to pope.

Then the pontiff and the deacon salute the Holy Element with bowed head, and look at the same so that if there be too many fragments he may cause some of them to be put in the aumbry.

Pope and deacon bow to Holy Element.

[49] After this the pontiff passes on, but before he comes to the choir the bearers of the candlesticks divide, four going to the right and three to the left; and the pontiff passes between them to the upper part of the choir and bows his head to the altar.

- Candle bearers divide, four right and three left.
- Pope passes between to foot of altar, bows head.

He then rises up and prays and makes the sign of the cross on his forehead, after which he gives the kiss of peace to one of the hebdomadary bishops and to the archpresbyter and to all the deacons.

- Pope arises and makes sign of cross on forehead.
- Pope gives kiss to one bishop, archpresbyter, all deacons.

[50] Then, turning toward the precentor, he signs to him to sing, *Glory be to the Father, and to the Son,* etc.; and the precentor bows to the pontiff and begins it.

Pope signals precentor to begin Gloria Patri.
[Pope kneels before altar during penitential seasons.]

Meanwhile, the ruler of the choir precedes the pontiff to set his faldstool before the altar, if it should be the season for it; and, approaching it, the pontiff prays thereat until the repetition of the verse [i.e., the anthem for the entry].

[51] Now when *As it was in the beginning* is said, the deacons rise up to salute the sides of the altar, first two and then the rest by twos, and return to the pontiff.

And then the latter arises and kisses the Gospel book and the altar and, going to his throne, stands there facing eastwards.

Deacons salute sides of altar two by two and return to pope. Pope
- rises,
- kisses Gospel book and altar,
- and goes to throne facing east.

9.   [52] Now, after the anthem is finished, the choir begins, *Lord, have mercy.*

But the precentor keeps his eye on the pontiff, so that the latter may sign to him if he wishes to change the number of the Kyries, and bows to him.

Choir begins Kyrie.

Choir sings until pope signals to stop.

[53] When they have finished, the pontiff turns himself round toward the people and begins, *Glory be to God on high,* if it be the season for it, and at once turns back again to the east until it be finished.

Then, after turning again to the people, he says, *Peace to you,* and, once more turning to the east, says, *Let us pray,* and the Collect follows.

At the end of it he sits, and the bishops and presbyters sit in like manner.

Pope turns toward people and begins Gloria, then turns back to east.
Pope turns to people to bid Collect, then turns east to pray it. Pope sits on throne.

10.   [55] Meanwhile the district subdeacons go up to the altar and place themselves at the right and left of the altar.

Then the pontiff signs to the bishops and presbyters to sit.

Subdeacons go to right and left of altar. Pope signals bishops and presbyters to sit.

[56] Now, as soon as the subdeacon who is going to read perceives that the bishops and presbyters are sitting down after the pontiff, he goes up into the ambo and reads the Epistle.

Subdeacon goes to ambo to read Epistle.

[57] When he has finished reading, a chorister goes up into the same with the grail and sings the respond.

And then *Alleluia* is sung by another singer, if it should be the season when *Alleluia* is said; if not, a tract; if when neither one nor the other is appointed, only the respond is sung.

Chorister goes to ambo to sing Gradual. Alleluia is sung by another. (Where?)

11. [59] Then the deacon kisses the pontiff's feet, and the latter says to him in an undertone, *The Lord be in your heart and on your lips.*

Then the deacon comes before the altar and, after kissing the Gospel book, takes it up in his hands; and there walk before him [to the ambo] two district subdeacons, who have taken the censer from the hand of the subdeacon-attendant, diffusing incense.

> Deacon kisses pope's feet.
>
> Deacon
> • kisses Gospel book,
> • takes it from altar, and
> • goes to ambo, preceded by two subdeacons with incense . . .

And in front of them they have two collets carrying two candlesticks.

On coming to the ambo, the collets part before it, and the subdeacons and the deacon with the Gospel book pass between them.

> . . . preceded by two acolytes with candles. Candle bearers part at ambo; deacon and subdeacons pass between.

[61] The subdeacon who is not carrying the censer then turns toward the deacon and offers him his left arm on which to rest the Gospel book, so that the former may open it with his right hand at the place where the mark for reading was put; [62] then, slipping his finger into the place where he has to begin, the deacon goes up to read, while the two subdeacons turn back to stand before the step coming down from the ambo.

> • Deacon opens book, resting on subdeacon's arm.
> • Deacon takes it up into ambo to read.
> • Subdeacons stand at descending step.

[63] The Gospel ended, the pontiff says, *Peace to you* and then *The Lord be with you.*

Answer is made, *And with your spirit;* and he says, *Let us pray.*

> Pope bids prayers (now missing).

[64] When the deacon is come down from the ambo, the subdeacon who first opened the Gospel book previously takes it from him and hands it to the subdeacon-attendant, who stands in his rank.

> • Deacon descends from ambo.
> • Deacon gives book to subdeacon, who gives it to attendant. Attendant takes book to choir to be kissed.

Then the latter, holding the book before his breast, outside his *planet,* offers it to be kissed by all who stand [in the quire] in the order of their rank.

[65] And after this a collet is ready on the step by the ambo with the case, in which the same subdeacon puts the Gospel book so that it may be sealed.

But the collet of the same district as that to which the subdeacon belongs carries it back to the Lateran.

- Acolyte stands at ambo with case for book.
- Subdeacon puts it in case.

12. [67] The deacon in the meantime returns to the altar, where a collet stands holding a chalice with a corporal lying on it; raising the chalice in his left arm, he offers the corporal to the deacon, who takes it off the chalice and lays it on the right part of the altar, throwing the other end of it over to the second deacon in order to spread it.

- Deacon returns to altar.
- Deacon takes corporal from acolyte.
- Two deacons spread corporal on altar.

[68] Then there go up to the throne the chancellor and the secretary, and the chief counselor, with all the district officials and notaries; but the subdeacon with the empty chalice follows the archdeacon.

Various officials go up to throne.

13. [69] The pontiff now goes down to the place where the notables sit, the chancellor holding his right hand and the chief counselor his left; and he receives the loaves of the princes in the order of their "promotion" (?).

Pope goes to notables and receives their loaves.

[70] The archdeacon next receives the flasks of wine and pours them into the greater chalice, which is carried by a district subdeacon; and a collet follows him holding a bowl outside his *planet,* into which the chalice, when full, is emptied.

- Archdeacon receives flasks of wine.
- He pours them into chalice.
- Chalice is emptied into bowl when full.

[71] A district subdeacon takes the loaves from the pontiff and hands them to the subdeacon-attendant, who places them in a linen cloth held by two collets.

Subdeacon hands loaves to attendant, who puts them in linen cloth.

[72] A hebdomadary bishop receives the rest of the loaves after the pontiff so that he may, with his own hand, put them into the linen cloth that is carried after him.

Hebdomadary bishop receives rest of loaves.

[73] Following him, the deacon-attendant receives the flasks of wine and pours them into the bowl with his own hand, after the archdeacon.

Subdeacon receives rest of wine.

[74] Meanwhile the pontiff, before passing over to the women's side, goes down before the confession, and there receives the loaves of the chancellor, the secretary, and the chief counselor. For on festivals they offer at the altar after the deacons.

Pope receives loaves before the confession.

[75] In like manner the pontiff goes up to the women's side and performs there all things in the same order as detailed above.

Pope receives loaves from women's side.

[76] And the presbyters do likewise, should there be need, either after the pontiff or in the presbytery.

Presbyters assist.

14. After this, the pontiff returns to his throne, the chancellor and the secretary each taking him by the hand, and there washes his hands.

- Pope returns to throne.
- He washes hands.

[77] The archdeacon stands before the altar and washes his hands at the end of the collection of the offerings.
Then he looks the pontiff in the face, signs to him, and, after the pontiff has returned his salutation, [the archdeacon] approaches the altar.

Archdeacon washes hands before altar.

At signal from pope . . .
. . . archdeacon approaches altar.

[78] Then the district subdeacons, taking the loaves from the hand of the subdeacon-attendant and carrying them in their arms, bring them to the archdeacon, who arranges them on the altar.
The subdeacons, by the bye, bring up the loaves on either side.

- Subdeacons take loaves from attendants.
- They bring them on either side to archdeacon.
- Archdeacon arranges them on altar.

[79] Having made the altar ready, the archdeacon then takes the pontiff's flask of wine from the subdeacon-oblationer and pours it through a strainer into the chalice; then the deacons' flasks and, on festivals, those of the chancellor, the secretary, and the chief counselor as well.

Archdeacon pours wine from pope's flask (and others) through strainer into chalice.

[80] Then the subdeacon-attendant goes down into the choir, receives a ewer of water from the hand of the ruler of the choir, and brings it back to the archdeacon, who pours it into the chalice, making a cross as he does so.

- Attendant gets ewer of water from choir.
- He brings it to archdeacon.
- Archdeacon pours it into chalice, making sign of cross.

[81] Then the deacons go up to the pontiff; on seeing which, the chancellor, the secretary, the chief of the district counselors [sic], the district notaries, and the district counselors come down from their ranks to stand in their proper places.

- Deacons go up to pope.
- Those with pope take places.

15. [82] Then the pontiff, arising from his throne, goes down to the altar and salutes it and receives the loaves from the hands of the hebdomadary presbyter and the deacons.

Pope
- goes to altar,
- salutes it,
- and receives loaves from presbyter and deacons.

[83] Then the archdeacon receives the pontiff's loaves from the subdeacon-oblationer and gives them to the pontiff.

- Oblationer gives pope's loaves to archdeacon.
- Archdeacon gives them to pope.

[84] And when the latter has placed them on the altar, the archdeacon takes the chalice from the hand of a district subdeacon and sets it on the altar on the right side of the pontiff's loaf, the offertory veil being twisted about its handles.

- Pope places loaves on altar.
- Archdeacon takes chalice from subdeacon.
- He puts it to right of pope's loaf with offertory veil twisted about handles.

Then he lays the veil on the end of the altar and stands behind the pontiff, [85] and the latter bows slightly to the altar and then turns to the choir and signs to them to stop singing..

- Archdeacon lays veil on end of altar
- He stands behind pope.
- Pope bows.
- Pope signs to choir to stop singing.

¶ And then is said the Prayer over the Offerings, in an undertone. *Receive, O Lord, we beseech you, the prayers of your people, with the offerings of sacrifices; that they, having been consecrated by the Easter mysteries, may contribute to our eternal healing by your working in us; through our Lord Jesus Christ, who with you and the Holy Spirit, lives and reigns, one God,*

Pope says *Oratio super oblata* in an undertone.

¶ At the end of this prayer the pontiff says in a loud voice, *For ever and ever.*

Answer: *Amen.*

16. [86] The offertory being finished, the bishops stand behind the pontiff, the senior in the midst, and the rest in their order: the archdeacon standing on the right of the bishops, the second deacon on their left, and the rest in order arranged in a line. [87] And the district subdeacons go behind the altar at the end of the offertory and face the pontiff, so that when he says, *For ever and ever,* or *The Lord be with you,* or *Lift up your hearts,* or *Let us give thanks,* they may be there to answer, standing upright, until the time when the choir begin to sing the angelical hymn, that is, *Holy, holy, holy.*

Subdeacons go "behind altar" and stand facing pope.

Pontiff, V: *The Lord be with you.*

R: *And with your spirit.*

V: *Lift up your hearts.*

R: *We lift them up unto the Lord.*

V: *Let us give thanks to our Lord.*

R: *It is meet and right.*

Pontiff: *It is very meet and right, reasonable and healthful, that we should at all times and in all places give thanks unto you, O holy Lord, almighty Father, eternal God; glorious in truth is it to praise you at all times, but specially on this day, when Christ our Passover was sacrificed for us, by whom the sons of light arise to eternal life, the courts of the heavenly kingdom are opened to the faithful, and by the law of blessed fellowship human things are changed to divine, for the death of us all is destroyed by the cross of Christ, and in his resurrection the life of every man has risen again; whom we own in his putting on of our mortality to be the God of majesty, and acknowledge to be God and Man in the glory of his godhead, who by his death has destroyed our death and by his resurrection has restored to us life. And therefore, with angels and archangels, thrones and dominations, and the whole company of the heavenly army, we sing the hymn of your glory, evermore saying,*

The Choir: *Holy, holy, holy, Lord of Hosts; heaven and earth are full of your glory.*

All bow.

[88] And when they have finished it, the pontiff rises alone and enters on the Canon.

Pope rises.

The bishops, however, and the deacons, subdeacons, and presbyters remain in the presbytery and bow themselves down.

17. [91] We have, by the bye, omitted something about the paten. When the pontiff begins the canon, a collet comes near, having a linen cloth thrown around his neck, and holds the paten before his breast on the right side [of the altar?] until the middle of the Canon.

Acolyte wearing linen cloth around neck holds paten before breast.

[92] Then the subdeacon-attendant holds it outside his *planet* and comes before the altar and waits there with it until the district subdeacon takes it from him.

Pontiff: *Therefore we humbly pray and beseech you, O most merciful Father, through Jesus Christ, your Son, our Lord, to accept and bless these gifts, these offerings, these holy and spotless sacrifices, which, in the first place, we offer to you for your holy Catholic Church, that you would be pleased to keep it in peace, to guard, unite, and govern it throughout the whole world, together with your servant our pope N.*

Remember, O Lord, your servants and handmaidens, and all here present, whose faith is evident and whose devotion known to you; who are offering to you this sacrifice of praise, for themselves and all their friends, for the redemption of their souls, for the hope of their salvation and their safety, who direct their prayers to you, everlasting God, living and true.

Joining in communion with, and moreover celebrating the most holy day of the resurrection of our Lord God Jesus Christ, according to the flesh; and venerating the memory, first of the glorious ever-virgin Mary, mother of the same our God and Lord Jesus Christ; and also of your blessed apostles and martyrs, Peter, Paul, Andrew, James, John, Thomas, James, Philip, Bartholomew, Matthew, Simon and Jude, Linus Cletus, Clement, Xystus, Cornelius, Cyprian, Laurence, John and Paul, Cosmas and Damian, George, Gregory, and all your saints, by whose merits and prayers grant that in all things we may be defended by the help of your protection, through the same Christ, our Lord.

Graciously accept, O Lord, we beseech you, this oblation of our service and of your whole family, which we offer unto you, for these also whom you have vouchsafed to regenerate with water and the Holy Spirit, and to grant remission of all their sins order our days in your peace, and deliver us from everlasting damnation, and number us in the flock of your chosen ones; through Christ our Lord.

Vouchsafe, O God, we beseech you, to make this offering in every way blessed, available, valid, reasonable and acceptable, that it may become to us the body and blood of your dearly beloved Son, but our Lord God, Jesus Christ,

Who, on the day before he suffered, took bread in his holy and venerable hands, and raising his eyes heavenwards to you, O God, his almighty Father, gave thanks to you, and blessed, and brake it, and gave it to his disciples, saying, Take and eat this, for this is my body.

Likewise after supper he took this noble chalice into his holy and venerable hands, and gave thanks to you, and blessed it and gave it to his disciples, saying, Take and drink of this, for this is the chalice of my holy blood of the new and eternal testament, a mystery of faith, which shall be shed for you and for many, for the remission of sins.

As often as you do these things, do them for my memorial.

Wherefore, O Lord, we your servants and your holy people are mindful both of the blessed passion of the same Christ, your Son, our Lord God, and also of his resurrection from hell, and of his glorious ascension into heaven, and offer unto your excellent majesty of your own gifts and presents a pure sacrifice, a holy sacrifice, a spotless sacrifice, the holy bread of eternal life and the chalice of everlasting salvation.

Vouchsafe to regard these with favorable and gracious countenance, and accept them as you deigned to accept the gifts of your righteous child Abel, the sacrifice of our patriarch Abraham, and the holy sacrifice, the spotless offering that your high priest Melchisedech offered unto you.

We humbly beseech you, almighty God, to command these things to be borne by the hands of your holy angel to your heavenly altar in the sight of your divine majesty, that so many of us as from this altar of participation shall receive the most holy body and blood of your Son, may be filled with all heavenly benediction and grace; through Christ our Lord.

[89] Now when the pontiff says, *to us sinners, also,* the subdeacons rise up;

To us sinners, also, your servants, who trust in the multitude of your mercies, vouchsafe to grant some part and fellowship with your holy apostles and martyrs, with John, Stephen, Matthias, Barnabas, Ignatius, Alexander, Marcellinus, Peter, Perpetua, Agnes, Cecilia, Felicitas, Anastasia, Agatha, Lucy, and all your saints, into whose company we beseech you to admit us, not weighing our merits, but pardoning our offenses; through Christ our Lord,

- Subdeacons rise.
- Attendant takes paten to subdeacon before altar.

And when he says, *By whom all these things, O Lord,* the archdeacon arises alone.

by whom, O Lord, you ever create all these good things, hallow, quicken and bless them, and bestow them upon us.

Archdeacon rises.

When the pontiff says, *By him, and with him,* the archdeacon lifts up the chalice with the offertory veil passed through its handles, and, holding it, raises it toward the pontiff.

Then the latter touches the side of the chalice with the loaves, saying, *By him, and with him,* as far as, *For ever and ever. Amen.*

By him and with him, and in him, be to you, God the Father Almighty, in the unity of the Holy Spirit, all honor and glory, for ever and ever, Amen.

- Archdeacon lifts chalice with veil through handles.
- He raises it toward pope.
- Pope touches it with loaves.
- Pope sets loaves down.

Then the pontiff sets the loaves down again in their place, and the archdeacon puts the chalice down by them and removes the offertory veil from the handles of the same.

- Archdeacon puts chalice next to them.
- Archdeacon removes veil.

18. [93] But at the end of the canon, the district subdeacon stands behind the archdeacon with the paten.

Subdeacon stands behind archdeacon with paten.

Pontiff: *Let us pray. Being urged by healthful precept, and prepared by divine instruction, we are bold to say, Our Father, in heaven, hallowed be your name, your kingdom come, your will be done on earth as it is in heaven; give us this day our daily bread and forgive us our trespasses, as we forgive those who trespass against us, and lead us not into temptation,*

Answer: *But deliver us from the evil. Amen.*

Pontiff: *Deliver us, O Lord, from every evil, past, present, and to come; and at the intercession for us of the blessed and glorious and ever-virgin, Mary the Theotokos, and of your blessed apostles Peter and Paul and Andrew, and all saints, graciously give your peace in our days, that we, being aided by the help of your mercy, may ever be freed from sin and safe from all unquiet,*

[94] And when the pontiff says, *And safe from all unquiet,* the archdeacon turns round and, after kissing the paten, takes it and gives it to the second deacon to hold.

Archdeacon
- turns,
- kisses paten, and
- takes and gives it to deacon.

through our Lord Jesus Christ, your Son, who with you lives and reigns, God, in the unity of the Holy Spirit, for ever and ever.

Answer: *Amen.*

Pontiff: *The peace of the Lord be with you always.*

- Pope makes sign of cross three times over chalice.
- He drops *Sancta* into it.

[95] When the pontiff says, *The peace of the Lord be with you always,* he makes a cross with his hand thrice over the chalice and drops a consecrated fragment [reserved from the last Solemn Mass] into it.

Answer: *And with your spirit.*

[96] Meanwhile the archdeacon gives the kiss of peace to the chief hebdomadary bishop, then to the rest of the clergy in order, and then to the people.	Archdeacon gives kiss of peace • to hebdomadary bishop, • to rest of clergy, and • to people.
19. [97] Then the pontiff breaks one of the loaves on its right side and leaves the fragment that he breaks off upon the altar; but the rest of his loaves he puts on the paten that the deacon is holding [98] and returns to his throne.	Pope • breaks piece from right side of loaf, • leaves fragment on altar, • puts rest on paten (held by deacon), and • returns to throne.
[99] Immediately the chancellor, the secretary, and the chief counselor, with all the district officials and notaries, go up to the altar and stand in their order on the right and left.	All officials go to stand at right and left of altar.
The invitationer and the treasurer, and the notary of the papal vicar, when the choir sing *O Lamb of God,* go up and stand facing the pontiff so that he may sign to them to write down the names of those who are to be invited either to the pontiff's table, by the invitationer, or to the papal vicar's, by his notary; and when the list of names is completed, they go down and deliver the invitations.	Invitations to papal table are assigned and delivered.
[100] The archdeacon now lifts up the chalice and gives it to the district subdeacon, who holds it near the right corner of the altar.	• Archdeacon lifts chalice and gives it to subdeacon. • Subdeacon holds it near right corner of altar.

[101] Then the subdeacons-attendant, with the collets, who carry little sacks, draw near to the right and left of the altar; the collets hold out their arms with the little sacks, and the subdeacons-attendant stand in front, to make ready the openings of the sacks for the archdeacon to put the loaves into them, first those on the right, and then those on the left.

* Attendants and acolytes bring sacks to right and left.
* Archdeacon puts loaves into sacks.

[102] The collets then pass right and left among the bishops around the altar, and the rest [i.e., the subdeacons] go down to the presbyters, so that they may break the consecrated loaves.

* Acolytes take sacks to bishops to break bread.
* Attendants take sacks to presbyters to break bread.

[103] Two district subdeacons, however, have proceeded to the throne, carrying the paten to the deacons, so that they may perform the fraction.

Subdeacons take paten to throne to deacons for fraction.

[104] Meanwhile the latter keep their eyes on the pontiff so that he may sign to them when to begin; and when he has signed to them, after returning the pontiff's salutation, they make the fraction.

At signal from pope, deacons make fraction.

[105] The archdeacon, after that the altar has been cleared of the loaves, except the fragment that the pontiff broke off his own loaf and left on the altar (which is done so that, while the solemnities of mass are being celebrated, the altar may never be without a sacrifice), looks at the choir, and signs to them to sing, *O Lamb of God,* and then goes to the paten with the rest.

* Archdeacon signals choir to start Agnus Dei.
* Archdeacon joins others at paten for fraction.

¶ Then the choir sing during the fraction:

O Lamb of God, that takes away the sins of the world, have mercy upon us.

And the collets respond: *O Lamb of God, that takes away the sins of the world, have mercy upon us.*

[106] The fraction being finished, the second deacon takes the paten from the subdeacon and carries it to the throne to communicate the pontiff, [107] who, after

* Deacon takes paten to throne to communicate pope.

partaking, puts a particle that he has bitten off the Holy Element into the chalice that the archdeacon is holding, making a cross with it thrice and saying,

Pontiff: *May the commixture and consecration of the Body and Blood of our Lord Jesus Christ be to us who receive it for life everlasting.*

Answer: *Amen.*

Pontiff: *Peace be with you.*

Answer: *And with your spirit.*
        And then the pontiff is communicated with the chalice by the archdeacon.

20. [108] Then the archdeacon comes with the chalice to the corner of the altar and announces the next station: [¶ Then the archdeacon announces the next station, saying in a loud voice:]

Tomorrow the station will be at the Basilica of St. Peter the chief of the Apostles.

And the choir answer: *Thanks be to God.*
        And after he has poured a small quantity of the contents of the chalice into the bowl held by the collet, there approach to the throne, so that they may communicate from the pontiff's hand, first the bishops in order, [109] and then the presbyters in like manner, so that they may communicate after them.

¶ In administering the Sacrament of the Body is said to each communicant: *The Body of our Lord Jesus Christ avail to you for the remission of all sins, and for everlasting life.*

        [110] Then the chief hebdomadary bishop takes the chalice from the hands of the archdeacon, in order to ad-

- Pope bites off particle.

Pope places particle in chalice (held by archdeacon), making sign of cross.

Archdeacon communicates pope with chalice.

Archdeacon
- comes to corner of altar and
- announces next station.

- Archdeacon pours small amount of wine into bowl held by acolyte.
- Pope communicates bishops and presbyters at throne.

- Archdeacon communicates bishops

minister the species of wine to the remaining ranks down to the chief counselor.

and presbyters from chalice.
- Chief hebdomadary bishop takes chalice from archdeacon and communicates remaining clergy.

[111] Then the archdeacon takes the chalice from him and pours it into the bowl that we mentioned above; he then hands the empty chalice to the district subdeacon, who gives him the reed wherewith he communicates the people with the species of wine.

Archdeacon
- takes chalice,
- pours remaining contents into bowl, and
- takes reed from subdeacon and gives him empty chalice.

[112] But the subdeacon-attendant takes the chalice and gives it to the collet, who replaces it in the sacristy.

Attendant replaces chalice in sacristy.

[113] *And when the archdeacon has administered the cup to those whom the pope communicated, the pontiff comes down from his throne, with the chancellor and the chief counselor, who hold his hands, in order to communicate those who are in the places allotted to the magnates, [114] after which the archdeacon communicates them with the cup.

- Pope comes down to administer bread to magnates.
- Archdeacon administers cup to magnates.

¶ During the Communion of the people, the choir sing the Communion anthem and psalm.

Choir sings . . .

Choir: Christ our Passover is sacrificed for us, Alleluja, let us therefore keep the feast with the unleavened bread of sincerity and truth, Alleluja.

Communio

Subdeacons repeat: *Christ our Passover,* etc.

Choir: Psalm 139, beginning where they left off to sing the Gloria of the Introit.

Subdeacons: *Christ our Passover,* etc.

Choir: the next verse of the Psalm.

Subdeacons: *Christ our Passover,* etc.

And so on to the end or the signal to sing the Gloria.

Choir: *Glory be to the Father, and to the Son, and to the Holy Spirit.*

Subdeacons: *As it was in the beginning, is now, and ever shall be, world without end, Amen.*

Choir: *Purge out the old leaven that ye may be a new lump as you are unleavened.*

Subdeacons: *Christ our Passover,* etc.

After this the bishops communicate the people, the chancellor signing to them to do so with his hand under his *planet,* at the pontiff's formal request; and then the deacons administer the cup to them.

• Bishops and presbyters communicate remaining men.
• Deacons and presbyters administer cup.

[115] Next they all pass over to the left side of the church and do the same there.

Same for women.

[116] Moreover, the presbyters, at a sign from the chancellor, by command of the pontiff, communicate the people also, and afterwards administer the cup to them as well.

[117] Now as soon as the pontiff began to communicate the magnates, the choir immediately begins to sing the Communion anthem by turns with the subdeacons; and they go on singing until, when all the people have communicated, the pontiff signs to them to sing *Glory be to the Father,* and then, after repeating the verse, they cease.

Pope signals subdeacon to signal for choir to cease.

[118] The pontiff, directly after communicating those on the women's side, goes back to the throne and com-

municates the district officials in order, and those who
stand in a group, and on festivals twelve of the choir as
well.

But on other days these communicate in the presbytery.

[119] After all these the invitationer, and the treasurer,
the collet who holds the paten, he who holds the towel,
and he who offers water at the lavatory communicate at
the throne, and after the pontiff has communicated them
[120] the archdeacon administers the cup to them.

21. [121] Then a district subdeacon stands before the
pontiff so that he may sign to him; but the pontiff first
looks at the people to see if they have finished communicating and then signs to him.

[122] Then he goes to the pontiff's shoulder and looks
toward the precentor, making a cross on his forehead as a
sign to him to sing *Glory be;* and the precentor returns his
salutation and sings, *Glory be to the Father,* etc. *As it was in
the beginning,* etc., and the verse.

[123] At the end of the anthem the pontiff rises with
the archdeacon and comes before the altar and says the
Post-Communion Collect, facing eastwards.

Pope and archdeacon
come to altar and face
east (not turning to
people for salutation).

For at this part of the service, when he says, *The Lord
be with you,* he does not turn to the people.

Pontiff: *The Lord be with you.*

Answer: *And with your spirit.*

Pontiff: *Let us pray.*

And then he says the Post-Communion Collect:

*O Lord, pour forth upon us the spirit of your love; that of your
loving-kindness you may make us to be of one mind whom you have
refreshed and fed with these Easter Mysteries; through Christ our
Lord,* etc.

[124] At the end of the Collect, one of the deacons, appointed by the archdeacon, looks toward the pontiff for him to sign to him and then says to the people, *Go, the Mass is over!* and they answer, *Thanks be to God.*

¶ A deacon then says: *Go, it is over.*

Answer: *Thanks be to God.*

Deacon, at signal from pope, dismisses people.

[125] Then the seven collets carrying their candlesticks go before the pontiff, and a district subdeacon with the thurible, to the sacristy.

District subdeacon with thurible, seven candle bearers, and pope head toward sacristy.

[126] But as he goes down into the presbytery, first the bishops say, *Sir, bid a blessing;* and the pontiff answers, *May the Lord bless us!* and they answer, *Amen.*

Inside presbytery
- Bishops ask for blessing;
- then presbyters,
- then monks,
- then choir,
- then banner bearers,
- then acolytes,
Outside presbytery
- then crucifers,
- then junior sextons.

After the bishops the presbyters say the same, and then the monks; then the choir; then the military banner bearers (i.e., those who carry standards after them the bearers); after them the taperers; after them the collets who watch the gate (of the confession?); after them, but outside the presbytery, those who carry the crosses; then the junior sextons; and, this done, the pontiff enters the sacristy.

Pope enters sacristy.

22. [Ordo II] *Supplement, showing what things are done differently if the stational mass is celebrated by another bishop when the pope is unable to be present.*

First, that the deacons, and not the bishop who is celebrating that day, enter with the candlestick and thurible.

Second, that the bishop does not sit in the throne behind the altar.

Third, that he does not say the Collect behind the altar, but at the right side of it

Fourth, that the deacon, and not the bishop himself, makes the sign of the cross in the place where it is customary.

Fifth, that the chalice is not elevated by the archdeacon after the Canon where *By whom you dost create all these things, O Lord,* is said.

Sixth, when *The Peace of the Lord be with you always* ought to be said, the subdeacon-oblationer brings a fragment of the *Fermentum,* which has been hallowed by the pope, and gives it to the archdeacon, and he offers it to the bishop, who, making the sign of the cross with it thrice as he says, *The Peace of the Lord be with you always,* drops it into the chalice.

This also is done differently, for the pope does not break one of the loaves, but the bishop breaks one over the cloth on the altar that is called a corporal.

Then all communicate, save only the celebrant bishop, for he does not communicate himself by his own hand.

Another bishop puts a part of a loaf into his hand, and then he communicates himself from his own hand.

Likewise a presbyter does for a presbyter, and a deacon for a deacon.

Everything else the bishop does just as the pope.

In like manner also things are done by a presbyter when he celebrates masses at a station, except *Glory be to God on high,* for this is not said by a presbyter except at Easter.

Bishops who rule over cities perform all things as the pope himself.

The rite of concelebration on festivals

48.   On festivals, that is to say on Easter Day, Pentecost, St. Peter's Day, and Christmas Day, the cardinal presbyters assemble, each one holding a corporal in his hand, and the archdeacon comes and offers each one of them three loaves.

And when the pontiff approaches the altar, they surround it on the right and the left and say the Canon simultaneously with him, holding their loaves in their hands and not placing them on the altar, so that the pontiff's voice may be heard the more strongly, and they simultaneously consecrate the body and blood of the Lord, but the pontiff alone makes a cross over the altar.

Notes

1. INTRODUCTION

1. Of the four accounts of the Last Supper in the New Testament (five, if we include the Fourth Gospel), this "command" is included only in Luke 22:19 (after the bread) and in 1 Cor. 11:24 (after the bread) and 25 (after the cup).

2. Justin Martyr, *Dialogue with Trypho* 41, in Sheerin, *Eucharist,* p. 36.

3. Theodore of Mopsuestia, "Baptismal Homily IV," translated in Yarnold, *Awe-Inspiring Rites,* pp. 216–19.

4. Paul Jacobson, "Ad Memoriam Ducens," p. 192.

5. This is effectively argued for the Towneley cycle in Lepow, *Enacting the Sacrament.*

6. Young, *Drama of the Medieval Church*; Hardison, *Christian Rite.*

7. Bakhtin, *Toward a Philosophy*; see also Barthes, *Elements of Semiology*; Eco, *Limits of Interpretation.*

8. For a summary of the many approaches to "performance theory," see Carlson, *Performance.*

9. See especially Austin, *How to Do Things*; Searle, *Speech Acts*; and the language model of Noam Chomsky.

10. See the work of Victor Turner, especially *Dramas, Fields, and Metaphors,* and Kenneth Burke, especially *A Grammar of Motives.*

11. See Bakhtin, *Toward a Philosophy*; Heidegger, *Being and Time*; Whitehead, *Process and Reality.*

12. Chambers, *Medieval Stage,* vol. 2, pp. 2–3.

13. See Young, *Drama of the Medieval Church*; Hardison, *Christian Rite*; Flanigan, "Roman Rite"; Wickham, *Medieval Theatre*; James M. Gibson, "Quem Quaeritis in Presepe"; and Muir, *Biblical Drama.*

14. See especially Stevens, *Words and Music*; and articles in Crocker and Hiley, *Early Middle Ages.*

15. In Koziol, *Begging Pardon and Favor,* see especially ch. 9, "How Does Ritual Mean."

2. Performing Liturgical Interpretation in the Medieval West

1. See Chambers, *Medieval Stage,* vol. 1, pp. 1–22.

2. See Hardison, *Christian Rite.*

3. See the discussion in Chambers, *Medieval Stage,* vol. 2, pp. 7–14, and in Young, *Drama of the Medieval Church,* vol. 1, pp. 178–97.

4. Reprinted in translation in Nagler, *Sourcebook of Theatrical History,* pp. 39–41.

5. Chambers, *Medieval Stage,* vol. 2, p. 16.

6. See Brockett, *History of the Theatre,* pp. 105–25.

7. Craig, *English Religious Drama,* p. 154.

8. Ogden, "Drama in the Medieval Church."

9. Such an appropriation of liturgical ceremony for use in the court may have begun in the anointing with oil of Pepin III by St. Boniface (on behalf of Pope Zachary) as early as 751.

10. Schnusenberg, *Relationship.*

11. Hardison, *Christian Rite,* p. 216.

12. Flanigan, "Liturgical Drama."

13. See Lerer, "'Represented now in yower syght,'" for the development of this aspect of performance.

14. Young, *Drama of the Medieval Church*; Flanigan, "Liturgical Drama"; Rankin, *Music of the Medieval Liturgical Drama.*

15. For this concept, see the discussions of M. Maus, "Essai sur le don," and G. Duby, *Guerriers et paysans, VII–XII siècles: Premier essor de l'économie européénne,* in Chauvet, *Symbol and Sacrament,* pp. 100–105.

16. MacGregor, *Fire and Light,* p. 382.

17. Bishop, *Liturgica Historica,* p. 1.

18. "24. Et vadunt ad secretarium dioconi scilicet et subdiaconi in planetis et accendent duo regionarii per unumquemque faculas de ipso lumine, quod de VI feria absconditum est, et veniunt ad altare." Andrieu, *Les Ordines Romani,* vol. 3, p. 272.

19. The basic source for these rubrics is Ordo XXVIII (c. 800) because both Ordo XXXI and Ordo XXXII (end of the ninth century) appear to be based on it. See discussions in ibid., vol. 3, pp. 482 ff. and 514. Ordo XXVIII itself seems to derive from the earlier (eighth century) Ordines XXIV, XXVI, and XXVII. Ibid., p. 381.

20. Ibid., pp. 403–4, reprinted in Appendix A below.

21. The only variant seems to be that represented by Ordo XXIX (c. 870–90), in which the reading of Genesis precedes the blessing of the paschal candle. This

would appear to be a practice derived from the source of Ordo XXIX, namely Ordo XXVII (750−800), which may contain the more primitive Roman practice of lighting two candles that are borne before the bishop or abbot and placed at each corner of the altar before the reading of the lessons. Ordo XXVII implies that this was the practice in the city of Rome, where there was no blessing of the candle, as opposed to that in the suburbicarian churches. Thus it is interesting, again, to see in Ordo XXIX the layering of practices from Roman ordines and from those containing more strictly Frankish material.

22. Amalarius of Metz, *Liber officialis,* p. 112.

23. Martini, *Il Cosiddetto Pontifical di Poitiers,* p. 214.

24. Ibid., p. 216.

25. MSS Paris, Bibliothèque Nationale, MS lat 1240. See Young, *Drama of the Medieval Church,* p. 204.

26. Reprinted in translation in Nagler, *Sourcebook of Theatrical History,* pp. 39−41.

27. Vogel, *Pontifical romano-germanique,* pp. 93−101.

28. Amalarius of Metz, *Liber officialis,* pp. 121−22.

29. For a discussion of the semiotics of culture that underlies this study, see Garcia-Rivera, *St. Martin de Porres,* pp. 30−39, and Schreiter, *Constructing Local Theologies,* pp. 56−73.

30. Schreiter, *Constructing Local Theologies,* pp. 85−91.

31. Rom 5:14: "Yet death exercised dominion from Adam to Moses, even over those whose sins were not like the transgression of Adam, who is a type of the one who was to come."

32. Southern, *Saint Anselm,* p. 48.

33. "The Story of the Holy Rood," in Morris, *Legends of the Holy Rood,* pp. 62−86.

34. Thomas Aquinas, *Summa theologica,* Q77, iii.

35. "There was much grumbling at Beverley in 1411 because certain well-to-do persons *(generosi),* who did not practice any trade or handicraft, had hitherto escaped the payments of contributions to the civic function; and the municipal authorities were constantly called upon to adjust and readjust the responsibility for this and that pageant with the fluctuations of prosperity among the various occupations. But on the other hand, the plays were the cause of much and profitable resort to those fortunate towns which possessed them. The mercers' guild at Shrewsbury found it necessary to impose a special fine upon those of its members whose business avocations required them 'to ride or goe to Coventrie Faire' at Corpus Christi tide, and so to miss the procession of the guilds at home." Chambers, *Medieval Stage,* vol. 2, p. 110.

36. Foster, *Northern Passion,* vol. 1, p. 81.

37. Lumiansky and Mills, *Chester Mystery Cycle,* pp. 271−72.

38. The Last Supper is referred to as "Christ's maunde" as early as the fourteenth century (see *OED*).

39. Rubin, *Corpus Christi,* p. 34: "In tracing the design of the eucharist and the mass, one reaches a point in the late thirteenth century when all was said and

done—not intellectually but in terms of the construction of a pastoral edifice, one which was conveyed through guide-books, the synodal legislation, the sermons, and *exempla,* collected in the thirteenth century as never before. Although theologians continued to disagree about the eucharist throughout the Middle Ages, they were suspicious of any change in its pastoral design."

40. Ibid., p. 246.

41. Episcopal Church, *The Hymnal, 1982,* Hymn 329.

42. See the discussion in Pelikan, *Growth of Medieval Theology,* vol. 1, pp. 79 ff.

43. Jungmann, *Mass of the Roman Rite,* vol. 1, p. 129.

44. See the discussion in Craig, *English Religious Drama,* pp. 239–80, and Meredith, *Passion Play,* p. 9.

45. Meredith, *Passion Play,* p. 20. Both these works were popular enough to have been printed in the fifteenth century, and *The Golden Legend* was translated into French.

46. Ibid., p. 72.

47. There is an interesting mistranslation of the Latin Bible contained in Jesus' account. Whereas the Vulgate calls for the eating of unleavened bread with bitter herbs (literally "wild lettuce," *Lactucis agrestibus*), the play gives the directions as "bitter bread" with "the bitter suckling." The Latin word for "suckling" is *lactens,* which could have been misread for *lactuca,* "lettuce." This is of importance only in that finding a text with the same mistranslation would yield a clue as to the antecedents of this part of the play.

48. Fletcher, in "The N-Town Plays," p. 183, specifically attributes the exegesis of Exod. 12 found in the play to a gloss of Rabanus Maurus found in the twelfth-century *Glossa ordinaria* but probably available to the playwright in a Latin sermon, "Qui manducat hunc panum vivet in eternum," found in an MS in the Hereford Cathedral Library (O. III.5, fols. 21v–24).

49. Meredith, *Passion Play,* p. 75.

50. Ibid., p. 73.

51. Vorgrimler, *Sacramental Theology,* p. 160.

52. Rubin, *Corpus Christi,* p. 71.

53. Robert Pullen (d. c. 1146), quoted in Rubin, *Corpus Christi,* p. 71.

54. Meredith, *Passion Play,* p. 76.

55. Ibid., p. 78.

56. I rely for support for this notion of uniqueness on ibid., p. 21.

57. Ibid., p. 76.

58. Ibid., p. 77.

59. Ibid.

60. Ibid., p. 78.

61. Rubin, *Corpus Christi,* p. 110. Among the collections that would be of future benefit in examining the popular origins of the plays would be Caesarius of Heisterbach's *Dialogus miraculorum* (1224–40), James of Vitry's exempla from ser-

mons of 1227–40, Thomas of Cantimpre's *Bonum universale de apibus* (1256–61), and the *Legenda aurea* (c. 1255).

62. J. Berlioz and J. M. David, "Introduction bibliographique," *Mélanges de l'École Francais de Rome* 92 (1980): 15–31, quoted in Rubin, *Corpus Christi,* p. 115.

63. Davis, *Non-Cycle Plays and Fragments,* p. lxxiii.

64. MSS Trinity College, Dublin, F.4.20 Catalogue N.652, ff. 338^r–356^r, printed in Davis, *Non-Cycle Plays and Fragments.*

65. Davis, *Non-Cycle Plays and Fragments,* p. lxxiii.

66. Ibid., p. 70. I have modernized the English for the sake of comprehension.

67. Ibid., p. 72.

68. Swanson, *Religion and Devotion,* pp. 283–84.

69. Rubin, *Corpus Christi,* p. 118. See pp. 125–26 for further examples.

70. Davis, *Non-Cycle Plays and Fragments,* p. 73.

71. Ibid., p. 80.

72. Ibid.

73. Ibid., p. 83.

74. Ibid., p. 84.

75. See Chambers, *Medieval Stage,* vol. 2, p. 102.

76. Craig, *English Religious Drama,* p. 363.

77. Archdiocese of York Court of High Commission, 1576, in reference to the Wakefield plays, quoted in Craig, *English Religious Drama,* p. 360.

3. PERFORMING DRAMA, LITURGY, AND BEING-AS-EVENT

1. Judith Malina and Julian Beck, *Paradise Now,* pp. 5–6.

2. Brockett, *History of the Theatre,* p. 728.

3. Counsell, *Signs of Performance,* pp. 224–25.

4. Ibid., p. 209.

5. Carlson, *Performance,* 15. The quote within the quote is from Hymes, "Breakthrough into Performance."

6. See the discussion in Schechner, *Between Theatre and Anthropology,* p. 35.

7. Carlson, *Performance,* p. 15.

8. Bakhtin, *Rabelais and His World,* pp. 122–23, quoted in Carlson, *Performance,* p. 28.

9. Carlson, *Performance,* p. 15.

10. Carlson, *Performance,* p. 16; the quotes inside the quote are from Singer, *Traditional India,* p. xiii.

11. Carlson, *Performance,* p. 25.

12. Ibid., p. 18; the quotes inside the quote are from Bateson, *Steps to an Ecology,* p. 179.

13. Barba and Savarese, *Dictionary of Theatre Anthropology*, p. 10. See also the discussion in Carlson, *Performance*, p. 19.

14. Carlson, *Performance*, p. 19.

15. Ibid., p. 29, referring to Jacques Ehrmann, "*Homo Ludens* Revisited," in *Game, Play, Literature*, ed. Jacques Ehrmann (Boston: Beacon Press, 1968), p. 33.

16. Van Gennep, *Rites de Passage*.

17. Carlson, *Performance*, pp. 20–21.

18. Turner, *Dramas, Fields, and Metaphors*, p. 33.

19. Ibid., pp. 29–32.

20. Ibid. p. 38.

21. Ibid.

22. Ibid., p. 39.

23. Ibid.

24. Ibid., p. 41.

25. Ibid., p. 45.

26. Schechner, *Performance Theory*, p. 169.

27. Ibid., p. 170.

28. Ibid., p. 171.

29. Ibid., p. 172.

30. Ibid.

31. Jasper and Cuming, *Prayers of the Eucharist*, p. 23.

32. Carlson, *Performance*, p. 34.

33. Goffman, *Presentation of Self*, p. 22, quoted in Carlson, *Performance*, pp. 37–38.

34. Carlson, *Performance*, p. 38.

35. Ibid., pp. 38–39; the quotes inside the quote are from Bateson, *Steps to an Ecology*, p. 183.

36. Carlson, *Performance*, p. 42.

37. Ibid., p. 44.

38. For a complete discussion of church legislation and polemic regarding theater and drama from the first through the tenth centuries, see Schnusenberg, *Relationship*.

39. Carlson, *Performance*, p. 44, referring to Bruce Wilshire, *Role Playing and Identity* (Bloomington: Indiana University Press, 1982), pp. 280–81.

40. In Schechner, *Performance Theory*, p. 38.

41. Ibid., p. 51.

42. Ibid., p. 58.

43. See the discussion of anamnesis by Frank Senn in Fink, *New Dictionary of Sacramental Worship*, pp. 45–46.

44. Kavanagh, *On Liturgical Theology*, p. 74.

45. See the discussion in Nöth, *Handbook of Semiotics*, pp. 62–63.

46. Austin, *How to Do Things*, pp. 6–7.

47. See Austin's definitions in ibid., pp. 109 ff. To some extent I follow Carlson's discussion in *Performance,* p. 61.

48. See Burke, *Grammar of Motives.*

49. Barthes, *Elements of Semiology,* pp. 58 ff.

50. Reprinted in Eco, *Limits of Interpretation,* pp. 101–10, from a longer version in *Drama Review* 21 (March 1997).

51. Ibid., p. 103.

52. Ibid., p. 104.

53. Ibid.

54. Ibid., p. 110.

55. Ibid., p. 108.

56. Bakhtin, *Toward a Philosophy,* p. 58.

57. Ibid., p. 3.

58. Ibid., p. 13.

59. Ibid., p. 14.

60. Ibid., p. 15.

61. Ibid., p. 16.

62. Ibid., p. 18.

63. Ibid., p. 27.

64. Ibid., p. 28.

65. Ibid., p. 29.

66. Ibid., pp. 33–34.

67. Ibid., p. 37.

68. Ibid., p. 40.

69. Ibid., p. 42.

70. Ibid., p. 62.

71. Ibid., pp. 63–64.

72. Ibid., p. 74.

73. Ibid., p. 64.

74. See the discussion in Chauvet, *Symbol and Sacrament,* pp. 453–76.

75. Irwin's analysis, in *Context and Text,* of Prosper's actual argument is an important caveat against inappropriate use of this maxim as the key to all liturgical theology. As he demonstrates, Prosper, arguing against the semi-Pelagians, drew on the structure of the liturgy (the fact of intercessory prayers in the Mass) and not the supposed doctrinal content of any particular prayer.

76. Especially in Kavanagh, *On Liturgical Theology*; Lathrop, *Holy Things*; Irwin, *Context and Text*; and Chauvet, *Symbol and Sacrament.*

77. Chauvet, in *Symbol and Sacrament,* moves in the direction of avoiding this by placing linguistic theory into dialogue with Heideggerian philosophical categories and neo-Freudian theory. Lathrop, in *Holy Things,* also allows for nonverbal meanings in his theory of juxtaposition.

78. For the former, see Newman, *Worship as Praise*; for the latter, see Kilmartin, *Christian Liturgy*.

79. See Power, *Unsearchable Riches*; Chauvet, *Symbol and Sacrament*.

80. See Ringren, *Israelite Religion,* pp. 33 ff.

81. The fact that the term *metaphor* rather than *category* or *first principle* is used to describe the center of modern philosophy is itself indicative of a shift from causal, materialist thinking to thinking based on process and intersubjectivity.

82. For the basic works on speech act theory, see Austin, *How to Do Things*; and Searle, *Speech Acts*.

4. Constructing Sacrament

1. See especially Olson, *Tragedy* and *Theory of Comedy*. I am indebted for this entire approach to the late Hubert C. Heffner of the Indiana University Department of Theatre and Drama.

2. Both reprinted in Crane, *Critics and Criticism*.

3. Olson, "Outline of Poetic Theory," p. 9.

4. Aristotle, *On the Art of Poetry,* p. 35.

5. For a brief summary of the debates, see especially Hardison's "Interchapter" and "Epilogue."

6. Aristotle, *On the Art of Poetry,* p. 35.

7. Hubert Heffner, unpublished notes, 1970.

8. As we said at the beginning, imitations are to be distinguished under these three headings: means, object, and manner. Thus in one way Sophocles is the same kind of imitative artist as Homer, since they both imitate noble men; but in another sense he resembles Aristophanes, since they both imitate characters as acting and dramatizing the incidents of the story. It is from this, some tell us, that these latter kinds of imitations are called dramas: they present characters who "dramatize" the incidents of the plot. Golden and Hardison, *Aristotle's Poetics,* p. 6.

9. The most complete argument for locating catharsis in the structure of the play is found in Else, *Aristotle's Poetics,* pp. 423 ff. Else concludes: "Thus the catharsis is not a change or end-product in the spectator's soul, or in the fear and pity (i.e., the dispositions to them) in his soul, but a process carried forward in the emotional material of the play by its structural elements, above all by the recognition. For the recognition is the pay-off, to use a vulgar but expressive modernism; or, in more conventional figure, it is the hinge on which the emotional structure of the play turns. The catharsis, that is, the purification of the tragic act by the demonstration that its motive was not μιαρον [unclean, polluted], is accomplished by the whole structure of the drama, but above all by the recognition" (p. 439).

10. As an example of this perspective, it is not surprising that the structure of the Mass as it evolved in the West should have led to an exaggerated focusing on the

Liturgy of Communion as opposed to the Liturgy of the Word. The entire history of Western drama witnesses to a pattern of "rising and falling action" in which a dramatic build leads to an obligatory climax (Aristotle's *peripetaia* and *anagnorisis*) that is experienced as the center of greatest interest and involvement and is the structural keystone of the entire dramatic movement. This climax almost always takes place in the final third of the actual time of the action, thus allowing for a gradual buildup, a turning point, and a fairly rapid denouement. The early fixing of the order for eucharistic worship with the Liturgy of the Word preceding the Liturgy of the Table would, if this structure had any power either from some natural human rhythm or simply from conventional experience, tend to focus attention upon the table, to make it the climacteric point in the liturgy. Certainly the music and ceremonial that came to surround this moment (not to mention the silence in which it was finally engulfed) only served to reinforce this structural position. It does not seem unusual, then, even prescinding from theological considerations, that the very moment of discovery *(peripetaia)* and reversal *(anagnoresis)* would be sought in the debates over the moment of transubstantiation. One can only wonder how much theology has responded unconsciously to the deep structure of the rite in its discussions about what happens at the Eucharist.

11. See especially Ricoeur's splendid analysis of the religious function for the community of Greek tragedy in *The Symbolism of Evil,* pp. 211–31.

12. See particularly Pseudo-Germanus, *Expositio antiquae liturgiae Gallicanae,* and Amalarius of Metz, *Liber officialis.* Further application of this approach from a more contemporary point of view is found in Hardison, *Christian Rite.*

13. Young, *Drama of the Medieval Church,* p. 80.

14. Hardison, *Christian Rite,* p. 40. Conversely, some modern performance techniques have tried to break down the barrier between theater and ritual by claiming that the actors are not impersonating anyone but merely enacting themselves or enacting roles in an enactment that includes all of the so-called audience. Thus just as today the descriptive terms *ritual* and *liturgy* are being used to explain theater as performance, so for Amalarius theatrical or allegorical language was being used to explain the liturgy as enactment.

15. Aristotle's *Poetics* is concerned primarily with the structure of the drama, the dramatic action of the text organized around plot. Aristotle adverts to the theatrical or performance aspect of a tragedy only insofar as spectacle represents the dramatic manner from which the other parts are derived. Whether the tragedy is actually performed does not greatly affect the proper construction of the plot. Likewise, the tragic effect, the catharsis of fear, can take place in a reading of the play if it is properly constructed. The *Poetics,* that is, is a study of the drama rather than of the theater. It does not examine the manner in which gesture and movement and scenery, for example, are unified in causing the tragic effect. It does include a detailed analysis of the way in which the rhetorical elements of the diction, the verbal devices that will ultimately affect the actor's delivery, are part of the plot. Likewise, Aristotle

demonstrates in chapter 16 how the important element of dramatic discovery can depend upon visual signs or marks. Nevertheless, these discussions are subsumed under the architectonic function of the dramatic plot; they are not parts of a theory of theatrical performance.

16. Rayner, in *To Act, to Do,* presents a useful distinction among these three infinitives that are often confused in discussions of theater and drama. Following Aristotle's analysis of action in the *Nichomachean Ethics* and the *Rhetoric,* Rayner understands *to act* to indicate intention. "Intention, from Aristotle onward, is an 'animating' principle, distinguishing act from event, praxis from kinesis" (p. 13). Such acts, like the plots of drama, are tellable and therefore repeatable. They are essentially mimetic of some prior intention on the part of the doer. *To do* indicates only manifest behavior or motion without prior intentionality. It is actual and unrepeatable and therefore unmimetic. "If *to act* is the dimension of action that links acts and intents, then *to do* might be said to sever intentions and regard only the material or gestural conditions" (p. 21). Finally, *to perform* is distinguished by a rhetorical or pleasurable quality. Performance is for an audience or for some other and employs strategies and rhythms for effective utterance. "The performance dimension engages an audience with sensory qualities in an exchange that can best be called erotic" (p. 27). In these terms, the restored behavior of the liturgical act can be understood again as a symbol that joins act to word.

17. Ibid., p. 124.

18. Aristotle, *On the Art of Poetry,* pp. 41–46.

19. This is the process referred to by Chauvet, *Symbol and Sacrament,* as the second canon.

20. This service remains vestigially in the Rite One Holy Eucharist, as in many previous Anglican prayer books, as the "Prayer of Humble Access."

21. Lord Jesus Christ, you said to your apostles: I leave you peace, my peace I give you. Look not on our sins, but on the faith of your Church, and grant us the peace and unity of your kingdom where you live for ever and ever.

22. As, for example, in *Apostolic Tradition* 4 and 21 (Cumming, *Hippolytus*), although the former is at the ordination of a bishop and the latter at a baptism.

23. This is part of what Irwin discusses as the "context" of the text (see *Context and Text,* pp. 83 ff.). The idea of "context," however, has the disadvantage of being a language-analogy term that hides the very different unity of structure found in the action of a plot. We might know, for example, that the Prayer of Confession is embedded in two different contexts in the Prayer Book; but that alone would not reveal to us that this breaks the unity of the action and thus confuses the symbolic meaning.

24. Jacobson, *Ad Memoriam Ducens,* p. 192.

25. Chauvet, *Symbol and Sacrament,* asks a similar question of the revelation of God in the passion, death, and resurrection of Jesus. See pp. 449 ff.

26. Chauvet, *Symbol and Sacrament,* ch. 1.

27. Thus the great kenotic hymn of Philippians speaks of Jesus not grasping at equality with God. I take this, here, to mean that he does not attempt to opt out of the becoming that requires living-in-sacrifice. He does not attempt to live outside the process. In this act, he reveals that, in fact, neither does God.

28. "In the opening of Hugh's major work, *On the Signs [Sacramenta] of the Christian Faith,* he explains that there are two great signs of salvation: the creation and redemption of mankind. Hugh then goes on to describe the process and history of salvation. In one section of his book, he treats of the ceremonies which mediate salvation. These too, he calls *sacramentum.* Clearly the word *sacramentum* did not yet mean the same as the English word 'sacrament' in the sense of a particular rite. Nor did Hugh and his colleagues agree about what might be called a 'sacrament.' Some, for instance, included the anointing of kings and the rituals of knighthood among the *sacramenta* of the church." See Macy, *Banquet's Wisdom,* pp. 84–92, for this discussion.

29. Dix, *Shape of the Liturgy,* ch. 4.

30. The early tripartite division becomes obscured, however, with the addition of minor orders such as doorkeeper, exorcist, lector, and acolyte, and by the scholastic treatment of the episcopacy as a high-priestly office.

31. The classic question *Quid mus sumit?* captured the essence of this debate by proposing a clearly a-believing subject as opposed to the nonbelieving (the pagan) or wicked (Judas) subject.

32. Are there seven sacramental acts? Certainly—at least seven. There is no reason to exclude any of the traditional actions by which the church has enacted in specific circumstances the process-ion of the Trinity. If baptism enacts the drowning by which Christians enter the new intentional way of acting, freed from the death of isolation, then penance enacts the restoration and healing of the church so constituted through a touch. What should be apparent is that liturgy can happen wherever there is sacrament—that is, wherever anamnesis of Trinity brings the community's acts of loss-of-self for the sake of other to conscious intention— wherever, that is, human beings act out the love that is always and ever being acted out in us.

5. The Performance of *Ordo Romanus Primus*

1. Hardison, *Christian Rite,* pp. 67–68.

2. See Duffy, *Stripping of the Altars.*

3. Andrieu, *Les Ordines Romani,* vol. 2, pp. 38–64. See also Vogel, *Medieval Liturgy,* pp. 155–60.

4. For a detailed discussion of this stational liturgy, see Baldovin, *Urban Character of Christian Worship.*

5. See Andrieu, *Les Ordines Romani,* vol. 2, p. 92. "Pontifex vero, antequam transeat in partem mulierum, descendit ante confessionem et suscipit oblatas primicerii et secundicerii et defensorum."

6. Krautheimer, Corbett, and Frankl, *Corpus Basilicarum Christianarum Romae,* vol. 5, p. 260; Toynbee and Ward-Perkins, *Shrine of St. Peter.*

7. This reconstruction follows the edition of Ordo I found in Andrieu, *Les Ordines Romani,* vol. 2, pp. 67–108.

8. I am following here, as in what follows, the translation of the terms for the various ecclesiastical and civil orders made by Atchley in his *Ordo Romanus Primus.*

9. Several Italo-Germanic manuscripts in Andrieu's edition indicate that the candlesticks at this point are carried off to the place in which they first stood, namely, in a line through the middle of the church *(Et tunc tolluntur cereostata de loco in quo prius steterant, ut ponuntur in linea per mediam ecclesiam).* Could such an arrangement have acted as a placeholder to keep the processional path clear of people for the entrance rite? Andrieu, *Les Ordines Romani,* vol. 2, p. 85. See his discussion of the manuscript variants on pp. 3–37.

10. According to Hiley, *Western Plainchant,* "The date of the introduction of an offertory chant into Roman use is unknown" (p. 499). However, it appears in the Gregorian tradition from the late eighth century onward. Ordo I clearly alludes to it when it directs the archdeacon to signal the choir to stop singing (Andrieu, *Les Ordines Romani,* vol. 2, p. 95). Nothing specific is said about when it begins until the late eighth century Ordo IV (a Frankish adaptation of Ordo I), in which the offertory is begun after the altar has been spread with the corporal and the pope has washed his hands and gone down to receive the offerings of the people *(Diende descendit pontifex ad suscipiendum oblationes a populo et annuit archdeaconus scolae ut dicatur offertorium).* Andrieu, *Les Ordines Romani,* vol. 2, p. 161. In ninth-century Francia, where the Credo was chanted immediately after the Gospel, and where there was an actual offertory procession of the people, the *offertorium* was begun immediately following the celebrant's salutation *Oremus.* Andrieu, *Les Ordines Romani,* vol. 2, p. 219.

11. The "ascending" and "descending" described here would, as we have seen, be literal in the case of St. Peter's, where the *presbyterium* was accessed by stairs.

12. That the pope must "look back" *(respicit)* to the choir may be another indication that, at least in some stations, he has been facing away from the people and toward the apse.

13. Andrieu points out that in the primitive recension of this ordo the Canon was considered to have begun with the dialogue and Sursum Corda. *Les Ordines Romani,* vol. 2, p. 95 n. 88.

14. The *Nobis quoque* is a possible locus for this action if the Canon begins with *Te igitur* (as in the understanding of the compiler of the long recension). It is at the *Nobis quoque* that the subdeacons "rise up" and that a series of actions begin in preparation for the fraction and Communion. On the other hand, if the Canon be-

gins with the dialogue (n. 13 above), then the action described takes place at that point. "Les mots *quando inchoat canonem* nous reportant au début de la préface. C'est aussitôt après l'offertoire, lorsque les pains ont été disposés sur l'autel, que l'acolyte prend la patène à la tient jusqu'au milieu du canon, c'est-à-dire jusqu'au *Te igitur,* ainsi que nous le précise Amailaire: *medio canone, id est cum dicitur Te igitur* (*De eccles. Off.,* 1. III, c. 27; P.L., CV, 1146), Andrieu, *Les Ordines Romani,* vol. 2, p. 96 n. 91.

15. Even by the turn of the eighth century, and especially in the Frankish realms, the Canon becomes silent *(tacite)* at this point. Ordo I, however, seems to indicate only the beginning of this tendency. See Jungmann, *Mass of the Roman Rite,* vol. 2, p. 104.

16. The subsequent history of the commingling(s) in the Roman rite is complex and finally devolves to a single act at the Pax. See Jungmann, *Mass of the Roman Rite,* vol. 2, pp. 311–21.

17. Again, at this point, various manuscripts of the ordo reflect the varying architecture of the stational churches (and of the Frankish churches to which this order came to be adapted) adding, "[N]am in ista loco, 'cum Dominus vobiscum' dixerit, non dirigit ad populum" (For at this point of the service, when he says, "The Lord be with you," he does not turn to the people). Andrieu, *Les Ordines Romani,* vol. 2, p. 107 (translation from Atchley, *Ordo Romanus Primus*). Needless to say, at a basilica aligned as St. Peter's is, to face east would be to face the people.

18. For a discussion of the appropriation of city by the early church, see Baldovin's "The City as Church, the Church as City," in *City, Church and Renewal,* pp. 3–11, and also his *Urban Character of Christian Worship.*

19. See Bradshaw and Hoffman, *Making of Jewish and Christian Worship,* p. 83.

20. Kostof, *History of Architecture,* p. 264.

21. Ibid., p. 258.

22. Ibid., p. 265.

23. This is true to a lesser degree in the primitive stratum of this ordo when the Canon is still audible. It remains the vocal gesture of the pontiff into which, even early on, he "enters alone"; but the words would have, presumably, contextualized the bread for those able to hear them. We will, therefore, still look to the words of the Canon for the context of the matter even from the people's point of view.

24. Andrieu, *Les Ordines Romani,* vol. 2, p. 82.

25. Ibid., vol. 2, p. 91.

26. See n. 23, above.

27. Jacobson, *Ad Memoriam Ducens,* p. 233.

28. Ibid., p. 221.

29. See the description in Young, *Drama of the Medieval Church,* vol. 1, p. 82.

30. "Memento domine famulorum famularumque tuarum et omnium circum adstantium quorum tibi fides cognita est et nota devotio qui tibi offerunt hoc

sacrificium laudis, pro se suisque omnibus, pro redemptione animarum suarum, pro spe salutis et incolomitatis suae tibi vota sua aeterno deo vivo et vero." Deshusses, *Le sacramentaire Grégorien,* p. 87. The translation is taken from Jasper and Cuming, *Prayers of the Eucharist,* p. 164, as is the attribution of the *Communicantes* and *Nobis quoque* to Gelasius.

    31. "Supplices te rogamus omnipotens deus, iube haec perferri per manus angeli tui in sublime altare tuum, in conspectu divinae maiestatis tuee, ut quotquot ex hac altaris participatione sancrosanctum filii tui corpus et sanguinem sumpserimus omni benedictione caelesti et gratia repleamur." Deshusses, *Le sacramentaire Grégorien,* p. 90.

Bibliography

Primary Sources

Amalarius of Metz. *Liber officialis.* In *Amalarii episcopi opera liturgica omnia,* edited by
Ionne Michaele Hanssens. Studi e Testi 139. Vatican City: Biblioteca Apostolica
Vaticana, 1947.

Andrieu, Michel. *Le pontifical de Guillaume Durand.* Vol. 3 of *Le pontifical romain au
Moyen Âge.* Studi e Testi 88. Vatican City: Biblioteca Apostolica Vaticana, 1940.
———. *Les Ordines Romani du haut Moyen Âge.* Louvain: Spicilegium Sacrum Lo-
vaniense, 1951. Latin text; French commentary.

Aristotle. *On the Art of Poetry.* Translated by Ingram Bywater. Oxford: Clarendon
Press, 1920.

Atchley, E. G. Cuthbert F. *Ordo Romanus Primus.* London: Alexander Moring, De La
Mare Press, 1905.

Bradshaw, Paul F. *Ordination Rites of the Ancient Churches of East and West.* New York:
Pueblo, 1990.

Church of England. *The Alternative Service Book, 1980.* Oxford: Oxford University
Press, 1980.

Collins, Fletcher, Jr. *Medieval Music Dramas: A Repertory of Complete Plays.* Charlottesville: University Press of Virginia, 1976.

Cumming, Geoffrey. *Hippolytus: A Text for Students.* Bramcote: Grove Books, 1976.

Davis, Norman. *Non-Cycle Plays and Fragments.* London: Oxford University Press,
1970. Based on the edition of Osborn Waterhouse.

Deiss, Lucien. *Springtime of the Liturgy: Liturgical Texts of the First Four Centuries.* Collegeville, MN: Liturgical Press, 1979.

Dumas, A., ed. *Liber Sacramentorum Gellonensis.* Turnholti: Typographi Brepols, 1981.

Deshusses, Jean. *Le sacramentaire Grégorien.* Fribourg: Éditions Universitaires Fribourg Suisse, 1971.

Episcopal Church. *The Book of Common Prayer.* New York: Church Hymnal Corp., 1979.

————. *The Hymnal, 1982: According to the Use of the Episcopal Church.* New York: Church Publishing, 1985.

Gingras, George E., ed. *Egeria: Diary of a Pilgrimage.* New York: Newman Press, 1970.

Gréban, d'Arnoul. *Le mystère de la Passion.* Critical ed. Edited by Omer Jodogne. Brussels: Palais des Académies, 1965.

Jackson, Richard A. *Ordines coronationis Franciae: Texts and Ordines for the Coronation of Frankish and French Kings and Queens in the Middle Ages.* Philadelphia: University of Pennsylvania Press, 1995.

Jacobus de Voragine. *The Golden Legend.* Translated and adapted by Granger Ryan and Helmet Ripperger. New York: Longmans, Green, 1969.

Jasper, R. C. D., and G. J. Cuming. *Prayers of the Eucharist: Early and Reformed.* Collegeville, MN: Liturgical Press, 1990.

Lodi, Enzo. *Enchiridion Eucholigicum Fontium Liturgicorum.* Rome: C. L. V., Editioni Liturgiche, 1979.

Lumiansky, R. M., and David Mills, eds. *The Chester Mystery Cycle.* London: Oxford University Press, 1974.

Martini, Aldo, ed. *Il Cosiddetto Pontificale di Poitiers (Paris, Bibliotheque de l'Arsenal, Codex 227).* Rome: Casa Editrice Herder, 1979.

McNeill, John T., and Helena M. Gamer. *Medieval Handbooks of Penance: A Translation of the Principal "Libri Poenitentiales."* New York: Columbia University Press, 1990.

Meredith, Peter, ed. *The Passion Play from the N. Town Manuscript.* New York: Longman, 1990.

Mills, David. *The Chester Mystery Cycle.* Medieval Texts and Studies 9. East Lansing, MI: Colleagues Press, 1992.

Mohlberg, Leo Cunibert, ed. *Liber sacramentorum Romanae auclesiae ordinis anni circuli (Cod. Vat. Reg. lat. 316/Paris Bibl. Nat. 7193, 41/56) (Sacramentarium Gelasianum).* Rome: Casa Editrice Herder, 1960.

————. *Missale Gallicanum Vetus (Cod. Vat. Palat. Lat. 493).* Rome: Casa Editrice Herder, 1958.

Morris, Richard. *Legends of the Holy Rood.* Early English Text Society 46. 1881. Reprint, New York: Greenwood Press, 1969.

Nagler, A. M. *A Sourcebook of Theatrical History.* New York: Dover Publications, 1952.

Neale, J. M. *The Ancient Liturgies of the Galican Church.* New York: AMS Press, 1970.

Pseudo-Germanus. *Expositio antiquae liturgiae Gallicanae.* Edited by E. C. Ratcliff. London: Henry Bradshaw Society, 1971.

Roman Missal. *The Sacramentary.* New York: Catholic Book Publishing, 1985.

Rose, Martial. *The Wakefield Mystery Plays.* New York: W. W. Norton, 1961.

Sheerin, Daniel J. *The Eucharist.* Message of the Fathers of the Church 7. Wilming-
ton, DE: Michael Glazier, 1986.

Strothman, Werner. *Das Wolfenbutteler Tetraevangelium Syriacum.* Gottinger Orient-
forschungen. Wiesbaden: Otto Harrassowitz, 1971.

Vogel, Cyrille. *Le pontifical romano-germanique du dixieme siècle.* Studi e Testi 226, 227,
269. Vatican City: Biblioteca Apostolica Vaticana, 1963.

Whitaker, E. C. *Documents of the Baptismal Liturgy.* London: SPCK, 1960.

Wilson, H. A., ed. *The Gelasian Sacramentary (Liber Sacramentorum Romanae Ecclesiae).*
Oxford: Clarendon Press, 1894.

SECONDARY SOURCES

Aers, David, ed. *Culture and History, 1350–1600.* Detroit: Wayne State University
Press, 1992.

Alter, James. *A Sociosemiotic Theory of Theatre.* Philadelphia: University of Pennsylvania Press, 1990.

Alter, Jean. "From Text to Performance." *Poetics Today* 2 (1981): 113–40.

Apollonj Ghetti, B. M., A. Ferrua, E. Josi, E. Kirschbaum, L. Kaas, and C. Serafini.
Esplorazioni sotto la confessione di San Pietro in Vaticano. 2 vols. Vatican City: Tipo-
grafia Poliglotta Vaticana, 1951.

Artaud, Antonin. *The Theatre and Its Double.* New York: Grove Press, 1958.

Aston, Elaine, and George Savona. *Theatre as Sign System: A Semiotics of Text and Performance.* New York: Routledge, 1991.

Austin, J. L. *How to Do Things with Words.* 1962. Reprint, Cambridge, MA: Harvard
University Press, 1975.

Bakhtin, M. M. *Rabelais and His World.* Cambridge: MIT Press, 1965. Quoted in
Marvin Carlson, *Performance: A Critical Introduction* (New York: Routledge,
1996), p. 28.

———. *Toward a Philosophy of the Act.* Austin: University of Texas Press, 1993.

Baldovin, John F., S.J. "Accepit Panem: The Gestures of the Priest at the Institution
Narrative." In *Rule of Prayer, Rule of Faith,* edited by Nathan Mitchell and John
Baldovin. Collegeville, MN: Liturgical Press, 1996.

———. *City, Church, and Renewal.* Washington, DC: Pastoral Press, 1991.

———. *The Urban Character of Christian Worship.* Rome: Pontificium Institutum Stu-
diorum Orientalium, 1987.

Balthasar, Hans Urs von. *The Glory of the Lord: A Theological Aesthetics.* 7 vols. Edited
by Joseph Fessio and John Riches. Translated by Erasmo Leiva-Merikakis. New
York: Crossroad, 1983–91.

Barba, Eugenio. *The Paper Crane: A Guide to Theatre Anthropology.* New York: Routledge, 1995.

Barba, Eugenio, and Nicola Savarese. *A Dictionary of Theatre Anthropology*. New York: Routledge, 1991.

Barthes, Roland. *Elements of Semiology*. New York: Hill and Wang, 1967.

Bateson, Gregory. *Steps to an Ecology of Mind*. San Francisco: Chandler, 1972.

Baumstark, Anton. *Comparative Liturgy*. Revised by Bernard Botte. English ed. by F. L. Cross. Westminster, MD: Newman Press, 1958.

Beadle, Richard. *The Cambridge Companion to the Medieval English Theatre*. Cambridge: Cambridge University Press, 1994.

Bell, Catherine. *Ritual Theory, Ritual Practice*. New York: Oxford University Press, 1992.

Benamou, Michel, and C. Caramello. *Performance in Postmodern Culture*. Milwaukee: Center for Twentieth Century Studies, 1977.

Bishop, Edmund. *Liturgica Historica*. Oxford: Clarendon Press, 1918.

Bossy, John. *Christianity in the West, 1400–1700*. Oxford: Oxford University Press, 1985.

Bourdieu, P. *Ce que parler veut dire: L'economie des échanges linguistiques*. Paris: Fayard, 1982.

Bouyer, Louis. *Eucharist: Theology and Spirituality of the Eucharistic Prayer*. Notre Dame: University of Notre Dame Press, 1968.

———. *Liturgical Piety*. Notre Dame: University of Notre Dame Press, 1955.

Bradshaw, Paul F. *The Search for the Origins of Christian Worship*. New York: Oxford University Press, 1992.

Bradshaw, Paul F., and Lawrence A. Hoffman, eds. *The Making of Jewish and Christian Worship*. Notre Dame: University of Notre Dame Press, 1991.

Brockett, Oscar G. *History of the Theatre*. 5th ed. Boston: Allyn and Bacon, 1967.

Bryan, George B. *Ethelwold and Medieval Music-Drama at Winchester: The Easter Play, Its Author, and Its Milieu*. Berne: Peter Lang, 1981.

Burke, Kenneth A. *A Grammar of Motives*. Berkeley: University of California Press, 1969.

———. *The Philosophy of Literary Form*. New York: Vintage Books, 1957.

Bynum, Caroline Walker. *Fragmentation and Redemption: Essays on Gender and the Human Body in Medieval Religion*. New York: Zone Books, 1992.

———. *Holy Feast, Holy Fast: The Religious Significance of Food to Medieval Women*. Berkeley: University of California, 1987.

Caillois, Roger. *Man, Play, and Games*. Translated by Meyer Barash. New York: Free Press, 1961.

Calloud, Jean. *Structural Analysis of Narrative*. Philadelphia: Fortress Press, 1976.

Cannadine, David, and Simon Price. *Rituals of Royalty*. Cambridge: Cambridge University Press, 1987.

Cargill, Oscar. *Drama and Liturgy*. 1930. Reprint, New York, Octagon Books, 1969.

Carlson, Marvin. *Performance: A Critical Introduction*. New York: Routledge, 1996.

———. *Theories of the Theatre*. Ithaca: Cornell University Press, 1984.

Castelli, Elizabeth A., Stephen D. Moore, Gary A. Phillips, and Regina M. Schwartz, eds. *The Postmodern Bible: The Bible and Culture Collective*. New Haven: Yale University Press, 1995.

Chambers, E. K. *The Medieval Stage*. 2 vols. Oxford: Oxford University Press, 1903.

Chambers, Ross. "Le masque et le miroir: Vers un théorie relationnelle du théâtre." *Études Litteraires* 13 (1980): 397–412.

Chauvet, Louis-Marie. *Symbol and Sacrament*. Collegeville, MN: Liturgical Press, 1995.

Clark, Barrett H. *European Theories of the Drama*. New York: Crown Publishers, 1947.

Collins, Fletcher. *The Production of Medieval Church Music-Drama*. Charlottesville: University Press of Virginia, 1972.

Corbon, Jean. *The Wellspring of Worship*. New York: Paulist Press, 1988.

Counsell, Colin. *Signs of Performance*. New York: Routledge, 1996.

Craig, Hardin. *English Religious Drama*. Oxford: Clarendon Press, 1955.

Crane, R. S., ed. *Critics and Criticism*. Chicago: University of Chicago Press, 1957.

Crocker, Richard, and David Hiley. *The Early Middle Ages to 1300*. Vol. 2 of *New Oxford History of Music*, 2nd ed. New York: Oxford University Press, 1990.

Cuming, G. J. *A History of Anglican Liturgy*. London: Macmillan, 1969.

Davidson, Audrey Ekdahl, ed. *Holy Week and Easter Ceremonies and Dramas from Medieval Sweden*. Kalamazoo: Medieval Institute Publications, Western Michigan University, 1990.

Davidson, Clifford, C. J. Gianakaris, and J. H. Stroupe, eds. *Iconic and Comparative Studies in Medieval Drama*. Kalamazoo: Medieval Institute Publications, Western Michigan University, 1974.

Davidson, Clifford, and John H. Stroupe. *Drama in the Middle Ages*. New York: AMS Press, 1991.

De Torro, Fernando. *Theatre Semiotics: Text and Staging in Modern Theatre*. Toronto: University of Toronto Press, 1995.

Derrida, Jacques. *Writing and Difference*. Translated by Alan Bass. Chicago: University of Chicago Press, 1978.

Dix, Gregory. *The Shape of the Liturgy*. Westminster, MD: Dacre Press, 1945.

Downing, Marjorie D. Coogan. "The Influence of the Liturgy on the English Cycle Plays." PhD diss., Yale University, 1942.

Duffy, Emon. *The Stripping of the Altars: Traditional Religion in England, 1400–1580*. New Haven: Yale University Press, 1992.

Dumiege, Gervais. *Histoire du conciles oecuméniques*. Paris: Éditions de l'Orante, 1965.

Dumoutet, E. *Corpus Domini: Aux sources de la piete eucharistique medievale*. Paris: Beauchesne, 1942.

Eco, Umberto. *The Limits of Interpretation*. Bloomington: Indiana University Press, 1990.

Ehrmann, Jacques. "*Homo Ludens* Revisited." In *Game, Play, Literature*, edited by Jacques Ehrmann. Boston: Beacon Press, 1968. Quoted in Marvin Carlson, *Performance: A Critical Introduction* (New York: Routledge, 1996), p. 29.

Elam, Keir. *The Semiotics of Theatre and Drama*. London: Methuen, 1980.

Else, Gerald F. *Aristotle's Poetics: The Argument*. Cambridge, MA: Harvard Unversity Press, 1957.

Esslin, Martin. *The Field of Drama*. London: Methuen, 1987.

Evreinoff, Nicholas. *The Theatre in Life.* Translated by Alexander Nazaroff. New York: Brentano's, 1927.

Fagerberg, David W. *What Is Liturgical Theology? A Study in Methodology.* Collegeville, MN: Liturgical Press, 1992.

Fink, Peter E., S.J., ed. *The New Dictionary of Sacramental Worship.* Collegeville, MN: Liturgical Press, 1990.

Fish, Stanley. *Is There a Text in This Class?* Cambridge, MA: Harvard University Press, 1980.

Flanigan, C. Clifford. "Liturgical Drama and Dramatic Liturgy: A Study of the *Quem Queritis* Easter Dialogue and Its Cultic Context." PhD diss., Washington University, 1973.

———. "The Roman Rite and the Origins of the Liturgical Drama." *University of Toronto Quarterly* 43 (1974): 263–84.

Fletcher, Alan J. "The N-Town Plays." In *The Cambridge Companion to Medieval English Theatre,* edited by Richard Beadle. Cambridge: Cambridge University Press, 1994.

Foreville, Raymonde. *Latran I, II, III et Latran IV.* Histoire des Conciles Oecumeniques 6. Paris: Éditions de L'Orante, 1965.

Foster, Frances A. *The Northern Passion.* Early English Text Society. London: Kegan Paul, Trench, Trubner, 1913.

Fry, Northrop. *Anatomy of Criticism.* Princeton: Princeton University Press, 1957.

———. *Fools of Time: Studies in Shakespearean Tragedy.* Toronto: University of Toronto Press, 1967.

———. *A Natural Perspective: The Development of Shakespearean Comedy and Romance.* New York: Harcourt, Brace, and World, 1965.

———. *The Secular Scripture: A Study of the Structure of Romance.* Cambridge, MA: Harvard University Press, 1976.

Garcia-Rivera, Alejandro. *St. Martin de Porres: The "Little Stories" and the Semiotics of Culture.* Maryknoll, NY: Orbis Books, 1995.

Gibson, Gail McMurray. *The Theatre of Devotion.* Chicago: University of Chicago Press, 1989.

Gibson, James M. "Quem Quaeritis in Presepe: Christian Drama or Christian Liturgy." *Comparative Drama* 15, no. 4 (1981): 343–65.

Goffman, Erving. *The Presentation of Self in Everyday Life.* Garden City, NY: Doubleday, 1959.

Golden, Leon, trans., and O. B. Hardison. *Aristotle's Poetics: A Translation and Commentary for Students of Literature.* Tallahassee: Florida State University Press, 1981.

Grimes, Ronald L. *Beginnings in Ritual Studies.* Lanham, MD: University Press of America, 1982.

Guiver, George. *Company of Voices.* New York: Pueblo, 1988.

Gwilliam, G. H., et al. *Studia Biblica: Essays in Biblical Archeology and Criticism.* Vol. 1. Oxford: Clarendon Press, 1885.

Hanawalt, A. H., and K. L. Reyerson. *City and Spectacle in Medieval Europe.* Minneapolis: University of Minnesota Press, 1994.

Hanawalt, Barbara, and K. L. Reyerson, eds. *City and Spectacle in the Middle Ages.* Minneapolis: University of Minnesota Press, 1994.

Hanawalt, Barbara, and David Wallace, eds. *Bodies and Disciplines: Intersections of Literature and History in Fifteenth-Century England.* Minneapolis: Uiversity of Minnesota Press, 1996.

Hardison, O. B. *Christian Rite and Christian Drama in the Middle Ages.* Baltimore: Johns Hopkins University Press, 1965.

———. "A Commentary on Aristotle's Poetics." In *Aristotle's Poetics: A Translation and Commentary for Students of Literature,* translated by Leon Golden, commentary by O. B. Hardison. Tallahassee: Florida State University Press, 1981.

———. "Epilogue: On Aristotelian Imitation." In *Aristotle's Poetics: A Translation and Commentary for Students of Literature,* translated by Leon Golden, commentary by O. B. Hardison, pp. 281–96. Tallahassee: Florida State University Press, 1981.

———. "Interchapter: The Catharsis Clause of Chapter VI." In *Aristotle's Poetics: A Translation and Commentary for Students of Literature,* translated by Leon Golden, commentary by O. B. Hardison, pp. 133–37. Tallahassee: Florida State University Press, 1981.

Harper, John. *The Forms and Orders of Western Liturgy from the Tenth to the Eighteenth Century.* Oxford: Clarendon Press, 1991.

Harris, John Wesley. *Medieval Theatre in Context: An Introduction.* New York: Routledge, 1992.

Hassan, Ihab. *The Dismemberment of Orpheus: Towards a Postmodern Literature.* Madison: University of Wisconsin Press, 1971.

———. "The Question of Postmodernism." In *Romanticism, Modernism, Postmodernism,* edited by Harry R. Garvin. Lewisburg: Bucknell University Press, 1980.

Hatchett, Marion J. *Commentary on the American Prayer Book.* New York: Seabury Press, 1980.

Heffner, Hubert, and Samuel Sellman. *Modern Theatre Practice.* New York: Appleton, Century, Crofts, 1959.

Heidegger, Martin. *Being and Time.* San Francisco: Harper, 1962.

Helbo, André. *Theory of Performing Arts.* Amsterdam: Benjamins, 1987.

Hiley, David. *Western Plainchant: A Handbook.* New York: Oxford University Press, 1995.

Hillgarth, J. N., ed. *Christianity and Paganism, 350–750.* Philadelphia: Uiversity of Pennsylvania Press, 1969.

Hoffman, Lawrence A. *Beyond the Text: A Holistic Approach to Liturgy.* Bloomington: Indiana University Press, 1987.

Hughes, Andrew. *Medieval Manuscripts for Mass and Office.* Toronto: University of Toronto Press, 1982.

Huizinga, Johan. *Homo Ludens.* New York: Beacon Press, 1950.

Hymes, Dell. "Breakthrough into Performance." In *Folklore: Performance and Commu-nication,* edited by Dan Ben-Amos and Kenneth S. Goldstein. The Hague: Mou-ton, 1975. Quoted in Marvin Carlson, *Performance: A Critical Introduction.* (New York: Routledge, 1996), p. 15.

Irwin, Kevin W. *Context and Text: Method in Liturgical Theology.* Collegeville, MN: Liturgical Press, 1994.

Isambert, F. A. *Rite et efficacité symbolique.* Paris: Cerf, 1979.

Jacobson, Paul. "Ad Memoriam Ducens: The Development of Liturgical Exegesis in Amalar of Metz's 'Expositiones Missae.'" PhD diss., Graduate Theological Union, 1996.

Jansen, Steen. "Esquisse d'une théorie de la forme dramatique." *Languages* 12 (1968): 71–93.

Jansen, William H. "Classifying Performance in the Study of Verbal Folklore." In *Studies in Folklore in Honor of Distinguished Service Professor Stith Thompson.* Bloom-ington: Indiana University Press, 1957. Quoted in Marvin Carlson, *Performance: A Critical Introduction* (New York: Routledge, 1996), p. 15.

Jungmann, Joseph A. *The Early Liturgy to the Time of Gregory the Great.* Notre Dame: University of Notre Dame Press, 1959.

———. *The Mass of the Roman Rite.* 2 vols. 1951 and 1955. Reprint, Westminster, MD: Christian Classics, 1992.

Kantorowicz, Ernst. *The King's Two Bodies: A Study in Medieval Political Theology.* Prince-ton: Princeton University Press, 1957.

Kavanagh, Aidan. *On Liturgical Theology.* New York: Pueblo, 1984.

———. *The Shape of Baptism.* New York: Pueblo, 1978.

Kaye, Nick. *Postmodernism and Performance.* New York: St. Martin's Press, 1994.

Kelly, Henry Ansgar. *The Devil at Baptism: Ritual, Theology, and Drama.* Ithaca: Cornell University Press, 1985.

Kilmartin, Edward J., S.J. *Christian Liturgy: Theology and Practice.* Vol. 1. *Systematic The-ology of Liturgy.* Kansas City: Sheed and Ward, 1988.

Kirby, Michael. "Nonsemiotic Performance." *Modern Drama* 25 (1982): 105–11.

Kostof, Spiro. *A History of Architecture: Settings and Rituals.* New York: Oxford Uni-versity Press, 1995.

Kowzan, Tadeusz. "La signe au théâtre." *Diogéne* 61 (1968): 59–90.

———. *Littérature et spectacle.* The Hague: Mouton, 1975.

Koziol, Geoffrey. *Begging Pardon and Favor: Ritual and Political Order in Early Medieval France.* Ithaca: Cornell University Press, 1992.

Krautheimer, Richard, Spencer Corbett, and Wolfgang Frankl. *Corpus Basilicarum Christianarum Romae.* 5 vols. New York: Institute of Fine Arts, New York Uni-versity, 1937–77.

Kretzmann, Paul Edward. *The Liturgical Element in the Earliest Forms of the Medieval Drama.* Minneapolis: Bulletin of the University of Minnesota, 1916.

Kucharek, Casimir. *The Byzantine-Slav Liturgy of St. John Chrysostom.* Allendale, NJ: Alleluia Press, 1971.

Langer, Suzanne. *Feeling and Form.* New York: Charles Scribner's Sons, 1953.

Lathrop, Gordon W. *Holy Things: A Liturgical Theology.* Minneapolis: Fortress Press, 1993.

Lepow, Lauren. *Enacting the Sacrament: Counter-Lollardy in the Towneley Cycle.* Rutherford: Fairleigh Dickinson University Press, 1990.

Lerer, Seth. "'Representyd now in yower syght': The Culture of Spectatorship in Late Fifteenth-Century England." In *Bodies and Disciplines: Intersections of Literature and History in Fifteenth-Century England,* edited by Barbara A. Hanawalt and David Wallace. Minneapolis: University of Minnesota Press, 1996.

Lessing, Gotthold Ephraim. *Laocoön.* New York: Bobbs-Merrill, 1962.

MacAloon, John J., ed. *Rite, Drama, Festival, Spectacle.* Philadelphia: Instutute for Study of Human Issues, 1984.

MacGregor, Alistair J. *Fire and Light in the Western Triduum.* Collegeville, MN: Liturgical Press, 1992.

Macy, Gary. *The Banquet's Wisdom: A Short History of the Theologies of the Lord's Supper.* New York: Paulist Press, 1992.

Maldonado, Luis, and David Power. *Symbol and Art in Worship.* New York: Seabury Press, 1980.

Marranca, Bonnie. *The Theatre of Images.* New York: Drama Book Specialists, 1977.

Marshall, Paul V. *Prayer Book Parallels.* 2 vols. New York: Church Hymnal Corp., 1989.

Martimort, A. G., ed. *The Church at Prayer.* 4 vols. Collegeville, MN: Liturgical Press, 1986.

Mazza, Enrico. *The Origins of the Eucharistic Prayer.* Collegeville, MN: Liturgical Press, 1995.

McCall, Richard D. "Anamnesis or Mimesis? Unity and Drama in the Paschal Triduum." *Ecclesia Orans* 13 (1996): 315–22.

———. "Theopoetics: The Acts of God in the Act of Liturgy." *Worship,* forthcoming.

McGee, Timothy James. *The Liturgical Origin and Early History of the Quem Quearitis Dialogue.* Pittsburgh: University of Pittsburgh Press, 1974.

McKeon, Richard. "The Philosophic Bases of Art and Criticism." In *Critics and Criticism,* edited by R. S. Crane. Chicago: University of Chicago Press, 1952.

McKitterick, Rosamond. *The Frankish Church and the Carolingian Reforms, 789–895.* London: Royal Historical Society, 1977.

Merz, Michael. *Liturgisches Gebet als Geschehen.* Liturgiewissenschaftliche Quellen und Forschungen. Munster: Aschendorff, 1988.

Minnis, A. J., and A. B. Scott, eds. *Medieval Literary Theory and Criticism c. 1100–c. 1375.* Oxford: Clarendon Press, 1988.

Mitchell, Leonel L. *The Meaning of Ritual.* Harrisburg: Morehouse, 1977.

Mitchell, Nathan. *Cult and Controversy: The Worship of the Eucharist outside Mass.* Collegeville, MN: Liturgical Press, 1982.

Mitchell, Nathan, and John Baldovin. *Rule of Prayer, Rule of Faith.* Collegeville, MN: Liturgical Press, 1996.

Muir, Lynette R. *The Biblical Drama of Medieval Europe.* Cambridge: Cambridge University Press, 1995.

———. "The Mass on the Medieval Stage." *Comparative Drama* 23 (1989–90): 314–31.

Murphy, John L. *The General Councils of the Church.* Milwaukee: Bruce, 1960.

Myrc, John. *Instructions for Parish Priests.* Edited by Edward Peacock from Cotton MS Claudius A. II. 1868. Reprint, New York: Greenwood Press, 1969.

Nagler, A. M. *The Medieval Religious Stage.* New Haven: Yale University Press, 1976.

———. *A Sourcebook of Theatrical History.* New York: Dover Publications, 1952.

Nelson, Janet L. "The Lord's Annointed and the People's Choice." In *Rituals of Royalty,* edited by David Cannadine and Simon Price. Cambridge: Cambridge University Press, 1987.

Newman, David R. *Worship as Praise and Empowerment.* New York: Pilgrim Press, 1988.

Nocent, Adrien. "Gestures, Symbols and Words in Present-Day Western Liturgy." In *Symbol and Art in Worship,* edited by L. Maldonado and D. Power. New York: Seabury Press, 1980.

Nöth, Winfried. *Handbook of Semiotics.* Bloomington: Indiana University Press, 1990.

Ogden, Dunbar. "Drama in the Medieval Church: Public Enactment or Hidden Rite." *On Stage Studies* 18 (1995): 44–53.

Ohmann, Richard. "Literature as Act." In *Approaches to Poetics,* edited by Seymour Chatman. New York: Columbia University Press, 1973.

———. "Speech Acts and the Definition of Literature." *Philosophy and Rhetoric* 4 (1971): 10–15.

Olson, Elder. "An Outline of Poetic Theory." In *Critics and Criticism.* edited by R. S. Crane. Chicago: University of Chicago Press, 1952.

———. *The Theory of Comedy.* Bloomington: Indiana University Press, 1968.

———. *Tragedy and the Theory of Drama.* Detroit: Wayne State University Press, 1961.

Osborne, Kenan B., O. F. M. *Reconciliation and Justification: The Sacrament and Its Theology.* New York: Paulist Press, 1990.

Paterno, Salvatore. *The Liturgical Context of Early European Drama.* Potomac, MD: Scripta Humanistica, 1989.

Patte, Daniel. *What Is Structural Exegesis?* Philadelphia: Fortress Press, 1976.

Pavis, Patrice. *Languages of the Stage.* New York: Performing Arts Journal Publications, 1982.

———. "Problems of a Semiology of Theatrical Gesture." *Poetics Today* 2 (1981): 65–94.

———. *Voix et images de la scène.* Lille: Presses Universitaires de Lille, 1985.

Pelikan, Jaroslav. *The Growth of Medieval Theology (600–1300).* Vol. 3 of *The Christian Tradition.* Chicago: University of Chicago Press, 1978.

Petrey, Sandy. *Speech Acts and Literary Theory.* London: Routledge, 1990.

Pfister, Manfred. *The Theory and Analysis of Drama.* Cambridge: Cambridge University Press, 1988.

Pierce, Joanne M. "Early Medieval Liturgy: Some Implications." *Worship* 65 (November 1991): 509–22.

Pinell, Jordi M. *La benediccio del ciri pasque i els sues textos.* Barcelona: Tallers Grafics Maria Galve, 1958.

Porter, Joseph A. *The Drama of Speech Acts.* Berkeley: University of California Press, 1979.

Power, David N. *The Eucharistic Mystery.* New York: Crossroad, 1995.

———. *Unsearchable Riches: The Symbolic Nature of Liturgy.* Collegeville, MN: Liturgical Press, 1984.

Procter, F., and W. H. Frere. *A New History of the Book of Common Prayer.* New York: Macmillan, 1901.

Rahner, Karl. *The Church and the Sacraments.* London: Burns and Oates, 1963.

———. "The Theology of the Symbol." In his *Theological Investigations IV.* Baltimore: Helicon Press, 1966.

Rankin, Susan, ed. *Music in the Medieval English Liturgy: Plainsong and Mediaeval Music Society Centennial Essays.* New York: Oxford University Press, 1993.

———. *The Music of the Medieval Liturgical Drama in France and in England.* New York: Garland, 1989.

Rayner, Alice. *To Act, to Do, to Perform.* Ann Arbor: University of Michigan Press, 1994.

Read, Alan. *Theatre and Everyday Life: An Ethics of Performance.* London: Routledge, 1993.

Reichel, Oswald. *Solemn Mass at Rome in the Ninth Century.* London, 1895.

Riche, Pierre. *The Carolingians: A Family Who Forged Europe.* Translated by Michael Idomir Allen. Philadelphia: University of Philadelphia Press, 1993.

Ricoeur, Paul. *The Symbolism of Evil.* New York: Harper and Row, 1967.

Ringren, Helmer. *Israelite Religion.* Philadelphia: Fortress Press, 1966.

Rouet, Albert. *Liturgy and the Arts.* Collegeville, MN: Liturgical Press, 1997.

Rozik, Eli. "Categorization of Speech Acts in Play and Performance Analysis." *Journal of Dramatic Theory and Criticism* 8, no. 1 (1993): 117–32.

———. "Plot Analysis and Speech Act Theory." In *Signs of Humanity,* edited by Gerard Deledalle. Berlin: Mouton de Gruyter, 1992.

———. "Speech Acts and the Theory of Theatrical Communication." *Kodikas/ Code* 12 (1989): 41–55.

Rubin, Miri. *Corpus Christi: The Eucharist in Late Medieval Culture.* Cambridge: Cambridge University Press, 1991.

Russell, James C. *The Germanization of Early Medieval Christianity.* New York: Oxford University Press, 1994.

Sagovsky, Nicholas. *Liturgy and Symbolism.* Grove Liturgical Study 16. Bramcote: Grove Books, 1978.

Schechner, Richard. "Approaches to Theory/Criticism." *Tulane Drama Review* 10, no. 4 (1966): 20–53.

———. *Between Theatre and Anthropology*. Philadelphia: University of Pennsylvania Press, 1985.

———. *Performance Theory*. New York: Routledge, 1988.

Schmid, Herta, and A. Van Kestern, eds. *Semiotics of Drama and Theatre*. Amsterdam: Benjamins, 1984.

Schnusenberg, Christine. *The Relationship between the Church and the Theatre Exemplified by Selected Writings of the Church Fathers*. Lanham, MD: University Press of America, 1988.

Scholes, Robert. *Structuralism in Literature: An Introduction*. New Haven: Yale University Press, 1974.

Schreiter, Robert J. *Constructing Local Theologies*. Maryknoll, NY: Orbis Books, 1985.

Searle, John R. *Speech Acts: An Essay in the Philosophy of Language*. Cambridge: Cambridge University Press, 1969.

Seasoltz, R. Kevin. *Living Bread, Saving Cup: Readings on the Eucharist*. Collegeville, MN: Liturgical Press, 1987.

———. "Non-verbal Symbols and the Eucharistic Prayer." In *New Eucharistic Prayers*, edited by F. C. Senn, pp. 214–36. New York: Paulist Press, 1987.

Semaine d'études liturgiques. *Gestes et paroles dans les diverses familles liturgiques*. Conferences Saint-Serge xxive semaine d'études liturgiques. Rome: Centro Liturgico Vincenziano, 1987.

Sequeira, A. Ronald. "The Rediscovery of the Role of Movement in the Liturgy." In *Symbol and Art in Worship*, edited by L. Moldonado and D. Power. New York: Seabury Press, 1980.

Smoldon, William L. *The Music of the Medieval Church Dramas*. New York: Oxford University Press, 1980.

Southern, R. W. *Saint Anselm: A Portrait in a Landscape*. Cambridge: Cambridge University Press, 1990.

Stevens, John E. *Words and Music in the Middle Ages: Song, Narrative, Dance, and Drama, 1050–1350*. New York: Cambridge University Press, 1986.

Stevenson, Kenneth. *Eucharist and Offering*. New York: Pueblo, 1986.

Stuhlman, Byron. *Eucharistic Celebration, 1789–1979*. New York: Church Hymnal Corp., 1988.

Swanson, Robert N. *Religion and Devotion in Europe, c. 1215–c. 1515*. Cambridge: Cambridge University Press, 1995.

Taft, Robert. *Beyond East and West*. Washington, DC: Pastoral Press, 1984.

———. *The Liturgy of the Hours in East and West*. Collegeville, MN: Liturgical Press, 1986, 1993.

Talley, Thomas J. *The Origins of the Liturgical Year*. Collegeville, MN: Liturgical Press, 1986.

Tellenbach, Gerd. *The Church in Western Europe from the Tenth to the Early Twelfth Century*. Cambridge: Cambridge University Press, 1993.

Thurian, Max. *L'eucharistie: Memorial du Seigneur, sacrifice d'action de grâce et d'intercession*. Neuchâtel: Delachaux-Niestlé, 1963.

Toynbee, Jocelyn M. C., and J. B. Ward-Perkins. *The Shrine of St. Peter and the Vatican Excavations*. New York: Longmans, Green, 1956.

Turner, Victor. *Dramas, Fields, and Metaphors*. Ithaca: Cornell University Press, 1974.

Tyrer, John Walton. *Historical Survey of Holy Week*. Oxford: Oxford University Press, 1932.

van Gennep, Arnold. *Rites de Passage*. Paris: É. Nourry, 1908. Translated by M. B. Vizedon and G. L. Caffee as *The Rites of Passage* (Chicago: University of Chicago Press, 1960).

Veltrusky, Jiri. "Contribution to the Semiotics of Acting." In *Sound, Sign, and Meaning,* edited by Ladislav Matejka, pp. 533–606. Ann Arbor: University of Michigan Press, 1976.

———. "The Prague School Theory of Theatre." *Poetics Today* 2, no. 3 (1985): 225–35.

Vergote, A. *Interpretation du language religieux*. Paris: Seuil, 1974.

Vogel, Cyrille. *Medieval Liturgy: An Introduction to the Sources*. Revised and translated by William Storey and Niels Rasmussen. Washington, DC: Pastoral Press, 1986.

Volp, Rainer. *Zeichen: Semiotik in Theologie und Gottesdienst*. Munich: Kaiser, 1982.

Von Allmen, J. J. *Celebrer le salut: Doctrine et pratique du culte chretien*. Paris: Cerf-Labor et Fides, 1984.

Vorgrimler, Herbert. *Sacramental Theology*. Collegeville, MN: Liturgical Press, 1992.

Wainwright, Geoffrey. *Doxology: The Praise of God in Worship, Doctrine, and Life*. New York: Oxford University Press, 1980.

———. *Eucharist and Eschatology*. New York: Oxford University Press, 1981.

Wegman, Herman. *Christian Worship in East and West: A Study Guide to Liturgical History*. Collegeville, MN: Liturgical Press, 1990.

Weil, Louis. *Sacraments and Liturgy, the Outward Signs: A Study in Liturgical Mentality*. Oxford: Basil Blackwell, 1983.

Weston, Jesse L. *From Ritual to Romance*. Princeton: Princeton University Press, 1920, 1993.

White, James F. *Documents of Christian Worship*. Louisville: John Knox Press, 1992.

Whitehead, Alfred North. *Process and Reality*. New York: Free Press, 1979.

Wickham, Glynne. *The Medieval Theatre*. 3rd ed. Cambridge: Cambridge University Press, 1987.

Wimsatt, William K., and Cleanth Brooks. *Literary Criticism: A Short History*. New York: Vintage Books, 1957.

Yarnold, Edward. *The Awe-Inspiring Rites of Initiation*. Collegeville, MN: Liturgical Press, 1994.

Young, Karl. *The Drama of the Medieval Church*. 2 vols. Oxford: Clarendon Press, 1933.

Index

actions, differentiation by intention, 96
"Actuals: A Look at Performance
　　Theory" (Schechner), 60
Adam (play), 13
aesthetic seeing, 71
aesthetic theories and bridge to
　　theological truth claims, 67
allegorical commentaries on the Mass,
　　85, 108. *See also* Amalarius of Metz;
　　Honorius of Autun
Amalarius of Metz, 12, 14, 85, 94, 134
　　Liber officialis, 107
　　liturgical exegesis method, 2
　　paschal candle interpretation, 19, 21
anamnesis, 2, 87, 94, 95
　　actualization and, 60
　　church as part of, 100–102
　　liturgical prayer and, 60–61
　　versus mimesis, 61
　　of Trinity as object of liturgy, 95
Andrieu, Michel, 109, 110
Antiochene eucharistic prayers, 99
Aristotle, 6
　　categories defining a made thing, 79
　　definition of tragedy, 81–83
　　—as model for differentiation of
　　　types of performance, 79, 80

audience. *See* performer and audience
Augustine, 9
Austin, J. L., 44, 63–64, 66, 76

Bakhtin, Mikhail, 3, 60
　　on carnival, 45
　　once-occurrent Being-as-event, 63
　　Toward a Philosophy of the Act, 67–71
Barba, Eugenio, 48–49
Barthes, Roland, 3, 64
Bateson, Gregory, 48
　　on performance as marked, 48
　　"A Theory of Play and Fantasy," 58
Bauman, Richard, 48
Baumstark, Anton, 19
Bede, 2
behavior versus performance, 45
Benedictine monks, *Quem quaeritis*
　　and, 10
Berengar of Tours, 13, 22, 23, 29
Berger, Peter, 59
biblical text, interpretation of, 22
Bishop, Edmund, 17
bread
　　intention symbolized by, 90, 96–97
　　in *Ordo Romanus I,* 119–20, 126–29
　　—*Sancta,* 113, 119

RICHARD D. MCCALL
is associate professor of liturgy and church music at
the Episcopal Divinity School.